MW00532001
TO CARLA,
WITH LOVE
X
BEST WISHES!
12-3-18

"*Gold in the Cracks* is an invitation to pick up the broken pieces of your life, embrace your emotional scars, and transform your life. Your scars are proof that despite life's hard knocks, you have emerged strong and beautiful. It is time to embrace your imperfections and find happiness. Let Rani St. Pucchi be your guide as you go on your journey to find the treasure within by making peace with your past."

—**Jack Canfield**, coauthor of the *Chicken Soup for the Soul*® *series* and *The Success Principles*™

"Responsibility is the key to freedom. Although our genetic and environmental conditioning may be responsible for our habitual way of thinking or paradigm, we are responsible for changing it. *Gold In The Cracks* is a beautiful guide to living the life you were meant to live. But, it won't happen by accident. You must take responsibility and choose it."

—**Bob Proctor**, Master Success Coach, best-selling author of *You Were Born Rich*

"*Gold in the Cracks* takes you on a journey to prove that your broken pieces are where your treasure lies."

—**John Gray**, author of *Men are from Mars, Women are from Venus*

"In *Gold in the Cracks*, Rani St. Pucchi invites you to embrace your past in order to create a magnificent future. She shows you how to pick up the broken pieces of your life and transform any emotional scars into something beautiful. Despite life's adversities, you can emerge strong, at peace, and happy."

—**Marci Shimoff**, #1 NY Times best-selling author, *Happy for No Reason* and *Chicken Soup for the Woman's Soul*

"In *Gold in the Cracks*, Rani St. Pucchi takes readers on a journey to reconcile with their past so they may embrace their present and go forth to live intensely. Step by step, she holds the reader's hand and shows how they are in fact more valuable for having faced all the challenges and the ups and downs of life. Rani inspires us to embrace our imperfections, to accept our beautiful selves and transform our lives. This is a book everyone must read and a plan all readers must follow. I highly recommend it!"

—**Dr. Pankaj Naram**, referred by National Geographic as a Master Healer

"My heartfelt congratulations to Rani St. Pucchi for another brilliant work, *Gold in the Cracks*! Rani inspires and leads me to a contemplative and silent place where I am able to deeply reflect on my own journey to great success and true, lasting love. *Gold in the Cracks* is beautifully written for one to see that age is truly only measured by our past experiences and through them we evolve in revolutionary growth. Rani brings out our Heavenly Father's majestic work on each one of us, His very own Divine creations. She is amazing and motivating and at the same time gives comfort to the reality of being aware of what our own life's choices are for directing our inner journey. Rani's *Gold in the Cracks* seeps into my heart like an angel. Using her recipe each and every day promises to bring everyone the tools to accomplish their own consistent Excellence." With love,

—**Lady Angelle Grace Wacker**, chairman, Swiss American Chamber of Commerce

"Rani St. Pucchi has a poignant and very timely message that she shares beautifully in her book, *Gold in the Cracks.* At a time when many are willing to settle for a mediocre life, stuck in their history and the stories they tell themselves, Rani holds her readers by the hand and shows them how, by picking up all the scattered pieces of their life, they can repair their 'brokenness' and become beautiful and whole again. An exciting new world awaits the reader! I highly recommend this book."

—**Sandra Biskind**, #1 international best-selling author of *CODEBREAKER: Discover the Password to Unlock the Best Version of You*

"Rani St. Pucchi's book *Gold in the Cracks* offers a golden blueprint to recover your broken places and meld them into a beautiful work of life. Having helped thousands of women, she eloquently guides you to 'draw confidence from your most difficult experiences instead of letting your experiences draw confidence from you.' I highly recommend."

—**Deborah Sandella**, PhD, RN, #1 international best-selling author, *Goodbye Hurt & Pain, 7 Simple Steps to Health, Love and Success.*

"Rani St. Pucchi's new book, *Gold in the Cracks*, is a must read for people of all ages and stages. We all have a story, a past, broken pieces of ourselves which when reframed, can become our gold and our legacy. How we choose to live through our story is completely up to us. Rani pulls from her darkest times and finds her gold, and in turn has created a step-by-step guide to help us find gold in our cracks, to reframe our pain into our power, our dark into our light, to live our most passionate life. This book is her legacy, her gift, her gold."

—**Kathleen Seeley**, founder and CEO, Massively Human Leadership.

"You will be transfixed by the transformative power of Rani St. Pucchi's book, *Gold in the Cracks*. Shift and expand your view of your life's journey where not only fulfilled dreams but every challenge, shattered experience, and bump can be transformed into the beautiful human being that you are."

—**Dr. Anita Sanchez**, international trainer, speaker, author, *The Four Sacred Gifts.*

"Having known Rani for several years, we can unequivocally say that she is determined to share her message and support others in living their best lives. Her dedication to inspiring the world around her continues in her latest book, *Gold in the Cracks*. In it, Rani helps us see how, though we may fall down in life, each hardship we've suffered gives way for the light to shine in. And if we're aware of this and allow ourselves to see life through this perspective, we see each experience as a blessing. Because it truly is."

—**Jodi Chapman and Dan Teck**, cocreators of the best-selling 365 book series.

"*Gold in the Cracks* is a personal journey that reveals an artful way for people to repair the pieces of their broken past and restore the faith in their abilities to design a beautiful life."

—**Tony Jeton Selimi**, human behavior specialist, international best-selling author of *A Path to Wisdom.*

"We all have wounds, scars, and cracks. But the question is: Will we let our cracks define us and break us or be the source of our healing and transformation? In this beautiful book, *Gold in the Cracks*, Rani St. Pucchi uses her vast experience of coaching over twenty thousand women and walks us through the step-by-step process of examining our broken bits and then choosing to put them back together so we can feel whole again. This is not a book to read, but a plan to follow. Highly recommend."

—**Lourds Lane**, founder of the global educational nonprofit, The SuperYou FUNdation.

"Having known Rani St. Pucchi for numerous years and watching her saintly response to adversities in her own life, I am convinced after reading *Gold in the Cracks* that she is the expert who can guide us to the best way to heal our life and bring light to the cracks. In her new book, *Gold in the Cracks,* Rani helps us lift ourselves to a higher level, to see the good in the bad, and find light at the end of the tunnel. You will be rewarded as you implement the steps by the beauty Rani brings to you as she helps guide you to live the life you are meant to live. Get ready for your beautiful journey with Rani St. Pucchi. Read and grow."

—**Chanda Montroy**, De Luz, Temecula, CA.

"*Gold in the Cracks* is a poignant journey to embrace imperfection, to see the best in everything we do. This book is a true testament to living a fulfilling life without always looking for the perfect business, perfect partner, perfect road map, or perfect life. Rani St. Pucchi inspires her readers to seek the truth in a world sometimes stimulated by perfectionism. We are all a work in progress, and Rani's book teaches us simple strategies in creating a worthwhile existence by ceasing to compete with or judge one another. *Gold in the Cracks* will change your view on the notion of imperfection and assist you in seeking beauty with every encounter you face."

—**Pashmina P.**, international best-selling author of *The Cappuccino Chronicles* series.

"In her book, *Gold in the Cracks*, Rani St. Pucchi delivers a message that is supremely powerful—being broken does not mean we are less valuable! In fact, in those very moments of loss or despair, we can discover an internal choice. That choice is to connect with what is truly valuable about ourselves—the intrinsic value that has always existed within us. Through Rani's courageous journey and determination to be master of her circumstances, she gives us the inspiration and steps we need to achieve our own mastery. This inspirational, yet practical book, will not leave you where it found you; it will lead you on a journey to a place where you will feel whole."

—**Kelsey Price**, independent artistic talent representative.

"*Gold in the Cracks* is a powerful story about resilience. The author, my childhood friend, relives her tale of a tumultuous life and imparts her knowledge on how to rise from the ashes even when there seems to be no hope. Rani's powerful message stems from her deep love for transformation and living in the present moment. There is no day but today. An excellent book that will take you on a soul quest and remind you how to look at life through the eyes of beauty, even when something is flawed."

—**Laxmi Dialdas Lam,** grandmother, mother, childhood friend and entrepreneur.

"*Gold in the Cracks* is a phenomenal story, an empowering journey from being broken to becoming a winner in life. Rani St. Pucchi embodies wisdom in her pages as she reveals the philosophy that although we are all flawed in some way we have the ability to rise, move forward, and become the best version of ourselves. An inspiring work that is sure to make the reader feel empowered."

—**Natalie Glebova**, Author, I Am Winning, A Guide to Personal Empowerment, former Miss Universe 2005

ALSO BY

RANI ST. PUCCHI

Your Body, Your Style:
Simple Tips on Dressing to Flatter Your Body Type

The Soulmate Checklist:
Keys to Finding Your Perfect Partner

Your Bridal Style:
Everything You Need to Know to Design
the Wedding of your Dreams

Gold in the Cracks:
Move from Shattered to Whole and Reveal Your Light
by Rani St. Pucchi

ISBN 978-0-9978809-0-8

Library of Congress Control Number: 2018953928

Book interior designed by Rani St. Pucchi

Published by

St. Pucchi

P.O. Box 27254
Los Angeles, CA 90027
www.stpucchi.com

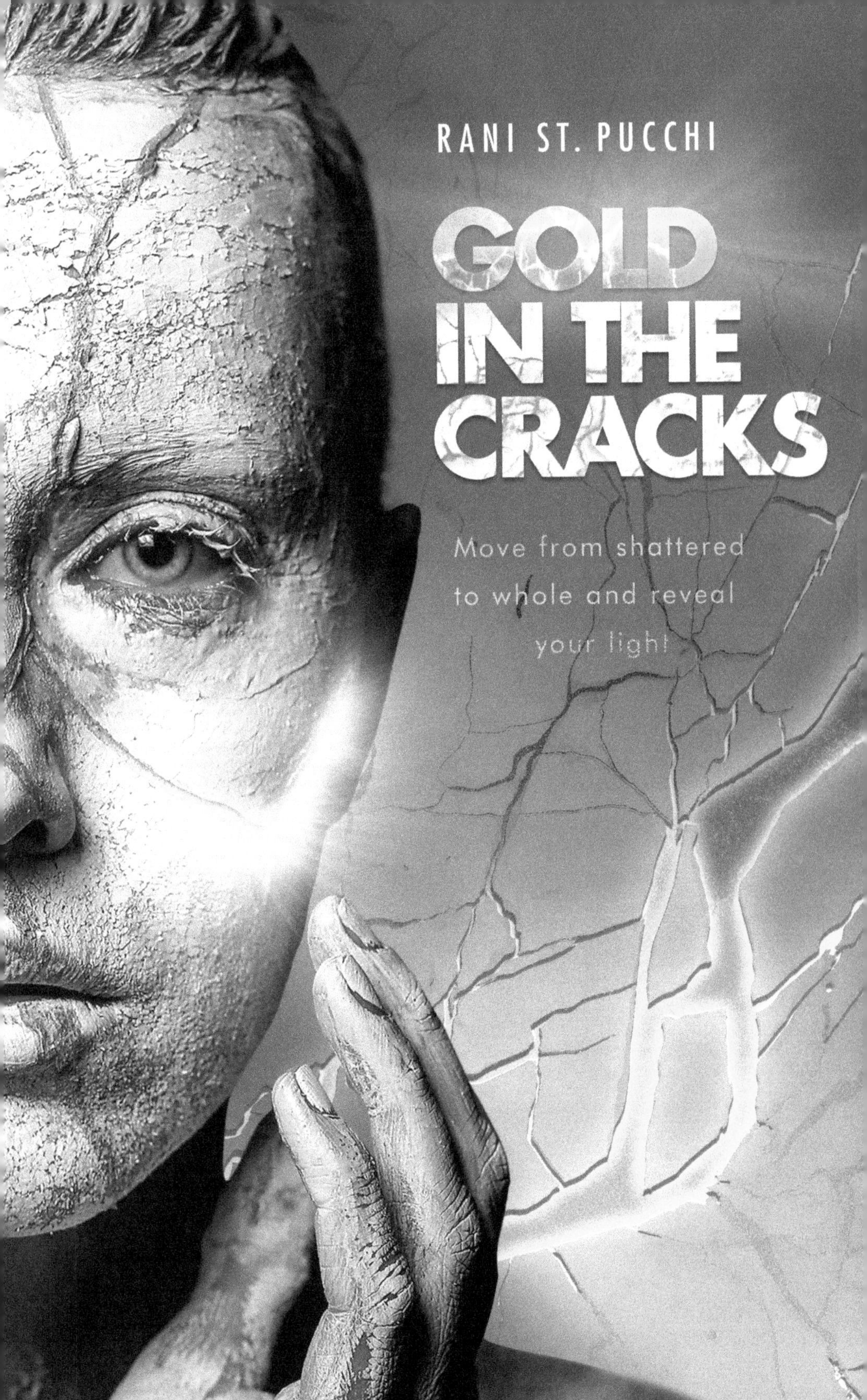
RANI ST. PUCCHI
GOLD IN THE CRACKS
Move from shattered to whole and reveal your light

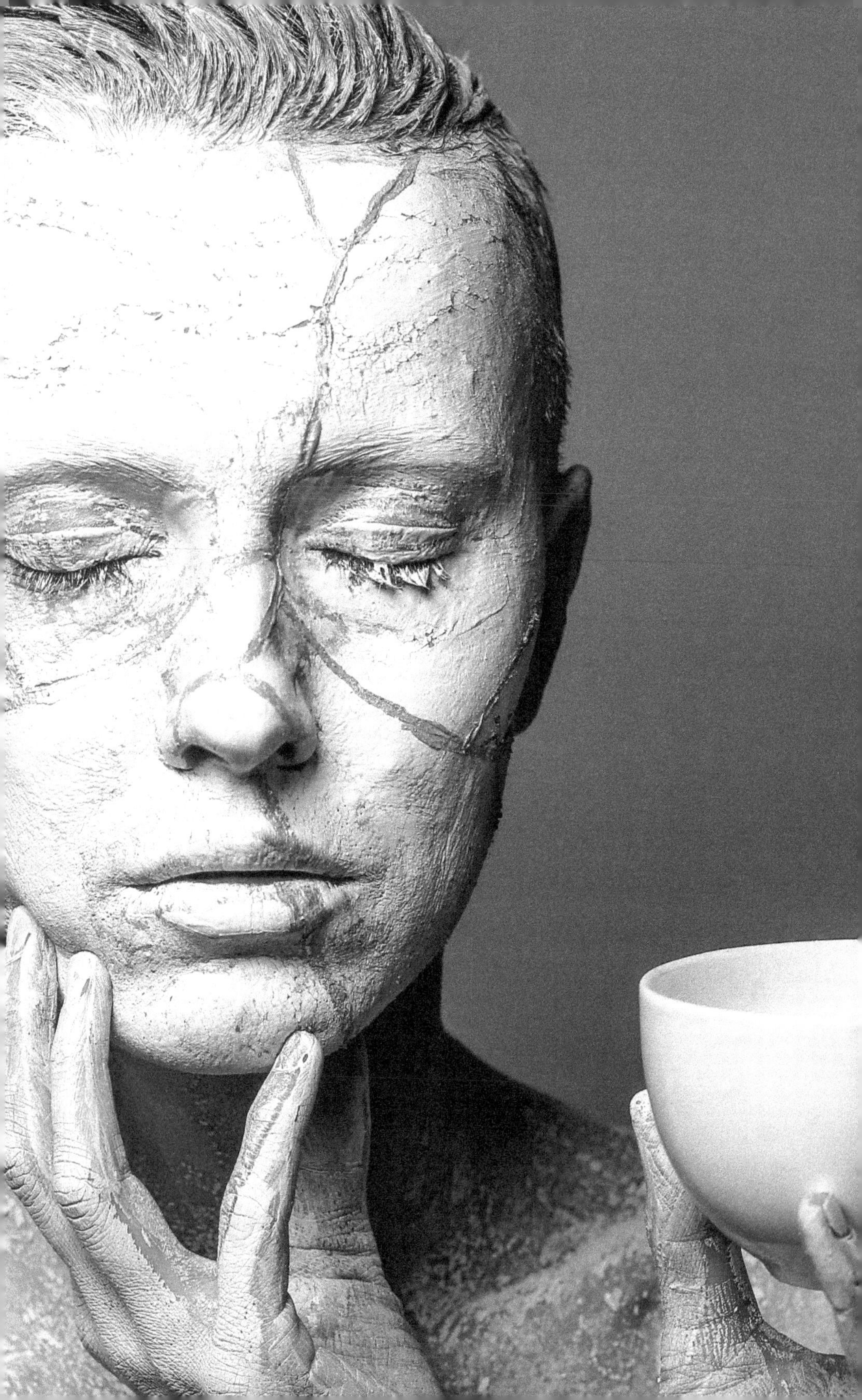

Your joy is your sorrow unmasked.
And the selfsame well from which your laughter rises was oftentimes filled with your tears.
And how else can it be?
The deeper that sorrow carves into your being, the more joy you can contain.
Is not the cup that holds your wine the very cup that was burned in the potter's oven?
And is not the lute that soothes your spirit, the very wood that was hollowed with knives?
When you are joyous, look deep into your heart and you shall find it is only that which has given you sorrow that is giving you joy.
When you are sorrowful look again in your heart, and you shall see that in truth you are weeping for that which has been your delight.

Some of you say, "Joy is greater than sorrow," and others say, "Nay, sorrow is the greater."
But I say unto you, they are inseparable.
Together they come, and when one sits alone with you at your board, remember that the other is asleep upon your bed.

Verily you are suspended like scales between your sorrow and your joy.
Only when you are empty are you at standstill and balanced.
When the treasure-keeper lifts you to weigh his gold and his silver, needs must your joy or your sorrow rise or fall.

—Kahlil Gibran

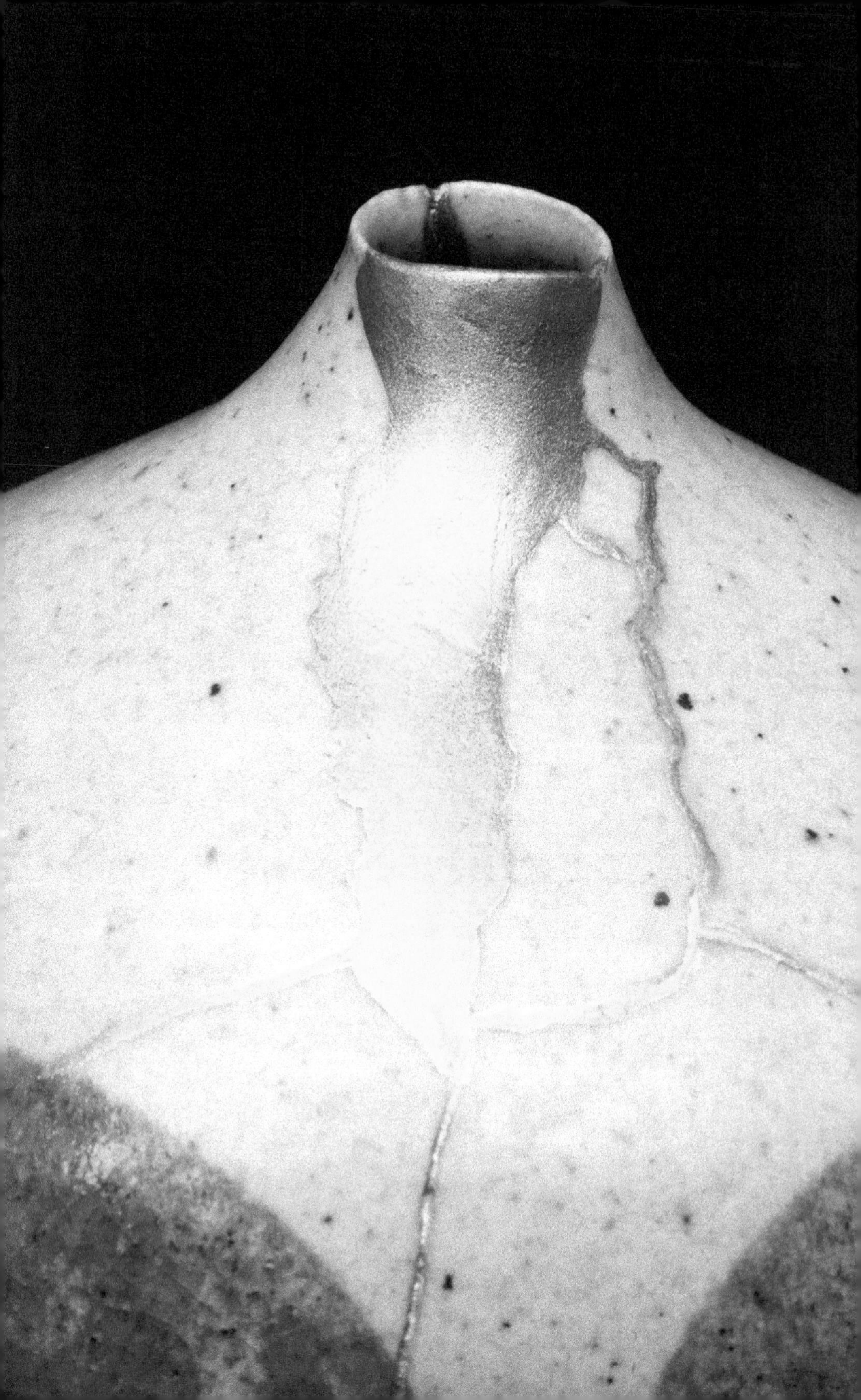

DEDICATION

Dedicated to those who feel they are broken, who try to smile despite the pain they feel, who dare not ask questions of others, and to those who have never been asked. This book will offer you the golden repair to feel whole, vibrant, and happy again. Your golden seams are beautiful reminders of a life well lived. I'm excited to share this journey with you and offer you my heart and abundant blessings.

*Gold in the Crack*s is my gift to you.

PART III: WHERE THE MAGIC HAPPENS

PART IV: THE ART OF REPAIRING AND LETTING GO

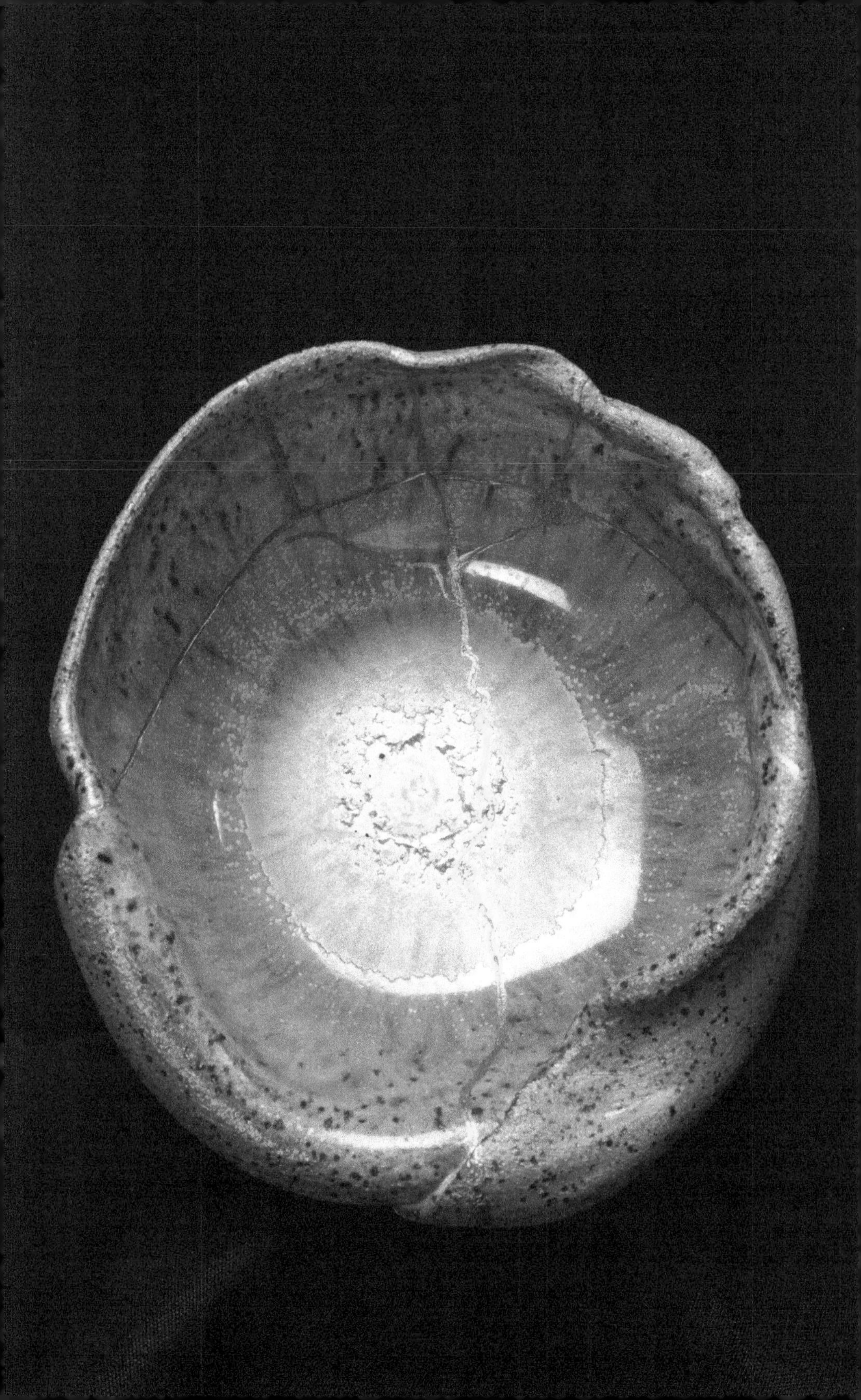

INTRODUCTION

A Personal Statement

> "The wound is the place where the Light enters you."
>
> —*Rumi*

It was the summer of 1989, and I was showing my St. Pucchi bridal collection at the World Fashion Fair in Osaka, Japan. At dinner one evening, a Japanese client handed me a beautifully wrapped gift. That gift remained in its original wrapping cloth, called *furoshiki, f*orgotten for more than two decades all through my move from Dallas to Los Angeles in 1999 until February 2017, when I finally unpacked the last remaining boxes.

They say the teacher appears when the student is ready, not a minute sooner and not a second later. Apparently, this was the right time as my attention was now drawn to the beautiful gift. I gently peeled off the furoshiki and opened the carved, wooden box that revealed a gorgeous jade bowl with golden veins running through it. My first thought was *what a beautiful piece of art.* On second glance, I thought the gold veins did not make much sense as they were haphazard and to the naked eye looked like a river flowing through cracks. *How interesting,* I thought. I picked up the note that was tucked inside the bowl; it read, "May you become a kintsugi master," and it went on to explain the meaning of *kintsugi* as "golden rejoining."

Kintsugi art dates back to the late fifteenth century. Legend has it that the craft commenced when Japanese shogun Ashikaga Yoshimasa sent his favorite tea bowl—a *chawan*—that was cracked back to China for repair. Upon its return, Yoshimasa was displeased to find that it had been mended with unsightly metal staples. Clearly this was less than esthetically pleasing. The shogun immediately tasked Japanese craftsmen to come up with an alternate, more pleasing method of repair. And thus kintsugi was born.

How fascinating! This evoked intriguing thoughts because beholding the artistry of kintsugi, I could immediately see its transformative power. The bowl in my hand was more beautiful for having been broken. While the original form was forever destroyed, the essence of its beauty not only survived, it had been enhanced. And I thought, *if such astounding beauty can emerge from shards of a shattered bowl that was once pristine, could a similar transformation also be possible with the parts of us we believe are shattered beyond repair to create a stunning masterpiece?* In other words, can putting the pieces of one's broken life back together help transform and lead to a total reinvention of the self in which the shattered pieces are alchemized into a beautiful, thriving masterpiece?

Kintsugi gives new life, healing, and rebirth to damaged or aging ceramic objects by celebrating their flaws and history. I learned that the repair is done with lacquer dusted with powdered gold, silver, or platinum. The cracks are filled in with gold. As a philosophy, kintsugi treats breakage as part of the history of an object and focuses on its hidden beauty with the understanding that rather than something to disguise, the piece is more beautiful because it has been broken. The

Japanese believe that when something has suffered damage and has a history, it becomes more valuable.

However, from what I've since learned from a kintsugi master, what is not apparent is the time and patience it takes to gather the broken pieces and fill in the cracks. Each crack is unique, and to fill it properly and make it stronger, one must figure out which kind of lacquer is best to use and continuously monitor, adjust, and refine the tiny details. It feels as if the broken bowl is talking to you as you touch and feel each broken piece with the hands of your heart, the lacquer running through it like bloody veins, and the gold adding to its beauty. There's an intention that's expressed as you invest time, energy, and intelligence to fix something that will be a part of your life, which perhaps you might use to consume food or drink. The kintsugi master is essentially expressing that a broken vessel deserves more than just being forgotten and replaced and is worth the investment of time so that it can continue to exist.

Similarly, we are all trying to heal emotional wounds and rebuild our lives so we can become stronger. Kintsugi teaches us that nothing lasts, nothing is finished, and nothing is perfect. We are all works in progress, and each scattered piece of our lives is precious and worth embracing.

Living a kintsugi life is to be unafraid of taking risks and getting damaged. Shutting ourselves off from the world to protect ourselves so we can live without suffering is the kiss of death, because then we are resigned to *surviving* instead of *living intensely*. The key is to embrace all our broken pieces and create something beautiful and whole.

It's unrealistic to expect life will always be wonderful. Inevitably, despite taking the utmost care, fragile things such as a favorite bowl will occasionally break. Suffering— whether it be through illness, job loss, heartbreak, tragedy, or the loss of a loved one—is part of life, and adversity a collateral element of living. Ceramics are fragile, strong, and beautiful all at once, just like people. Ceramics and life can break apart into a thousand pieces, but that's not reason enough for us to stop living passionately. Painful experiences can in fact make us into more determined individuals ready to face the world with optimism.

We can be broken in so many places that it becomes impossible to concentrate on everything that needs to be fixed. Because we don't have time to fix everything, we must choose which parts deserve our attention and what tools to use as we fix, refine, and polish ourselves. We must engage our minds and give meaningful intention to strengthen and make whole, and more beautiful, the parts of our lives that are precious. Filling in the cracks with gold is to add beauty to something that was broken, and like a piece of art that enriches your life every day, the repaired vessel also brings joy. It serves as a reminder of how it was broken and the effort it took to fix the broken parts so that you value it even more now that it was broken and repaired.

As you go through life, be prepared for the inevitable, and when challenging times occur, apply the philosophy of kintsugi. Instead of sweeping problems under the metaphorical rug, put yourself back together and embrace the challenges you face as being part of life's journey and acknowledge that it's your scars that make you a strong and interesting person. Your imperfections are your story; they show how far you've come.

Never underestimate what has happened nor trivialize the consequences of adversity. Being too stoical is not kintsugi living. There's a difference between repairing and patching up. Fixing a broken bowl is not recycling; it's creating value. It's about not forgetting our past but to keep going and putting forward the best part of ourselves. If we don't take the time needed to repair and reflect on life's challenges, we're at risk of miring ourselves in self-pity and victimization. In the words of Hemingway: "*The world breaks everyone, and afterward, some are strong at the broken places.*"

Many people talk about feeling "broken" after enduring heartbreak, grief, and trauma. It's time we rethink our philosophy of life and remember there's an entire art dedicated to filling in the cracks of broken things with lacquered gold, an art form that proves that even the broken and damaged history of an object is beautiful and should be treasured. I love the concept of kintsugi. It's such a wonderful metaphor for life.

The same is true for *your* life. Every wrinkle is a road map of your life journey; every scar is a solemn decoration, a perception that writes timeless poetry upon flesh and mind, like the stroke of a painter's brush dipped in golden paint, creating art that is timeless despite the wrinkled grooves, deep creases, torn and broken parts. For that is where true beauty emerges.

And just like the shattered pieces of pottery, my heart, too has been broken into many pieces. I have faced more valleys than mountains along my life journey. All I know for sure is that I'm full of wounds and cracks—and still standing. From every wound there's a scar, and every scar tells a story, a story that says I have survived and continue to fill in my scars and shattered pieces and adorn them with gold. I love my life now, but it wasn't always this way.

I was raised in a culture that not only had its own set of beauty standards but also viewed remarks about one's appearance in public as perfectly acceptable. All through my childhood, I was constantly told there was something wrong with me. My complexion was too dark, I was too scrawny, too clumsy; I could never do anything right. Everyone compared me with my siblings. It's no surprise I grew up with low self-worth.

As the youngest of six, I somehow got lost in the shuffle and had to assert myself to get noticed. I always pretended nothing others said to me or about me was a big deal, and even though I wanted to cry, I swallowed my tears and pretended to smile. I didn't want others' pity. It was bad enough that they made fun of me because of the color of my skin because I was the darkest in the family. I imagined placing invisible bandages over my emotional hurts to cover them. My parents shipped me off to a Catholic convent at the age of nine, and when the nuns pinched me for every innocent mistake I made, whether it was hitting the wrong piano key or falling down the stairs, I just covered up the bruises and scars so no one could see them. Somehow, things always seemed better with Band-Aids because I didn't have to look at the scars anymore. I admit I got so used to using them that there were times I wore Band-Aids so that other people would cut me a little more slack!

Because I was so focused on showing that I was strong and perfect, I suffered. My decades of crippling self-sabotaging patterns resulted in a ton of *I wanted to say no, but I had to say yes* situations in life along with abusive relationships, because I felt I was not good enough, that I didn't deserve. Life threw more curves through the years, and I followed the same pattern. When my father beat me because I refused to be forced into an arranged marriage, I suffered in silence. When he "won" and married me off to an abusive man who hit me—breaking my nose and bruising my body, cursing me, and finding faults with everything I did or said—I just hid in shame. When my children were taken away from me, I slapped invisible Band-Aids on my heart. When my livelihood was stolen and all my finances and resources were taken away, I suffered in silence and stepped away from the world.

For the longest time, my happiness meter was at an all-time low, but I never questioned my inner voice. I believed it was protecting me from harm even though it often reduced me to self-loathing. My life was fraught with anxiety and sadness, physical and emotional trauma, but I kept going, never pausing to let my wounds heal.

That was no way to live. Life is hard when your heart is always racing with anxiety and worry, wondering when the next shoe will drop, when you will be traumatized again. I climbed and scrambled out of the abyss without actually dealing with the root of the problem, the actual wounds, not moving any further than to the edge of the abyss that I was in before. I could still see down into this abyss, and it was a fearful place to be. I had yet to learn how to mend my brokenness, to gain awareness that it was possible to fill in the cracks and wounds with gold, that I could show strength within my weakness and beauty within ugliness. I was not aware that my scars could be turned into something beautiful.

The journey of healing and reclaiming my self-worth was a long one. I made a daring move far away from my family to live across the world from those who would cage me so I could heal myself. Turns out I was still not getting far enough away. I was not solving anything. Because wherever you go, there you are! I was always on thin ice, my state of being was always very fragile. At times, I took enough medication to numb my pain to where I could be strong and start to really focus on living my life. But my ups were not even reaching the lowest levels of most people's downs, and I lost my will to live.

The Universe must have heard me, because then the car accident happened.

It was March 30, 2015. I remember the day so well. A colleague invited me to have lunch with her and insisted we take her car. On the way back, she attempted to run a red light at an intersection. In a split second, three cars were involved in the crash. Her car was totaled. She scrambled out unscathed. Where I was sitting, the airbag deployed and hit me in the chest, and my chest caved in. I managed to wrench my door open and stumble out, collapsing on the curb at the corner of the street. I couldn't breathe. Moments later, the ambulance took me on a stretcher to the nearest hospital.

Taking each breath was a laborious effort, and for eight months I was unable to even lie down. Breathless, my life flashed before me. Suddenly, I had the strongest desire to live fully, love completely. I felt there was so much that I still had left undone on this earth. I no longer wanted to crawl through life waiting breathlessly for someone to rescue me. I realized I am my own rescue. I sent love to my body, thanking every cell, every limb, every organ for being there for me. So many things could have gone wrong but for the grace of God.

Those eight months gave me the opportunity to do some soul searching. I spent the time assessing every area of my life, revisiting, reviewing, and reflecting on every person, event, and incident that had happened in my life that had brought me to this place of "playing small." I was no longer afraid. I wanted to make sense of my life—accept what was, let go of what I could not change, take 100 percent responsibility for my own part in it—then clear and heal myself, my past, and move on to live the life that had been waiting for me. I was ready to mend the cracks and patch together the shattered pieces of my life and fill them in with gold. I knew it would not be easy, but I was willing to be patient and put in the effort.

Life can throw us challenges and tough lessons, pain and sorrow. Unless we face these head on and walk through them rather than around them, patiently piece them together and fill them in with gold; unless we take the time and make the effort, the lessons will come back to haunt us again and again. We must find the courage to face our challenges—acknowledge, accept, and master them.

You don't have to wait for something drastic to happen to propel you to make a move.

Having experienced the love and light on the other side and having assisted many to embrace their own true worth, I can promise you that it absolutely can be done. The minute you let go of the need to please everybody, the moment you shed the layers of worrying about how others see you, you will start to see your own brokenness and appreciate your own magnificence.

There is a very good reason you are here today. When I was first guided to compose and offer these lessons, I asked the Universe how I could present these principles in a way that others could grasp easily and not have to go through the decades long journey like I did. Intuitively,

I knew that there were two distinct issues that needed to be addressed: overload and confusion. So, I've kept this book really simple and used language that you can follow easily. I present a framework that if you follow will change your current limiting beliefs and help you embrace your past.

It's a three-step process. The first step is to *identify the limiting belief.* To do this, you will have to go back in time. This in my opinion is the hardest step of all because your beliefs are embedded in your subconscious. Somewhere, someone, or some event triggered it in you, and you have to dive deep to bring it to the surface.

The second step is to *weaken the existing limiting belief* because if you don't weaken the belief first, it's very hard to put a new belief on top of it and have it succeed. Compare that to a mildewed wall. Let's say you want to put new wallpaper on this wall. If you don't clean the mold off the wall first, then the mold will continue to grow underneath the new wallpaper. So, as you go through this second step, ask yourself, *this belief that I have, is this really true?*

Finally, in the third step, you must *replace that old belief* with one that is not going to limit you. This can be done with the help of affirmations, visualizations, and even vision boards. But you MUST go through the first two steps because this third step will not work otherwise.

By visiting your past, putting your thoughts on paper, and answering the questions in this book, you can bring to light events that have conditioned you, that affect how you live today and the decisions you make. You are able to pick up the broken and shattered pieces and identify your limiting beliefs as you bring them to the surface and forgive those who have hurt you and let go so you may get to a place where you're finally clear about what exactly happened and know your truth. You get to choose how your story ends.

The past has a tendency to hold us back from living a great life. Now you have a choice: either to leave your best creativity, productivity, and impact on the table of broken dreams by staying stuck in the past and continuing to stay angry at those who have hurt you and wronged you, or you can forgive and get busy following your vision and changing the world.

Now is the only sphere of life that you can live in. Not the past, not the future. Just the present. To illustrate this point, just imagine that you stop breathing now and attempt to survive on the air you breathed in the past or the air you are about to inhale in the future. Is that even possible?

You cannot live that way because you can only live with now. But people tend to forget that. The past is memory. If it is memory, it is unreal. A failed businessman's remembrance of his past glory will not make him rich. The future is vision. Vision is anticipation.

The future can only become real when it becomes now. The past is important, so is the future. The past is memory that nourishes your now, and the future is the vision that makes your now meaningful. Even then, only now is real. Live in the moment!

Are you willing to go on this journey with me and move from your past to the now?

Don't waste another day waiting on the sideline like I was and wishing your life would become better, that things would magically turn around. You may be working with the Law of Attraction like I was, hoping and praying, staying positive, visualizing and affirming that things are just going to get better soon. It wasn't until I was willing to own my stories, turn toward the pain of my past, and dig into my feelings instead of pretending, perfecting, and disowning my pain; it wasn't until I found the courage to reckon with my past and rumble with the truth of all that had happened that I learned who I really was. I no longer wanted to deny my story but rather to defy the ending. Owning my stories of failure gave me the power to write a daring new ending.

Lasting change is an inside job. Improving any area of life requires us to go within and look at what beliefs are guiding us. If you want to raise your level of happiness, you must go within to see what's making you unhappy and deal with it. If you want to raise your self-esteem, you must check with yourself and change the things you believe about yourself that keep you from liking who you are. Whether you like it or not, YOU are 100 percent responsible for YOU.

Have you ever wished someone else would make the change *for* you? Here's the thing about waiting for the change to happen *to* you: When you approach things this way, nothing actually changes. Instead, you're highly likely to unconsciously create a similar situation in your next job/project/relationship in order to learn the lesson.

Or, you can skip the encore by being the one to take full control of your life, the one to take action, the one who is the master of your own destiny. *You* get to choose.

Kintsugi can teach us so much. Kintsugi is about embracing damage, of letting things break so they can come back together again in an incomparable beauty formerly impossible. Who I am is hardly damaged—I believe it was always meant to be this way. But it most certainly calls for breaking. Maybe it's my Oriental roots; maybe it's the romantic in me. But it's our fault lines and cracks that turn porcelain into gold.

I was mended together, and the cracks became these golden veins that pulled everything together. Just like a bowl when it is damaged, my cracks are not hidden, and the bowl hasn't been thrown away. Instead, the brokenness is embraced as the cracks and broken pieces are united and laced with gold.

We have plenty of brokenness in our lives, and it's up to us to pick up our pieces and our tools and perform kintsugi on ourselves and not let our past keep us shattered. Our decision to patch ourselves makes the broken bowl more beautiful than the pristine one, not because of how perfect it is, but because of how broken it was. Remember that your brokenness can be mended together with gold, and your life can end up being more beautiful just by the act of mending.

I believe that being broken and having failures can only be viewed as positive *after* you are healed. It is my hope that the kintsugi idea leaves a positive impression on your brain and gives you the courage to be whole again.

I agree with Hemingway, that the world breaks everyone and afterward many are strong in the broken places. Like a piece of broken pottery, we're all a little broken, and that's okay. Oftentimes, we think because we're broken from having gone through challenges in life we are of lesser value than those whose lives seem to be smooth and effortless, filled with love.

You don't necessarily have to have experienced hardship to feel that your world is too broken for you to fix it with some sort of magic glue. It doesn't really work like that, but if you can come to an understanding that every single person on this earth is fighting some sort of battle and putting on a brave face, then it behooves you to show up for the world and for the less fortunate in your full potential.

Somehow, we all know what it is to be broken and repaired, and because of that, we are so much more beautiful if we enhance our flaws and our similarities and allow ourselves to share our vulnerability. That is how we become a human family; that is how we build a golden path in a world where humanity is the language and compassion is the rule. Isn't that the most beautiful thing to create?

So when you feel broken and worried about how to get back to where you were, think about this and how a master potter can reconstruct what was broken into a masterpiece worth more than it was before. The repair is not carried out to disguise but rather to illuminate the damage, a celebration of strength. Even though broken, you are beautiful.

Kintsugi saved me. Although shattered into tiny bits, I still have the spirit of kintsugi. Slowly but surely, I have been able to put each of my broken pieces together, holding them gently, not so loose that I may fall again, not so hard that I get crushed, just perfect. I fuse them together with gold, all the golden gossamer that I had stored in my heart. Broken as I have been, I wear the broken pieces beautifully.

On the days when I feel ashamed of my scars, my mind only registering how ugly they are rather than the proven beauty of my survival, I see my kintsugi bowl and remind myself how much more I am than an object; that my survival, my journey, my scars deserve to be treasured, too. Those imperfections I used to hide from the world, I've now decorated them. I'm stronger in the places where I've been broken, and I feel more beautiful, too!

Put kintsugi to work in your life. Let it inspire you when you're dealing with the times you feel broken in life and find the gold to mend yourself. Reframe your story. Heal from your past and own all your parts. Remember that your wounds and imperfections are your beauty and that all beautiful things carry distinct imperfections; that breakage and mending are honest parts of your past that you don't need to hide.

My goal in writing this book is to provide you the tools and strategies to get to know your true self, and from that knowledge to overcome adversity, embrace your past, and rebuild your life as an authentic kintsugi master. Embrace the philosophy behind kintsugi and honor your imperfections. Instead of trying to conceal the damage of your broken pieces, or even throwing them out altogether, mend the pieces and fill in the cracks with streams of gold; transform the damage into your most valuable asset. Like broken pieces of ceramic, this shift from useless to priceless makes each piece singularly unique. Given that we each have a past filled with our own stories, this isn't a bad philosophy to live by.

Your wounds and healing are a part of your history, a part of who you are. The beauty of any object lies in the flaws of that object. Every beautiful thing is damaged. You are that beauty. We all are.

Like the broken pottery mended with gold, may you, too live a kintsugi life.

Dance

when you're broken open.

Dance, if you've torn the bandage off.

Dance in the middle of the fighting.

Dance in your blood.

Dance when you're perfectly free.

—Rumi

How to Get the Most out of this Book

The book you are holding in your hands is written with the intention to help you discover your gifts, the valuable treasures and potential that lie within you, and to bring all the scattered pieces of your past together to reveal your true beauty.

Filling *Gold in the Cracks* means embracing our flaws and imperfections to create an even stronger, more beautiful work of art. Just as every break in a piece of pottery is unique, so is our brokenness. Instead of wondering how we can repair our brokenness, let's look at the four-hundred-year-old kintsugi technique and appreciate how we, too can highlight our *scars* as part of our life design. Kintsugi teaches us an important lesson: Sometimes in the process of repairing things that are broken and shattered, we actually create something more unique, beautiful, and resilient.

Many of us grow up believing we should emphasize the inherent positives about ourselves. But what if we also emphasized the negatives, the parts we've had to work so hard to fix or improve? If we did it just right, would the negatives still look negative after all? These are some of the questions that come to mind as we ponder and repair our brokenness —not to achieve perfection, but to dare to reinvent ourselves and not hide the cracks.

Living a kintsugi life means finding value in the missing pieces—the cracked and the chipped—bringing to light the scars from our life experiences, finding new purpose through aging and loss, seeing value and beauty in imperfection, and loving ourselves, our family, and friends, even with and despite the flaws. It is human nature to break down when things consistently fall apart, but let's celebrate our brokenness and imperfections and strengthen ourselves through kintsugi. Let's take advantage of the opportunities presented by life instead of wasting time mourning what it inevitably takes from us; let's appreciate the pure beauty of life—a chipped vase, a quiet, rainy day, the impermanence of all things—and take comfort in the natural beauty around us.

Perhaps some unfair things have happened to you, but neither your past nor those incidents define you or determine your future. It's not what happens *to* you but what happens *in* you that matters most. Draw confidence from your experiences instead of letting your experiences drain confidence from you.

Understanding the value of who you are and what you are capable of requires you to invest in yourself. You must learn to love yourself so you can share that love with others. No matter where you are in your life today, you have the potential to have better relationships, to overcome obstacles, and have increased confidence. When you tap into those treasures within, you will be amazed at the impact and influence you'll have on the world around you.

We all, it seems, want to repair our cracks, our brokenness. The aim of *Gold in the Cracks* is to show you the way to do just that, not only honestly, but also artfully.

Life is full of ups and downs, and things don't always go according to plan. No matter what obstacles you may face, you have a choice to put the pieces together and create something wonderful. Celebrate your imperfections. Instead of striving for an impossible ideal, embrace your strengths and focus on your potential. Learn to love yourself, nourish yourself from the inside out, fuel your body with a simple and healthy lifestyle, and take care of yourself as you would a best friend.

Are you ready to reinvent yourself? If so, it's time to leave the past behind, the damage, the scars left by life's hard knocks, and make room for the bright future that is waiting for you. Embrace the destiny that lies ahead. Honor the space between "no longer" and "not yet," and let this book guide you to reveal what is holding you back so you can see your life with a fresh new perspective, beyond where you are at the present moment, to the new options and opportunities that are waiting for you.

As you go through the pages in this book, I ask that you take your time to think deeply, savoring each and every one of the concepts, stories, questions, and resources that I share with you. Connect with kintsugi. Have a conversation with the book. Be honest and open-minded as you revisit your past. Being honest with yourself allows you to face your history, to acknowledge and accept weaknesses and flaws squarely, and to stop them from becoming your obstacles. Without honesty, the ego takes over, and you can lose touch with your deepest longings, letting your knowledge and desire get in the way of who you think you are and the actual being who has the God-given potential to be who you can become. By default, you then become who you *think* you are rather than who you naturally are.

Unless you function from total awareness, history will continue to multiply its tragedies as you try to fit into the mold and narrow expectations others set for you, to trade in your desires and joy for social approval and economic success. And of course, that society is you, and so the cycle continues as you raise another generation with the same expectations that were thrown at you. On the flip side, when you're utterly convinced of who you are and what drives you, you become creative and purposeful, and from that place you're able to make choices that give your life a bigger meaning.

Remember that the beauty of any object lies in its flaws. Mistakes and damages, or failures, are just lessons learned that have made you who you are today—stronger, more beautiful, and more aware. True beauty is a study in contrasts, so something can only be seen to embody perfection if it also embodies a corresponding degree of imperfection.

There is only one person who can dream your dreams, only one person alive who can kill those dreams, and only one person who can make your dreams come true. That person is YOU! You have the final say. It's time to wake up to the REAL you and live your life in accordance with your deepest longing.

Gold in the Cracks is a neutral tool that allows you to comfortably ask and answer questions about your friends, partners, family, colleagues, chance acquaintances, and yourself. However you choose to use the book—as a journal, a communication tool, as a ritual for transformation—try to answer the questions spontaneously. As you travel through the book, one thing is certain: You will make discoveries about others and yourself.

This is not a book you read; it's a plan you follow. This book is all about your responsibility as you face your possibility. It is a resource to help you repair your life independently and without compromising. By diving into your past, you are able to identify your limiting beliefs, to reconcile with all that happened no matter how big or small, acknowledge everything, including your responsibility about everything that happened, then step into an exciting new world you've never known before.

Join me on a trip I know very well. I've been there; I've hit rock bottom, been trampled on, and gone through the wringer several times, and having done this work, I've come out on the other side with great clarity and wonder. I can vouch that had I not met with success as I walked through the steps I'm inviting you to take, I would not be writing this book. The process works if you work at it. A new dream will emerge from the shadows of yesterday.

I invite you to contemplate, meditate, and peruse this book in a way that lifts you to a state of wonder. It's not enough to just read the book. You must engage with the material, and above all, you must take action. The best thing to do is to honor yourself by embracing whatever emotions surface and allow yourself to feel. The more you avoid facing negative emotions, the more that energy gets trapped in your system. Your emotions are inner communications indicating to you whether what you're doing is aligned with your truth or not. Don't deny them and don't keep them bottled up longer than they need to be. Now you have the tools. Now you can emerge and recognize the beautiful you that is waiting to be loved.

Go through this book. Do the work. Find your own voice. Rewrite your story.

THE LESSONS

Each part of this book, each idea and image, reflects yet another way you can become an individual by following your inner calling and living in accordance with your heart's deepest desires. Each idea, each set of questions, is meant to be a building block in creating new thoughts, beliefs, and behaviors so you can enjoy the rich rewards that come with emerging from the shadows of yesterday and today to become a beautiful, bright light on your tomorrows.

Step by step, you are taken on a path on this important journey to know yourself, because when you choose a path, you are choosing what you want to contemplate so that your journey is focused. Remember, you can't fix your parts without treating the whole. So please don't skip any of the steps.

The book is divided into four parts.

PART I is all about you. It's meant to make you aware of where you are right now. You must know your starting point in order to clearly see the direction to go forward. Here, I invite you to jot down the facts about yourself, your family, your fears, and your struggles through the years to remember what gives you joy, what your favorite things to be, do, and have are. You'll then reflect on all that you have just recalled and documented and what that means to you now. Don't let the space on the pages confine you. Feel free to use these prompts as a starting place and continue your journaling in a notebook or on your computer. The prompts are meant to get you out of your head and into your heart. Take the time to complete these exercises.

PART II focuses on clarifying your path and your beliefs in the most important areas of your life: your personal life, including health and fitness, emotional and spiritual aspects; your relationships, romantic or otherwise; and your professional life, which covers your career, financial situation, and leadership role. This will help clarify where you are, your goals, and the direction of your life. It will help measure your growth, reinforce your values and your vision. Learning new ways of thinking, doing, and being is imperative for personal growth and wellness. However, too much unfocused information is overwhelming and usually cannot be implemented in any meaningful way. To make real change, information comes first, action second.

PART III is where the magic happens. Now you are aware of your thoughts, beliefs, and behaviors and can move into changing the false limitations you've placed upon yourself or were ingrained in you. Having clarified your past and your path, you now have usable information to create new empowering thoughts, beliefs, and behaviors and pave the way to clarify your legacy. Now you know for sure what you want in life and how to go about achieving your life aspirations.

PART IV invites you to repair and let go of the past as you create a working action plan for lasting, meaningful change. You have gained clarity about your dreams and your vision. It's time to set clear, realistic goals and actionable steps, make commitments, and follow through on your plan. Moving through your journey has helped you understand why you want to make these meaningful changes and the benefits of making them as well as how you can go about creating a fulfilled life. Finally, you can celebrate your wins and write your new, beautiful story, one that is aligned with your wishes and that brings you joy.

There are worksheets throughout the book for taking notes and journaling your thoughts, inspirations, and the progress you make. Write down whatever comes up so you may revisit your revelations at any time. You'll be so glad you did, as these exercises are a window to what you hold deep inside.

After each chapter, take a few minutes to pause and reflect. Take time to immerse yourself in positive affirmations. Feel free to skip or add others that feel authentic and resonate with you. Add feelings to your affirmations.

Affirmations are a simple but powerful tool to invite happiness into your life. They help quiet the constant negative chatter that runs through our minds and give us a happiness boost. Believe whatever you're affirming as if it is already true. Over time and with repetition, your go-to thoughts will become more positive, and you will see a profound shift in your life.

I hope you will visit this book and review your notes often. Highlight the takeaways that have the most meaning for you, and keep it near you to use for a long time. Make a decision and a commitment to change or improve at least one aspect of your life from each lesson in regard to thinking, behavior, or habit.

As you travel through the questions, you will make discoveries about others and yourself. Ultimately, this is a road map to your destination of personal happiness. Will you achieve that state of happiness, self-acceptance, self-confidence, self-esteem, and realize your self-worth? It's really up to you. I can only take you on the journey, but you must walk it. The answers already exist within you; you are the one in control.

If you keep following and stay fully engaged through the process, you will reach a place of love and appreciation of everyone and everything in your life. Every obstacle you've ever encountered will lead you to a profound realization; every person in your life, past and present, every challenge you've faced thus far will begin to make sense to you. My goal is to present you with a new viewpoint, a new reality about how to embrace the past and achieve happiness. You may ignore or skip some details and hold on to former beliefs, or you may fully embrace the validity of the information, factor it into your current perception of reality, and go forth and put it to great use. You have a choice. You hold the key.

Ultimately, this work is about you finding out about, and accepting, the real YOU.

Remember, it's the small steps taken every day that lead to transformative changes, so keep it simple and keep it fun. You really do have all you need within to make incredible, life-enhancing improvements to any and all areas of your life.

THE JOURNEY

Look ahead at your schedule and plan your start date. Try to maintain some sort of consistent routine so there is a flow of thought as you navigate through each chapter to recall and reflect and write down your answers.

It's impossible to do two things simultaneously and do them well. Like a kintsugi master working on a beautiful bowl piecing all the broken parts together, if you want to make something extraordinary, you need to focus all your attention on that task. In that precise moment that the master is delicately and slowly mending the shattered pieces, nothing exists other than him and his bowl. He knows that the resulting beauty lies in the attention he showers on his craft.

Your life is precious. Like the broken bowl, it, too needs your attention and focus as you bring together the broken pieces and shattered fragments—the hurt, pain, and brokenness—to create a beautiful work of art. What was broken is now beautiful. What was painful is now inspiring. What has suffered is now strong. The bowl is a projection of your soul, creativity, and mind. The texture of the bowl is a reflection of the journey through your history, through the spirituality of your life, and through all your relationships.

Contemplate this journey with the excitement of someone witnessing the birth of something unique. Fire, earth, and air come together, and with time, dedication, and patience you can at last see the result of all your work, love where you are and where you are going.

Before you start your journey, do the following:

- Set aside some quiet time and give undivided attention to experience maximum results.
- Turn off all distractions; find a private and quiet place and write down whatever immediate answers come up.

- Don't overanalyze or rationalize your answers. Think of and write down anything that comes to mind; don't edit, don't second-guess. The first answer that comes to mind is probably the best.
- Be specific whenever you can. Precise details will add authenticity and make your story come alive.
- Over time, some details get fuzzy, and even your most poignant memories can be contaminated by what you hear others say. This is not about what others have said. It's about retaining all the facts you need to trigger vivid recall. Because you lived them. You were there.
- Take time at the end of each group of questions to contemplate. Then answer the key questions in "Reflections."
- There is no need to rush. Take your time. There is no deadline, no alarm clock.
- Allow yourself no excuses. Keep going, no matter what! Yes, you can complete the process.
- The questions have been grouped together for a reason. Don't skip any since it will defeat the purpose.
- Choose a specific area to focus on daily.
- Commit to reading and working on at least a few pages daily at a specific time each day.
- Take notes using the worksheets provided in this book—you may be surprised how useful this is and how much you'll implement when you take the time to write down what comes up.
- Review your notes briefly and often.

- Commit to making at least one change in the next thirty days—you'll be clear on which change *that* will be once you've chosen your path.
- Be good to yourself and treat yourself compassionately throughout the process.
- Find a partner, ideally someone who's also working through the book to do the exercises with you (if that feels comfortable).

You hold in your hands an excellent means for preserving memories and discovering those aspects of yourself that you were perhaps not consciously aware of. Trust that the information you uncover will in some way lead to a greater sense of peace about yourself. Know that whatever you discover about yourself, you can handle with ease and acceptance.

Now you have the opportunity to meet the younger you, to know who you were and what your world was like. Let this book be your guide in expanding your awareness, as a catalyst to making positive shifts in your life, in your relationships, in your wealth, and in deepening your connection with your inner world and with the Divine. Let it serve not only as a source of information but for meditation as well and as a guide to steer you to take the steps so necessary and rewarding to make your life all that it can be. The answers will take you by the hand and lead you to where you want to go.

You will feel a sense of freedom as you journey inward to discover your authentic self, to discover hidden fears, and to gain a better understanding of who you really are, your values, your natural talents and abilities, your passions, what empowers you, inspires you, and what you truly love!

You will reach a place where your relationships will improve as you become more comfortable with yourself. Now you care less what others think of you, you don't need their approval, and the wrong people will leave your life creating space for the right ones to appear.

By looking inward, you harness your true capabilities and are able to tap into your natural talents and unique gifts you were born with and pursue a career that is more aligned with your passion, one that makes you happy.

Self-awareness contributes not only to improved mental health but also better physical health. You will begin to value yourself and take better care of your body, get out more, and function from a strong desire to give your body what it truly needs.

Thank you for making the decision to take care of you this year and for years to come. Changing one behavior, one thought, one belief can dramatically affect your life. Why? Because when we start taking action in a positive direction—even if it's just a small act—we begin to feel the benefits and become aware of what feels good. We feel empowered and realize that we are the ultimate decider and motivator in any situation or circumstance.

Make this fun, and remember, be kind to yourself. You are doing something magical!

Are you ready to clear your past so you can love your present? Are you ready to gather all the shattered and scattered pieces of your life and make them into a beautiful whole, to fix your wounds and heal your heart? Are you ready to fill your cracks with gold?

Are you ready to live the kintsugi life?

Let's begin.

PART I

IT'S ALL ABOUT YOU

PART I

INTRODUCTION

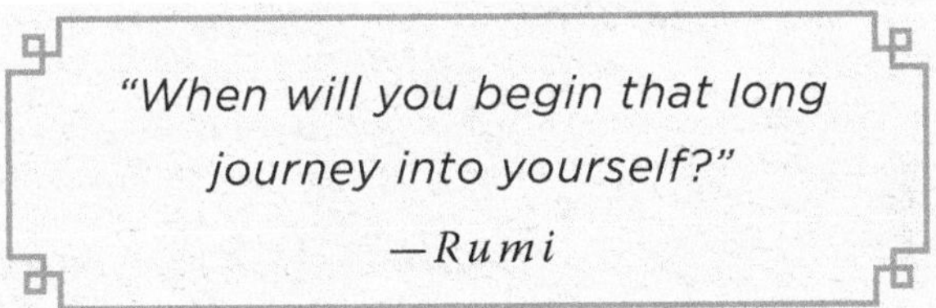
"When will you begin that long journey into yourself?"
—*Rumi*

Do you remember everything that happened to you before you were six years old? Well, science has proven that your subconscious mind does. Isn't that remarkable?

Every cartoon character, every song on the radio, every conversation you overheard your parents having at that time, all that got soaked into your mind like water into a sponge.

And what was the result?

A collection of dormant beliefs that have silently, but profoundly, influenced your ability to manifest abundance, wealth, and success in all areas of your life.

These same beliefs are also the reasons that you sometimes feel stuck in life. They are the reasons you feel at times like YOU are your own worst enemy, that YOU sabotage your own success. The big questions, then, are what kind of beliefs were implanted in you? How exactly are they blocking your success?

This is what you want to find out. These are what you're about to change by revisiting the past.

As little children, we believed that there were quick fixes for everything. If we pricked our fingers, if we bumped our heads even slightly, if we fell and saw tiny scars barely left on the surface of our skin, we reached for comfort from our parents and caretakers. Whether it's an old scar, a new scar, a blue scar, or a red scar, in a child's mind it can somehow be fixed. As we grow older, it's the emotional wounds that stick with us, and no matter how hard we try and suppress them, they continue to persist. Now, *we* must take full responsibility to fix these wounds.

Have you ever found yourself instinctively reacting to certain situations, saying certain things, giving into certain habits, or making certain choices that almost immediately leave you frustrated and disappointed in yourself and make you wonder, *why the heck did I do that?* It's not surprising seeing that these uncontrollable impulses are almost always caused by the subconscious triggers implanted in your mind from childhood, usually by parents, mentors, or friends who probably meant well and may not have even realized what they were doing.

What's most dangerous about such things is that they work in the background like a computer virus so you're not even aware that they're there or how they are holding you back and sabotaging your actions and successes.

Far too many people live a life without ever finding out about the "Unknown." The *Unknown* is a byproduct of experiencing the breakthrough that comes from getting to know yourself. There's a moment of epiphany when you go through your past, face your vices, your fears, your deep, limiting beliefs that have been stored deep in your heart and mind that have been holding you back. The challenge is that very few people are willing to take time out of their lives to experience breakthroughs that lead them to realize what their potential is.

Can you imagine living a life without ever knowing *your* full potential?

How many wounds and bruises have you covered in your life? How are you living in denial even today? Are you waiting for someone to tell you you're worthy? That you're deserving? Are you stuck in the limiting belief that you are not good enough? These are some of the questions I invite you to ask yourself.

As you grow in awareness, you will better understand why you feel what you feel and why you behave as you behave. This understanding gives you the opportunity and freedom to change those things you'd like to change about yourself and create the life you want. Without knowing who you are, self-acceptance and change are impossible.

In *Part I*, I invite you to go deep within to record the unique facts of your life history about yourself, your parents, your siblings, and those who were responsible for raising you as well as those you considered family.

Now, you are asked to revisit your life from your very beginning through the journey of childhood, adolescence, and young adulthood. With deliberate effort, names and events can be brought to the surface of your consciousness. Poignant bits of your past will pop up naturally as you track down the facts for your journal, and your senses will be heightened as you recall sounds, tastes, and smells associated with your past. Examples of these past sensual memories might include the perfume your mother wore, old nursery songs you sang, the sound of rustling leaves in your backyard, the warmth of the sun on your back as you played with your siblings, and so on.

What do you remember most about the way your body changed? If you are a woman, what do you remember about your first period? If you are a man, what do you remember about your voice changing? What was your relationship with your parents like during your teen years? Did you argue with them? On other fronts, did you face peer pressure to play hooky? Did you experience the wonder and exhilaration of falling in love for the first time?

Teen friendships, rejections, failures, and successes that had such a profound impact when you were growing up all of a sudden may not seem like such a big deal now. Adolescence no doubt brought with it an ambush of physical, emotional, and social changes, academic and social pressures. As you recall the teenager you once were, be gentle and kind to yourself and muster the courage to write candidly about the good and the not-so-wonderful times.

Walking back into your story, facing past disappointments and failures can be emotional to say the least. Our brains are hardwired to protect us, and that often makes us want to run, fight, hide out, and even blame others. On the flip side, recalling the wonderful, bygone days makes us nostalgic enough to want to reach out to those who made those times special. For help on this journey, talk to those you grew up with about the old days and compare notes so you can fill in the blanks.

As you describe yourself, try to be detached and see yourself as a stranger would see you and don't be critical. Accept the small and large details that make you unique and practice objectivity and self-acceptance. You are an individual and have your own naturally endowed gifts, unique physical traits, and mannerisms that are unlike anyone else in the world. Your life experiences, the choices you've made, your skills, habits, personal style, and quirks are shining expressions of the person you've chosen to be today. So make this an exercise in appreciating your individuality.

Then, as you pull up memories about your family, be generous with the details and don't hesitate to include your personal opinions. Record any sentiments, secrets, observations, behaviors, acts of kindness or lack thereof, and include any skepticism you may have, but do not leave anything out. Reminiscing often brings clarity. If you can't remember certain areas of your past, leave blank spaces and come back to them later.

Now may be a good time to organize a family reunion and get your answers! It may even be fun for you to research and get a clear picture by asking your family members to fill in the gaps.

Once you have a *before* snapshot of where you came from, what you experienced and lived through, you will have gained full awareness, recognition, and control of key areas of your life. Your journey into your successful future is then assured as you now make better and smarter decisions.

Analyze your way to a better YOU—and a brighter future!

"There is a candle in your heart, ready to be kindled. There is a void in your soul, ready to be filled. You feel it, don't you?"

—Rumi

CHAPTER ONE

Appreciating Your Individuality

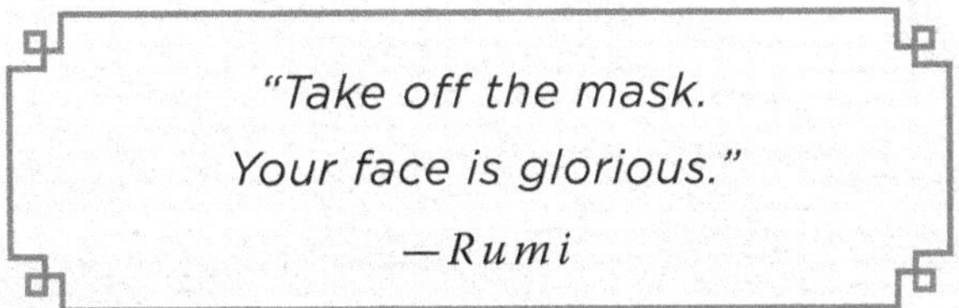

If I were to ask you *who are you,* how would you describe yourself?

You would likely have to refer to your own history, to a past that you've lived through and to which you are undoubtedly tied from which you find it difficult to escape. The question *who are you?* begs for facts about your life, the self-descriptors that are a part of you today.

Your mannerisms and physical appearance may have been inherited, but your life choices—your absolute favorite things to do, to have, to be—have made you who you are. They've shaped your character, personal style, skills, and preferences. You are unique, much more than a blueprint. There is no one like you in this whole wide world.

This is an exercise in appreciating and accepting your uniqueness, the large and small details that make you, YOU.

The answers to *who am I?, why am I here?, and where am I going?* may emerge through your responses to the prompts in this chapter.

As you describe yourself, try to see yourself with objectivity and self-acceptance. Don't be critical.

1. What is your full given name?

2. Who chose that name?

3. How do you like to be called?

4. Do you know who you're named after? Is there a significance or story to it?

5. How did you feel about your name growing up? How about now?

6. What's your current address?

7. Your current age: .... Height: .... Weight: ....

8. Date of birth: .... Place of birth: ....

9. Hair color: .... Eye color: ....

10. Distinguishing marks (such as birthmarks, tattoos, scars, moles):

....

....

11. Astrological sign: ....

12. Current profession: ....

13. Education: ....

14. What is your approximate annual income? ....
    a. Are you making more money than you expected to? ....
    b. Did you always think you would make more money? ....

15. What number of hours do you spend working each week? ....
    a. Are you happy with the time you spend? ....
    b. Do you wish it were less? ....

16. Do you own a pet? What kind? If you don't, would you like to own one?

....

17. Describe your overall physical appearance and your body parts:

Face: ....

Eyes: ....

Nose: ....

Lips: ....

Hair: ....

Nails: ....

Feet: ....

Legs: ....

18. What mannerisms distinguish you (the way you talk, some quirky habits)?

....

....

19. What is your signature style (way of dressing, accessories)?

....

....

20. Describe the following:

a. your favorite piece of clothing: ....
b. your favorite watch: ....
c. the perfume, cologne, or after-shave lotion you wear: ....
d. the car you drive or your favorite car: ....
e. your favorite flower: ....
f. your favorite smell: ....
g. favorite bedtime story: ....
h. favorite song or rhyme: ....

i. a taste that makes you melt: ....

j. a drink you often order: ....

k. your favorite dessert: ....

l. your favorite time of day: ....

m. your favorite room/ place in your house: ....

n. favorite color: ....

o. favorite TV show: ....

p. favorite actor: ....

q. favorite actress: ....

r. favorite hobby: ....

s. favorite singer: ....

21. What are some things you hide about yourself?

....

....

....

....

22. What is your best physical feature?

....

23. What's the most important thing on your nightstand?

....

24. What's hanging on your walls?

....

25. What is your most-prized possession?

....

26. What is your one strangest possession?

....

27. What occupies your time?

....

28. What's one book you love and highly recommend?

....

29. Which author has affected you the most?

....

30. Which magazine or newspaper do you prefer to read the most?

....

31. Which artist do you respect and admire most?

....

32. What's your favorite sport? Do you enjoy watching it or playing it?

....

33. What's one movie that you could watch over and over again?

....

34. What's your favorite city that you visited? What was so special about it?

....

35. What is your favorite country that you visited/ explored? What was so special about it?

....

....

36. Five things you absolutely love:

1. ....
2. ....
3. ....
4. ....
5. ....

37. Five things you dislike:

1. ....
2. ....
3. ....
4. ....
5. ....

38. What's your favorite motto, one you live by?

....

....

39. List the addresses of the three main residences you've lived in:

1. ....

   ....
2. ....

   ....
3. ....

   ....

40. What distinguishing features do you recall that were special in the neighborhoods you lived in?

41. List and describe places you've visited or vacationed at:

a. Which ones did you go to with family?

b. Which ones did you go to for business?

c. Which ones did you go to solo?

d. Which ones were most pleasurable? Why?

e. Which ones stand out most in your memory? Why?

....

....

f. Which ones caused you anxiety or displeasure? Why?

....

....

....

....

42. What is the first and last name of your very first best friend?

....

a. How did you meet and become friends?

....

....

....

....

b. Are you still friends? If not, why not?

....

....

....

....

43. Who is your best friend now?

....

a. What is she/he like?

....

....

b. How long have you known each other?

....

44. What's the earliest memory you have of yourself as a child?

45. Who babysat you and what were they like?

46. How did you view life when you were young?

47. Were you emotionally attached to an object such as a stuffed animal or a favorite blanket that brought comfort to you? Did you give it a name?

48. What was your favorite toy or game that you wish you still had today? Why?

49. Describe your first day in nursery school or kindergarten.

50. Do you remember an incident as a child that caused you to never do something, say something, or feel something ever again?

51. What scared you the most—the dark, clowns, that there might be something/someone in the attic or under the bed—and how did you overcome that fear?

52. What are your fondest memories about your childhood?

53. Name a smell that reminds you of your childhood.

54. Is there a memory you are still haunted by from your childhood? What is it?

55. Describe a time you felt especially valued and loved.

56. What was your proudest moment as a child and who did you share this moment with?

57. What were your three favorite books to read as a child?

1. ....
2. ....
3. ....

58. What were you really into when you were younger but now think is silly?

....

....

59. If you could change one thing about your childhood, what would that be?

....

....

....

60. What do you truly regret not doing? How would it have changed who you are today?

....

....

....

....

....

....

REFLECTIONS

Contemplate where you're at now.

Your busy life and constant stimulation by the external environment can leave you out of touch with yourself. Being constantly on the go provides a real challenge to step away long enough and take a good look at your inner world. Do you take the time to nourish yourself, to feed your mind, your soul? Do you meditate, exercise, and eat healthy? Pause and reflect on this and make a daily commitment to take steps, no matter how small, to nurture your being. Your mind is a profound device. It is capable of expanding your experience of life. Make your mind your friend.

How do you feel about your body? Perhaps your body looks different than you would prefer; maybe it's not quite as energetic, comfortable, or as youthful as you would like, or performs as well as you would wish. However, none of those conditions should prevent you from appreciating what a gift your body is. Are you grateful for your body? Your body deserves your gratitude. It lets you breathe, move, taste, see, hear, feel, create. It is a vehicle for your Spirit to experience life. Take a few minutes now to feel and reflect on what your body has to offer.

Take time to listen to your whole self. Sit quietly to practice listening for at least ten minutes daily. Your inner world is always trying to tell you something. Pay attention. Stop everything during this time and just be.

It's not easy to go back and recall memories, to confront the past and its limitations. Sometimes, the psyche locks the door to traumatic memories, and push as we might, we just can't get in. But deep listening and tapping into your inner being is a powerful tool that everyone possesses. All the answers you need are within. So take a journey within.

Self-exploration is like working out—uncomfortable at times, yet most rewarding. It gets easier when you're consistent and focused.

1. Sit for ten minutes now and just be with yourself without doing anything; no watching TV, falling asleep, or looking at your phone. Ask yourself, *what am I noticing about myself?* Write down what comes to mind.

....

....

....

....

....

....

....

....

2. What are your gifts? Reflect back to your childhood: What were your favorite things to play, what lit you up, what did you never get tired of doing? As an adult, what subjects light you up today with positive energy? Have you noticed how some people talk about a subject and suddenly they get color in their faces and their posture straightens? Pay attention to what makes *you* light up and write down what that is. This could very well be your gift, or one of them.

....

....

....

....

....

....

....

....

As a child, perhaps one of your favorite things to play was nurse or doctor, and you had a stethoscope and your own medical bag. Now, you may find yourself happy guiding others toward healthy products they should use or wanting to be a caretaker or a nurse. Perhaps your favorite thing to play was school, and you fantasized about being a schoolteacher one day. If teaching others energizes you, it is your gift!

There is genius in all of us. Find your inner genius!

Remember to pay attention to how your body feels and notice what lifts you up and what drains you. Try it and see what you discover about YOU.

Once you pinpoint your gifts and start living them, you'll feel your vibration increase and your life become happier, even your health will start improving. At that higher, happier vibe, notice all the wonderful people, things, and situations you attract into your life!

3. **What's in the memory box of your heart?** How do you see yourself? What do you believe about your own value and significance? Answer the following:

    a. What is your ideal identity? *I want to be perceived as:*

    ....

    ....

    ....

    ....

    b. What are your unwanted identities? *I do NOT want to be perceived as:*

4. If people label you and reduce you to the identities they believe of you, they may miss the opportunity to know how complex you are. *I have many strengths, including:*

5. What are your self-descriptors? Are they neat little labels you've accumulated over a lifetime? Do you have a list of self-definitions you use on a regular basis? They could be tags such as: "I'm shy," "I'm clumsy," "I'm forgetful," "I'm not a good writer," "I can't dance," and a whole slew of additional "I ams" that you may not even be consciously aware you've been using. Write down a typical list of thirty "I ams" that you often use to describe yourself.

1.

2.

3.

4.

5. ....

....

6. ....

....

7. ....

....

8. ....

....

9. ....

....

10. ....

....

11. ....

....

12. ....

....

13. ....

....

14. ....

....

15. ....

....

16. ....

....

17. ....

....

18. ....

....

19. ....

....

20. ....

....

21. ....

....

22. ....

....

23. ....

....

24. ....

....

25. ....

....

26. ....

....

27. ....

....

28. ....

....

29. ....

....

30. ....

....

Now go back and alongside each "I am," substitute with such sentences as, "Until today, I've chosen to be that way but . . . ", "I used to label myself as . . . , but . . . ."

You've grown accustomed to your self-definitions, but now you'll become more mindful about what you say about yourself to yourself and to others about yourself. Here are some steps to take:

a. Eliminate negative descriptors after the words "I am" (e.g., *not, won't, can't*, etc.) wherever you can and substitute with empowering words such as *I am talented, I am loved, I am successful.*

b. Let those close to you know what you're working on, and ask them to remind you whenever you slip back into your old ways.

c. Set behavioral goals to act differently. For example, if you are shy in public gatherings, introduce yourself to one person you may have otherwise avoided.

d. Keep a journal on your daily efforts—successes or setbacks—in eliminating your negative "I ams."

e. Each day for forty consecutive days, work on eliminating at least one negative belief about yourself.

f. Find something you've never done and set aside an afternoon for that activity. This will create new neural pathways in the brain and change your negative "I ams" to positive ones.

g. Change the following four sentences in your vocabulary permanently:

From	To
"That's me."	"That was me."
"I can't help it."	"I can change that if I work on it."
"I've always been that way."	"I'm going to be different."
"That's my nature."	"That's what I believed was my nature."

AFFIRMATIONS

Each day, repeat the following affirmations. Affirmations should be in the present tense and not based in the future. They should read, "I am" not "I will," and must have power and feelings attached to them. Visualize as you declare the words so you can picture already living what you affirm.

1. I love and accept myself just as I am.
2. I am grateful for my body.
3. My body is a vehicle for my Spirit to experience life.
4. I love and appreciate my body.
5. I honor and care for my body.
6. I delight in moving, stretching, and working my body.
7. I invite myself to fully experience everything I feel.
8. I thank my mind for its efforts to protect me.
9. Today I listen with my whole self.
10. I choose to stay in faith, focus on the good, and keep the right perspective.
11. I choose to live this day in gratitude, happy and content.
12. Joy fills my entire world.
13. I am surrounded by love. All is well.
14. I speak words of love to those in my life on a regular basis rather than assuming they know how I feel.
15. I look for ways to support the people in my life.
16. I am sensitive to the needs of others.
17. I am willing to adapt my plans and my ways to show respect and bring harmony to my home.
18. I let my family and friends know how valuable they are by giving them my full attention.
19. I attract only those who are in sync with me and who love me unconditionally.
20. Today I choose to give love.

FOOD FOR THOUGHT:
Kintsugi and Happiness

Are you happy?

When you look back over the course of your life, it will not be the successes, the pressure of deadlines, details of the profit and loss sheets, or the escalating cost of everyday living that you'll remember. It'll be the wonderful times you shared with your loved ones, the wonder of watching your children grow up, a special vacation at a beautiful location, the joy of walking on the beach, the first time you heard a favorite piece of music.

Pause and appreciate the beauty around you and the abundance that exists in even the smallest things. Even in times of crisis, look for something that is working in your life. Listen to what you are saying about yourself. What thoughts are constantly playing in your mind? Make sure your internal dialogue is working to your benefit.

Ask yourself, *what's right about my life?* not, *what's wrong with my life?*

We spend so much time thinking about what we are missing, what we have to get to make us happy. Life can pass us by if we constantly wait for the better job, a nicer house, more money, a more attractive partner, or a better car that we forget to live.

Live each moment, for tomorrow is promised to no one. Adopt a champion's attitude and mind-set and monitor your internal dialogue so you can achieve a healthy self-image that will cause you not only to rise higher but also inspire those around you to live at their best. Just as a stone tossed into a pond sends ripples across the water, your actions, words, and behavior also affect those closest to you.

Capture your memories in a journal. Tune into the here and now. A journal is a great tool to remind yourself daily to pay attention to the present. Reveal what you truly feel and don't edit, don't hold back. Get into the habit of writing down, drawing, or painting in your journal; express your thoughts and feelings in colors that capture those moments when you've felt alive, content, or joyful.

There may be instances when some of the things that brought you joy turn out to be a source of sadness as you recall times gone by. Go ahead and capture the moment while it's fresh so you can remember how you felt that day and treasure the memory. Have that be the prompt you need to shift your focus to a happy thought.

Applaud yourself. Applaud even the smallest accomplishments. Don't wait for others to validate you—validate yourself. There's always something good you can find about yourself if you look for it. Be your own cheerleader. Stop focusing on the wrong. As you begin reminding yourself of all the things you do right, your attitude will change, and before you know it, you'll start thinking, *I am pretty good!*

Each night before you go to bed, write down five things you are grateful for. They could be as simple as the bed you sleep in, the running water, your neighbor, your eyes that see, your ears that hear.

Start a *Joy Journal* and each day this year note down five things that have brought you joy. These could be as simple as something that made you smile, an act of kindness you experienced or heard about, an activity you enjoyed, a beautiful walk in nature, a butterfly. Try to express how you felt at that moment and add pictures you may have taken of the moment.

Appreciate your life. Take time to consider all the nonmaterial things that you have to be grateful for: your loved ones in your life; those who make you smile, laugh, feel loved, feel alive, and happy; music that moves you; the joy of a kiss; places you've visited; the air you breathe. Every day, look for five different things to appreciate. Remember, what you appreciate, appreciates you back.

The present moment is all you have. So don't waste another minute. Take all the scattered pieces and happy memories and piece them together. Use the kintsugi method to connect them with lacquer and polish them with gold. Make your happiness bowl whole again and allow it to be illuminated to show off its beauty and become part of your daily life.

Be happy.

"Everything that is made beautiful and fair and lovely is made for the eye of one who sees."

—Rumi

WHAT I WANT TO REMEMBER FROM THIS CHAPTER

DATE: ....

KEY POINTS: ....

....

....

....

....

....

....

....

....

....

....

TAKEAWAYS: ....

....

....

....

....

....

....

....

....

....

....

AUG 19 - 22

CHAPTER TWO

Memories of Your Family

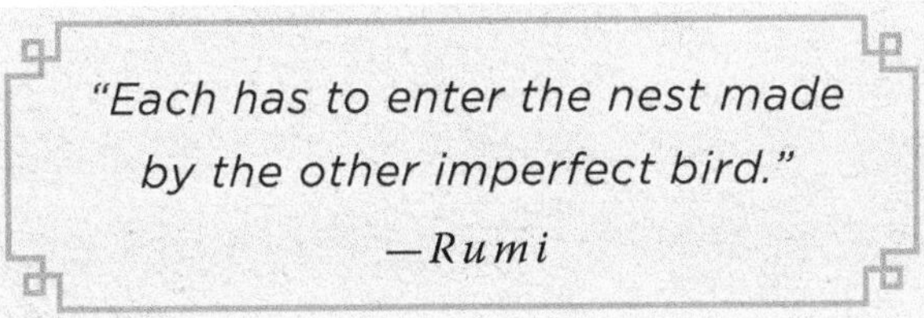

"Each has to enter the nest made by the other imperfect bird."
—*Rumi*

It's true that we don't get to choose the family we are born into. We are born where we are born out of pure chance. We don't get to choose our parents or our family environment, but we do get to choose how hard we're willing to work in order to make the best of what we're given.

We came into this world as blank slates and were shaped largely by those who took the responsibility to feed, shelter, and raise us. Our life course was set in motion by those we called our parents or guardians.

The quest for love and happiness begins in childhood where the close bond between baby and mother is instinctive, overwhelming, and based on survival. The kind of loving we receive influences the way our brain is wired and helps form our character. It has an impact on the choices we make in our teenage and adult years and the sort of relationships we forge.

In the early stages of life, love is all about looking for points of similarity and connection through constant communication. Personal differences and preferences are overlooked and even modified. Happiness is easily achieved through a simple exchange of a look or a kiss. But at some point, usually around the age of seven, the rhythm changes and real life comes into play, opinions are formed, and choices and compromises have to be made.

If we grew up in a family where criticism was the norm, then we're going to be critical as adults. If we grew up in a family where we were not allowed to express anger, then we are probably terrified of anger and confrontation. If we were raised in a family where we were manipulated by guilt, then we're probably going to behave the same way as adults and feel we have to be manipulative in some way to get what we want. As we grow up, we begin to live these false ideas and lose touch with our inner wisdom.

What was *your* childhood like? What did you learn from watching your mom and dad when you were growing up? Did they have a dynamic, loving relationship filled with passion? Did money come to them with grace and ease, or was it hard for them to earn a living? Were your parents happy and fulfilled? Or did they put their happiness on the backburner to take care of the family?

And how was the dynamic of your family? Was there a lot of love and laughter? Did you feel somewhat controlled and judged? What about anger, resentment, and blame? Were those emotions a big part of the equation?

What kind of family did you grow up in? Was it a great family where everyone was respected, where there was quality communication, trust and collaboration, where everyone's independence was valued?

Or did you grow up in a family that by all outward appearances was an ideal one, a role model in everyone's eyes except yours, the kind that deep down has all the characteristics of a toxic family? Were your family relationships about domination and submission, where children are there to satisfy the needs, egos, or the psychopathic deviancy of their elders, where envious and abnormal motivations were the norm?

Perhaps yours was a temporarily toxic family where certain specific circumstances, such as job loss, illness, or separation and divorce changed the trajectory of the family relationships to become chronically toxic, and consequently there was loss of balance and respect. If so, some siblings were brought up in a healthy environment and others in a toxic one, and because of that divergence, there was lack of empathy and understanding among family members.

It's possible that you are the most fortunate person in the world and had a wonderful family. In that case, congratulations! However, I assure you that for every happy family, there are thousands that are unhappy.

I ask these questions because what I've seen over the years is that the old paradigm of family creates a lot of pain and suffering for many and can leave indelible imprints. If after answering my questions, you see that there was some dysfunction in your family of origin, then there's a chance that you still have dysfunction in your life and possibly in your own family now.

Regardless of what type of hurts you may or may not carry from childhood, your journey is unique to you. Even when we face what appears to be the exact same type of loss or trauma as someone else, our experience is likely to be very different. This is because each person's personality, history, belief system, patterns of response, and emotional and psychological makeup are different. What completely shatters one person may be a minor setback to another and vice versa. Be gentle on yourself because comparing your experience to someone else's or basing it on societal norms—dealing with grief, for example—is counterintuitive.

Everyone has family patterns, and it's very easy to blame our parents, our family, and those we were surrounded with in our childhood for the present condition of our lives.

Your first step to overcoming your personal imprints is to know what they are. Awareness is the first step in the creation process. Your limiting beliefs become so ingrained in your psyche that it becomes almost impossible to move beyond them if you don't consciously bring them into your awareness and face them head on.

One of the most valuable gifts of this journey you're on is that as you do the work, you will heal from your experience of brokenness and heartache and emerge with a greater sense of compassion for others who are also hurting. But as valuable as this gift of empathy is, we must remember that each of us heals in our own way and at our own pace. Patience is key. We do more harm than good when we try to speed up our own or someone else's healing.

Like broken pieces of ceramic, no two damaged people are exactly alike. We break how we break and must likewise heal the way we need to heal. What matters is that we choose to do what is necessary to heal so that we can find and treasure the gold in the healing. All other methods are useless.

As little children, we are like seeds that thrive when placed in the right conditions. A seed is actually dormant if it remains tucked away in a drawer, but it is full of tremendous potential when planted in the right soil and given the water and nutrients it needs.

The same is true for the seeds inside you. Regardless of the family environment you were born into, you are full of tremendous potential. All you have to do is change your internal environment to allow the seeds to grow so they produce the harvest they were intended to produce. The seeds lie dormant until they are planted in the soil of your mind.

As you go through this chapter, I encourage you to open your mind and heart to allow your seeds to be brought to fruition. Your mature self will get an opportunity to meet the younger you, to expand your awareness of the present, and connect your past with the now. Your mature self will help you discover hidden aspects of yourself, clarifying the role each family member played in your life. This is a reminder to you of how much you've grown. By recalling your personal history, you have the opportunity to cultivate the seeds that may have been dormant.

Memories are fragile and often easily muddled. Over time, details can get fuzzy, and even your most poignant memories can be contaminated by what you hear others say. This chapter will set the record straight and help you retain the facts you need to trigger vivid recall. You know because you were there.

Begin to get to know yourself, discover and explore yourself to know what you're capable of. During the most vulnerable years of your life, people may have ignored you; overlooked your achievements and punished you; made you believe that you weren't capable; that you didn't know how to do things or which steps to take; and that you were worthless. All that would have wreaked havoc on your self-confidence, self-esteem, and self-worth.

Now you can reconcile with your grievances. Stop being afraid, stop worrying, stop running away without looking back. It's time to analyze instead of reacting. Your capacity for analysis is your best resource. Analyze people and learn to discern who you need to stay away from, who you should adopt a prudent and cautious attitude toward, and who to selectively share your life with. Holding onto past grievances is not the solution. When we hold onto our grievances, we are the ones who suffer because now we've given the situations and the people in our lives power over us and allowed these same situations and people to keep us mentally enslaved.

Sometimes, it's difficult to forgive because we see others as unworthy of being forgiven. Ask yourself, *does your condemnation accomplish anything or have any constructive effect whatsoever?* If not, see your condemnation for what it is, a waste of energy that corrupts your peace of mind.

Make up your mind to let go of all past hurts, to set yourself free from the needless cycle of pain, anger, and recrimination that keeps you imprisoned in your own suffering and prevents you from creating positive, affirming relationships with yourself and others. You are worthy of your love. Like self-worth, your worthiness of love is a fact. You are love and you are loved.

Your brothers and sisters, your parents and those close to you are worthy not only of your forgiveness but also of your love. Start making a conscious effort to love those who are easy to love, and then stretch a little more each day. As love moves through you with greater ease, your capacity increases, and you can begin to love even those who challenge you.

To rise beyond the limitations imposed by one's family requires inner work. Therefore, in the spirit of taking 100 percent responsibility for your life, it's important to take this journey within, to be willing to face your past, to practice self-acceptance, and to drop habits that no longer serve you.

Your collection of memories—some good, some not so good; some sentimental, some challenging; naughty anecdotes, acts of kindness—will become treasured and priceless gifts to be recorded for posterity. Regardless of your childhood, welcome all observations.

As you describe your family in this section, see them as a stranger would and state only the facts. Be as specific as you can when you answer the questions. Use both first and last names whenever possible. Try for as many exact dates, locations, addresses, and names as possible. This will give you an opportunity to know who you were and what your world was like. It will create a stream of information that is your life, your portrait, the person you were, and the person you are choosing to become all rolled up into one. Precise details will add authenticity and make your story come alive.

Your Father and His Family

1. Your father's full name: ....

2. Date of birth: ....

3. When and where was he born? ....

4. What does/did he do for a living? ....

....

5. What does/did he do for fun? ....

....

....

6. What are/were his skills or special talents?

....

....

7. Where is he now? ....

8. What do you know about his early upbringing?

....

....

....

9. Who were his siblings and what were they like as children? ....

....

....

....

10. What were the names of your paternal grandparents?

11. When and where were they born?

12. Did you know your paternal grandparents? If so, what do you remember about them?

13. Where did your paternal grandparents live when your dad was growing up?

14. What did they do for a living?

15. How much time did you spend with your paternal grandparents, and how involved were they in your upbringing?

16. What family legends do you know about? (Did they immigrate to this country? Did they do something that was out of the ordinary/memorable?)

....

....

....

....

....

17. Are there any secrets or skeletons lurking in your paternal family's closet? If so, describe.

....

....

....

....

Your Mother and Her Family

1. Your mother's full name: ....

2. Date of birth: ....

3. Your mother's maiden name: ....

4. When and where was she born? ....

5. What sort of work, if any, did she do before she was married? ....

....

6. What are/were her skills or special talents?

....

....

7. What are/were her favorite things to do?

....

....

....

8. Where is she now? ....

9. What were the names of your maternal grandparents?

....

....

10. When and where were they born?

....

....

11. Where did they live when your mom was growing up?

....

....

12. What did they do for a living? ....

....

13. How well did you know them? ....

....

14. How much time did you spend with your maternal grandparents and how involved were they in your upbringing? ....

....

....

15. What do you know about your mother's early upbringing? ....

....

....

16. Who were her siblings and what were they like as children? ....

....

....

....

17. What family legends do you know about? (Did they immigrate? Did they do something that was out of the ordinary/memorable?)

....

....

....

....

18. Are there any secrets or skeletons lurking in your maternal family's closet? Describe.

....

....

....

Your Siblings

1. How many siblings do you have? List their names and ages:

    1. ....
    2. ....
    3. ....
    4. ....
    5. ....
    6. ....

2. Where are you in the birth order (youngest, oldest, third, fourth)? ....

3. What's your relationship with each of your siblings?

....

....

....

4. Which one of your siblings is your favorite and why?

....

....

5. Which one of your siblings do you resent/don't get along with and why?

....

....

6. What was/is the biggest challenge in your relationship with your siblings?

....

7. **Do you remember the arrival of any younger siblings? How did you feel?**

8. **Do you believe your parents secretly favored one of your siblings?**

   a. What is your proof for this belief?

   b. How has this "favored status" affected the relationship between you and your parents?

9. **Where do you rank among your siblings in terms of success?**

10. **What traits do you and your siblings share in common?**

11. **What traits do you not share with your siblings?**

12. **Who in your family was considered to be:**

a. the black sheep? ....
b. creative? ....
c. high maintenance? ....
d. well behaved? ....
e. Mommy and Daddy's favorite? ....
f. smart? ....
g. good looking? ....

13. **How accurate were these labels?** ....

....

14. **What other labels were assigned to specific family members?** ....

....

....

15. **How did these labels influence each of them?**

....

....

....

16. **How did the particular label assigned to you influence you?** ....

....

....

Now answer the following questions:

1. Describe each of your parents the way you remember them as a child.

2. What do you know about how your parents met, fell in love, got married? How old were they when they got married?

3. If adopted, what were you told about your birth parents? When and what were you told about your adoption?

4. What have you been told about the first time your parents saw you and the day they brought you home? Were there any celebrations to welcome you (e.g., baptism, naming ceremony, or other family ritual)?

5. What have you gleaned about the circumstances around the time you were born? Were they advantageous or challenging?

6. What can you tell from photographs or memories about the home you were born into (e.g., rooms, crib, baby books, infant clothes, furniture, or other surroundings)? Describe in detail.

7. What kind of home were you raised in? Was it happy, peaceful, sad?

....

....

....

....

....

8. What is your earliest childhood memory?

....

....

....

....

....

....

....

....

9. Describe your best birthday. Describe your worst birthday.

....

....

....

....

....

....

....

....

10. Describe one of your:

a. most peaceful moments:

....

....

b. most embarrassing moments:

....

....

c. angriest moments:

....

....

11. What is your most beautiful memory of your parents? What is your most horrifying/sad memory of your parents?

....

....

....

....

....

....

....

....

....

....

....

12. When you were a child, did your parents spend:

a. enough time with you? ....

b. too much time with you? ....

c. not enough time with you? ....

13. What is/was your family's religious preference?

....

....

14. How often did you attend services, religious trainings, Sunday school, and what was that like?

....

....

....

....

15. Did your mother tell you she loved you enough? Did your father?

....

....

....

16. Do you think you said "I love you" enough to your mother? To your father?

....

....

....

....

17. What one important thing did you learn from each parent?

....

....

....

....

18. What was the biggest challenge in your relationship with each parent?

....

....

....

....

....

....

19. How did each of your parents compliment you? What specifically would he or she say? Did either or both of your parents ever criticize you? What specifically was said?

....

....

....

....

....

....

20. To your best knowledge, how do your parents perceive you today? How do you feel about your parents today?

....

....

....

....

21. If you could change one thing about each of your parents, what would it be?

....

....

22. Write about the memory or story from your childhood that you tend to exaggerate when telling others.

23. What is a routine you still remember from your childhood?

24. Write about your father:

a. I only wish he had:

b. I only wish I had:

25. Write about your mother:

a. I only wish she had:

b. I only wish I had:

26. What are some of the things your parents did that you've never forgiven? What would it take for you to forgive them?

27. Which one of your parents is your greatest role model? Why?

28. Write three traits and actions you most admire or consider positive about each of your parents. Write three traits you most dislike, hate, or consider negative about each of your parents.

29. What have your parents not done or are not doing that you think they could/should have done for you?

30. Which of your parents do you resent the most and least like to be around? Why?

31. What role did each parent play in disciplining your siblings and you, specifically?

32. What role did each parent play in supporting the household finances?

33. What did your parents want you to be growing up?

....

....

34. What was your interpretation of your parents' relationship when you were young?

....

....

....

....

35. What was each of your parent's main advice to you about life?

....

....

....

....

36. How would each of your parents describe the way you were as a child?

....

....

....

....

37. Which of your parents was running your life or burdening you the most?

....

....

38. Which of your parents do you feel left or abandoned you? How do you know that?

....

....

....

....

39. How did your parents react when things got tough at home?

....

....

....

....

....

....

40. Were you lectured, nagged, overprotected when you were little? How?

....

....

....

....

41. What were some things you were forbidden to do growing up?

....

....

....

a. Did you end up doing them anyway? ....
b. Why? ....

....

42. Did either one of your parents let you down when you were growing up? How?

43. Did either of your parents hit you when you were a child? Do you believe hitting a child is an appropriate form of discipline? Have you ever hit your children?

44. What were some unspoken rules you grew up with in your family?

45. If you are an only child, was there something you appreciated or resented growing up?

a. Did you ever discuss this with your parents?

b. How do you think being an only child affected the way you grew up?

46. What aunts, uncles, or cousins played an important role in your life? How? Which of your relatives was your favorite? Describe what they did that was appealing to you.

47. Is there a younger relative who looks up to you?

a. Why?

b. In what ways would you like to mentor or guide him or her?

48. What did your family members always say about you as a child?

a. How is their opinion different now that you are an adult?

b. How accurate or fair are they in your opinion?

49. How would you describe your early home life? (Compare it to a movie or TV sitcom, e.g., The Brady Bunch, Survivor, Friends, A Love Story, etc.)

50. Would you say your father is your friend? Your mother?

51. Who is/are the most important person(s) to you in your family?

a. Are you giving them the attention you want to give?

b. How can you spend more time with them starting today?

52. What are you grateful to your parents for right now?

....

....

....

a. Are you willing to let them know how you feel today? ....
b. What's stopping you? ....

....
c. What do you need to give yourself permission to express your truth? ....

....
d. How do you want to feel? ....

....
e. What's the WORST thing that could happen? ....

....
f. What's the BEST thing that could happen? ....

....
g. What really matters to you? ....

....

53. In what ways do you/would you try to be a better and more loving and caring parent than your parents were to you?

....

....

....

....

54. Are you truly happy today with the way you're showing up in your relationship with:

a. your parents? ....

b. your siblings? ....

c. your children? ....

d. your spouse? ....

55. Have you ever chosen to sever ties with a family member? ....

a. With whom and why? ....

....

b. Would you ever consider reconciliation? ....

c. What would have to happen for you to let go of the resentment? ....

....

d. What would have to happen for that person to deserve your forgiveness? ....

....

56. Did any family member cut you off from his or her life?

a. Explain what happened.

....

....

....

b. Would you accept his or her apology and reconcile? ....

....

c. What would have to happen for you to let go of the resentment? ....

....

d. What would have to happen for that person to forgive you? ....

....

57. Is there any family member with whom you have been too forgiving but who keeps on betraying/hurting you?

a. Who is it? ....
b. What happened? ....

....

c. Why do you think you must keep accepting the person back into your life? ....

....

d. Do you believe it's a lost cause? ....
e. Are you willing to disengage? ....

58. How much do you care about what your family thinks of you? ....

....

59. Do you ever hear your parents' words tumbling from your lips? What are they? What traits of your parents do you appreciate now that you are older?

....

....

....

....

60. If this were the last day of your life, what would you want closure or resolution on with your parents and other family members? How badly do you want this? Are you at peace with your family now? Explain.

REFLECTIONS

If you don't fit in with your family, you have nothing to be ashamed of, so don't feel bad about it. If you don't love your family, that's alright, too. There is no need to beat yourself up about it. You can't live with someone who harms you repeatedly, who is abusive, who steals, is a liar, manipulative, sexist, or homophobic. Don't feel guilty because that guilt that was instilled by your upbringing or your peers is the very thing that will keep you enslaved.

Most people suffer directly or indirectly because of their families, so you are not an exception after all. If others don't understand you or judge you, let it go. You have nothing to justify or explain. Start to write your own destiny, a new story that will empower you. It's time to reprogram your inner dialogue and replace the image you have of yourself. Consider this a huge life lesson that has now allowed you to move forward and be a better person, friend, or parent, someone who is respected and loved. Surround yourself with those who support you and carve out boundaries for those who are toxic.

In life, you will also encounter many parents who try to do their best for their children, but in spite of their efforts, their children still do not *feel* loved. This is heartbreaking indeed. When children don't feel loved, they do poorly in school, don't respond well to discipline, and are filled with anger. Advice from parents and elders is often taken as an affront.

Some parents may mean well but are sometimes controlling and opinionated without even realizing it. No one likes being told what to do. This applies to children and adults. We don't like to be fenced in and restricted. We don't want to be told what to think, what to wear, how to act, and so we retaliate. The resentments and childhood wounds are carried into our adulthood.

There is a young and wounded child in each of us trying to get our attention. The child asks for care and love, but often we do the opposite. We want to end our suffering by sending the child to a deep place inside and want it to stay there as far away as possible because we're afraid of the suffering. We numb ourselves by keeping ourselves constantly entertained—working, socializing, watching TV, using alcohol and drugs, hoping that the child will go away and the wounds will stay invisible. Running away, ignoring the wounded child, and covering the wounds with outside stimuli don't end the suffering; these fruitless efforts only prolong it. This child has been seriously wounded and needs us. Instead, we turn away.

Many wounded children grow up into adults who exhibit similar behaviors and traits to their own children. That's because inside every child is an emotional love tank. When the tank is full—meaning the child feels loved by his or her parents—the child grows up emotionally healthy. But when the love tank is empty, the child will grow up with many internal struggles. Loving children effectively requires parents to express their love in a language the child understands.

Psychologists say it takes ten words of praise to counter a single word of criticism. Are you careful about the way you express disapproval to others? How good are you at giving praise and compliments? Do you ever go out of your way to say nice things to those you love, to thank them for all the things that they do right? Perhaps start there to begin your healing.

Healing childhood wounds can take a lifetime if we let it. But it doesn't have to take that long. Healing these wounds involves a mind shift and a decision. You have a choice, but to make the right choice, you must bring your hurts to the surface and look at the story you've been telling yourself squarely and without bias.

Being stuck in a story for too long is akin to putting a Band-Aid on a problem that persists just so you can patch it and hide it. That is only a temporary solution that makes you strong for specific moments. You're only very *slowly* peeling the bandage off, and that slow process can hurt. The solution, then is to rip off the Band-Aid in one fell swoop so you can stop the pain and start the healing.

For a long-term solution, you must change your story. The six steps listed below will be your guide as you begin writing your new story.

The sense of not belonging in a family is one of the most dangerous hurts there is. It has the power to break hearts, spirits, and diminish self-worth. What does it mean to be a part of a family you "belong" to versus a family you merely "fit-in" with? The first one boosts confidence while the second one depletes it.

Too many of us suppress the past events and circumstances of our childhood because we are afraid that confronting those demons and digging them up will be traumatic and make us accountable. The wounded child is in each cell of our body. We don't need to look far into the past for that child. We only have to look deeply to get in touch with it. But just as the suffering is present in every cell of our body so are the seeds of awakened understanding and happiness. We just have to tap into these through the practice of mindfulness.

If we want to be accepted as we are, we must be willing to accept others as they are. We always wanted our parents to accept us totally, and yet often we are not willing to accept them as they are.

Acceptance is giving everyone, ourselves and others, permission to be authentic. It is arrogant to set standards for others; we can only set standards for ourselves. Even so, these must be more like guidelines than standards. The more we practice self-acceptance, the easier it is to drop habits that no longer serve us. It's easy for everyone to grow and thrive in an atmosphere of love. Let's strive to love others and to forgive past behaviors.

The first step is to learn to love and forgive ourselves.

1. Write a short letter to each of your parents (dead or alive) that they will never read. Share honest or deeply hidden feelings about your childhood experience and the role they played in those primary years of your life. Be honest; write down real thoughts and insights about how you felt they did their job of raising you as a child. Thank them and bless them.

....

....

....

....

....

....

....

....

....

....

....

....

....

....

2. **Write down a memory from your childhood.** A memory that's linked to an emotional state can be anchored to stay fresh indefinitely and further protected against loss. Tie your memory to the following sensory details and include as much feeling as possible:

a. sound: ....

b. taste: ....

c. smell: ....

d. sight: ....

e. touch: ....

f. good feeling: ....

g. bad feeling: ....

3. Call someone who knew you as a child and ask the person what you were like. Write down what you find out.

4. Make a blame list. In your list, detail everything about yourself that you dislike and whom or what you blame for your condition. The list may go like this:

What I dislike about me and my life	Who/What is to blame
I'm too clumsy.	Teacher, mother, heredity
I'm too shy.	Parents, girlfriend, my figure
I'm lousy at mathematics.	Deficient math genes, elementary teacher
I'm unhappy.	Stock market, divorce, illness, economy

Write down twenty things that you blame others for.

What I dislike about me and my life	Who/What is to blame
1.	
2.	
3.	
4.	
5.	
6.	
7.	
8.	
9.	
10.	
11.	

What I dislike about me and my life	Who/What is to blame
12.	
13.	
14.	
15.	
16.	
17.	
18.	
19.	
20.	

Read the list and see if you're any different now that you have appropriately doled out the blame to the precise people and things in your life.

What did you notice? It didn't change a thing. You are exactly the same. Whether someone is to blame or not, you stay exactly as you are unless *you* do something to correct the situation.

This exercise proves to you the futility of blaming others for the conditions of your life. Blame is a waste of time. It's a neat little device that people use whenever they don't want to take responsibility for something in their lives. Focusing on someone else as somehow being responsible for your situation means you're looking at others to determine your values. It makes others more important and powerful than you and sends a message that your own fulfillment is something outside of yourself. Looking outside of you for an explanation of how you should feel or what you should do is living a life of emotional servitude. Real change can only happen when *you* take responsibility for your own life.

5. **Make time for self-reflection.** Look at the life or situation you have now.

    a. What is it that you're dissatisfied with? Write these down. Now ask yourself what steps you can take to change things. When will you begin? Write your plan.

    ....

    ....

    ....

    ....

    ....

    ....

    ....

    ....

    b. What aspects of your life or situation make you happy? Write these down. Now give yourself space to reflect on these and be thankful that you are blessed.

    ....

    ....

    ....

    ....

    ....

    ....

c. What choices have you made in order to achieve what you covet that you now regret? Write these down. Can you find it within you to forgive yourself and move on?

....

....

....

....

....

....

6. Practice self-compassion. Be your own best friend and treat yourself with the same loving kindness and compassion you give to your best friend and family. Be happy in your own skin and accept yourself exactly as you are. Do the following this week:

a. Write a letter to yourself and describe aspects of yourself or your life that you're unhappy with. Explain your feelings fully; don't hold back. No one else will read this letter.

b. Now write a letter as if from an imaginary best friend to you, someone who knows you and understands you completely and is compassionate and fully accepting of your faults. What is this friend saying about the aspects you listed in your letter to yourself?

c. Accept the love and care as you read your friend's letter to you, and try to introduce this love, understanding, and compassion into your life.

AFFIRMATIONS

Using affirmations daily is a powerful way to bring happiness into your life. Affirmations shut down the negative chatter that runs through our minds and give us a happiness boost. Say the following affirmations to rise above family patterns:

1. I bless my family with love.
2. I love and respect my parents and know that they wish only the best for me.
3. My brothers and sisters are worthy of my forgiveness.
4. I allow others to be themselves.
5. I forgive myself for any way I may have obstructed my own happiness and potential.
6. I am worthy of my love.
7. I forgive myself for my fear.
8. I forgive myself for any time I have not treated myself with love and kindness.
9. I forgive myself for attacking the world.
10. My purpose today is to forgive the world.
11. I release the world from my control.
12. I forgive everyone who has ever caused me pain or harm.
13. All my relationships are enveloped in a circle of love.
14. I forgive myself for my anger.
15. I release all old hurts and forgive myself.
16. I let go of old family limitations and awaken to Divine Harmony.
17. All my relationships are harmonious.
18. I have compassion for my parents' childhood.
19. I release all criticism.
20. My heart is open. I speak only loving words.

FOOD FOR THOUGHT:
Kintsugi and Your Story

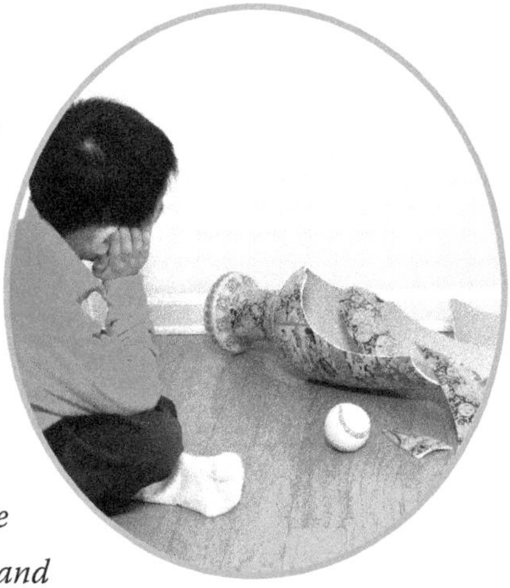

What is your story?

I'd like to share one with you of a child who runs away from home.

The young boy can't stand his mother any longer. She's been nagging him about his tardiness and his behavior for as long as he can remember. He's come to a conclusion that enough is enough, and it's time for him to run away from home for good.

So, off he goes on the road with only a few dollars in his pocket. Very soon, he runs out of the little money he has. Now hungry and cold, he stops by a food stall and begs for a bowl of rice.

The stall owner, a kind old man, gives the young boy a bowl of rice. The boy gulps down the rice in no time and is apparently deeply moved.

"Thank you very much, Sir!" says the boy. "You are so kind, unlike my mother!"

On hearing this, the old man chuckles. "I just gave you a bowl of rice and you thank me so profusely," says the old man. "Your mother has been taking care of you all these years, and you are full of complaints against her."

What the old man says jolts the young boy awake. He realizes all of a sudden that he's been taking the love his mother showered on him for granted. How ungrateful he is! Not only has he not recognized her love, but he has been full of discontent and ingratitude.

Having awakened to this fact, the young boy rushes home. The moment his mother sees him, she starts admonishing again. "Where have you been, you rascal!" she yells.

Everything, however, has changed now. The boy is no longer resentful. His mother's anger is now music to his ears because he realizes she had been worried about him and her anger reveals her underlying concern.

What have you been taking for granted?

Family dynamics are never easy. For some of us, our childhood may have been full of trauma and heartache, and we feel justified to behave as we do. For others, it may have been some things that were said or that we overheard as we were growing up, and we consequently told ourselves that we were not wanted or that we didn't matter.

Whatever the stories about others that we have in our heads, perhaps we can try to walk in their shoes and understand even a little of what they are going through. It may occur to us that they are doing the best they can given what they know and what their own childhood conditioning was.

We've all had the heartbreaking experience of watching a favorite mug or vase inadvertently slip from our hands and shatter on the floor. Maybe you tried to glue some of the pieces together only to realize that it was a lost cause—either too time-consuming or too expensive. Similarly in relationships, we have a tendency for zero tolerance and are inclined to give up. Follow the philosophy of kintsugi and repair your relationships. You may realize that the repaired pieces start to have greater meaning, more character, and become more valuable.

Whatever your story is, make peace with your past. It is time to accept what was and heal yourself, time to pick up all the childhood fragments, piece by piece, and make some sense of them as you put them back together. Like a kintsugi master, seal the cracks and adorn them with gold to create a beautiful masterpiece.

Change your story.

"Don't turn away.
Keep your gaze on
the bandaged place.
That's where the
light enters you."

—Rumi

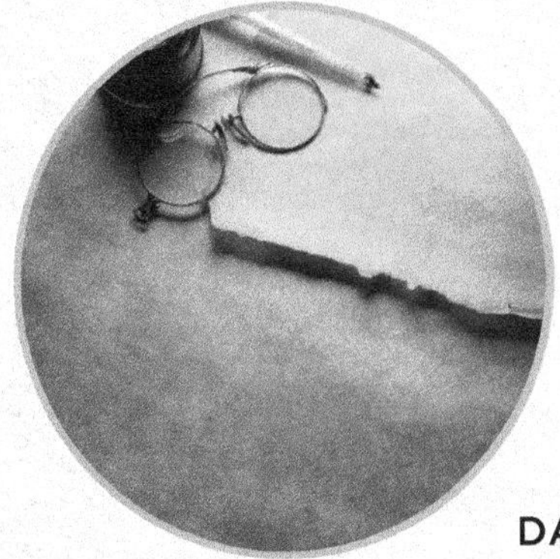

WHAT I WANT TO REMEMBER FROM THIS CHAPTER

DATE: ....

KEY POINTS: ....

....

....

....

....

....

....

....

....

....

TAKEAWAYS: ....

....

....

....

....

....

....

....

....

....

....

CHAPTER THREE

A Vulnerable and Tender Time

> *"Adolescence is a new birth, for the higher and more completely human traits are now born."*
>
> —*G. Stanley Hall*

Early adolescence is a tender time. It can be awkward and downright painful. Emotions run close to the surface or get stuffed far below; friends can be closer than ever or painfully absent. The capacity for reasoning grows by leaps and bounds.

Through friendships and mentoring relationships, we engage in the age-old question, who am I?, possibly doing the serious work of identity formation—gender identity, racial identity, religious identity. Looking good and finding a sense of belonging feel like urgent matters. We long for a place where we will find acceptance and affirmation, compassion, courage, inspiration, and a chance to make a difference.

This is the age when one develops default ways of responding to things. When faced with a situation in which one disagrees with an action, some withdraw emotionally in an attempt to avoid conflict;

others display their disagreement through disapproving silence instead of openly expressing their opinion or needs.

More is caught than taught. Children will catch what you say and replicate how you act. These characteristics are survival strategies learned by emulating those around them and adopted out of facing challenges they couldn't understand or adequately address at that age.

However these responses originated, they worked well for us at a time when our other options were limited so we kept using them over and over when similar situations arose. The problem is that these default responses often prove to be less helpful as we get older and have access to a wider array of options, skills, and understandings. Yet we continue to tell ourselves the same old stories without realizing we're doing so.

The tendency to shut down becomes even more pronounced over the years, especially at times when we feel broken and shattered. Our survival mechanism kicks in stronger than ever, pulling us unswervingly back into the same old ruts we've traveled so many times before.

From doing the work in this book, we realize that no matter how strong the old conditioning is, we do have other options; that life's broken places are in fact ideal opportunities on so many levels to start fresh and create something new. After all, if the life we've been familiar with has already crumbled around us, why not use the rubble to build something new and different instead of struggling to recreate what has already collapsed?

Rebuilding requires intentional effort, and it starts with first recognizing our default responses and storylines. Pay attention to how you respond to situations and notice the patterns. Soon you'll notice how they actually have appeared in your history. You'll see glimpses of your current behavior as you answer the questions in this chapter and will also have an opportunity to evaluate their usefulness at this stage of your life. Are they working for you now? Do they help you move through life in ways that are empowering? Do they contribute to your growth, help you become the person you want to be, uphold the values you hold most dear?

If they don't, you have the choice to begin to look at new options. This step has proven to be a challenge for many. Our default responses are so deeply ingrained that sometimes we can't begin to imagine an alternative way of thinking and behaving. What can be most helpful here is to look at people you know or admire who've emerged from challenges similar to yours and observe their responses so you can start to adapt as you assess your life.

So much of what happens in adolescence stays with you for years to come and directs your thoughts, beliefs, and ultimately your actions and behavior. The vulnerability you feel can be overwhelming. It's easy to get walloped in the awkward cycle of physical, emotional, and social change. Rejections, failures, and successes take a toll on self-confidence and have a profound impact on self-worthiness. Academic and social pressures, the rush of hormones, the exhilaration of new love, peer pressure, all seem overwhelming.

The focus is to create self-awareness, to know yourself and to be valued for who you are with all your gifts and quirks, to build social confidence, personal and religious/spiritual identity, and bonds of friendship that cross generations.

What do you remember about this time of your life? Be empathetic as you recall the answers to the following questions.

1. **How did you view life when you were young?**

2. **Do you remember an incident as a child that caused you to never do something, say something, or feel something ever again? How has that incident affected the way you've dealt with issues in your life?**

3. **How did you get along with your teachers in elementary and middle school?**

   a. Did that change in high school?

   b. What kind of teachers did you have an easy time getting along with?

   c. What kind of teachers did you have a difficult time getting along with?

4. Write about your favorite teacher.

5. Describe your first school friend.

6. Was it easy or hard for you to make friends?

7. Did you have imaginary friends in your life? Describe them.

8. Did you have any pets? What names did you give them, and which ones were your favorite?

9. **Did you learn to swim, ride a bike, skate? Describe when and how it felt.**

....

....

....

....

10. **The very first time you were punished for something, do you remember the reason why?**

....

....

....

....

11. **Describe the first naughty deed you ever committed.**

....

....

12. **Explain the first time you were caught red-handed doing something you shouldn't have done.**

....

....

a. What did you do? ....

....

....

b. How did you feel? ....

....

....

13. What have you gotten away with?

14. What might you be tempted to do if you knew you would never be caught?

15. Have you ever cheated on an exam? Explain what happened.

16. What do you regret/feel guilty about?

17. What do you regret not doing?

18. How many students were in your high school graduating class? ....

19. How would you describe yourself in high school? Were you a bully, nerd, fighter, loner, athlete, straight-A student, pothead, rocker, gangster? A combination of some of these?

....

....

....

....

20. Were you fearful, confident, or competitive? Give examples.

....

....

....

....

21. Did you struggle to fit in? If so, were you tempted to do what you knew was wrong to be accepted in your circle of friends? ....

....

22. What did it feel like entering a contest, participating in a debate, or running for a school office?

....

....

....

....

23. Were you concerned about your appearance, and if so, why?

....

....

....

....

a. How did you overcome your concerns? What remedies did you try? ....

....

....

b. To what lengths did you go to measure up to your friends and fit in? ....

....

....

24. What clothes did you wear and what was your style of dressing? Were you happy with your image?

....

....

....

....

25. Were you more, or less, mature than your classmates?

....

....

26. Did your body develop faster or more slowly than most of your friends? How did you feel about that?

....

....

....

27. **How much did you worry about being popular?**

....

....

28. **Whom did you sit with at lunch and hang out with after school?**

....

....

29. **Did you have a crush on a classmate? A teacher? A singer, movie star, or anyone else?**

....

....

30. **How would you describe your group of friends? Are you still in touch with any of them, and in what way?**

....

....

....

....

31. **Did your parents approve of your choice of friends?**

....

....

32. **Did you ever do drugs or alcohol in your youth?** ....

a. When was your first experience with drugs?

....

b. What was your attitude about drugs and alcohol?

....

....

c. Do you still do drugs? ....

d. How do you think it has affected the way you are as an adult today? ....

....

....

33. What is the most pressure you faced in a situation and how did you handle it?

....

....

....

....

34. What three events made the biggest impact on who you are today?

1. ....

....

2. ....

....

3. ....

....

35. What was your favorite music or band growing up?

....

a. How did that music or band influence the way you viewed the world? ....

....

b. Are you still a fan of that band and/or that type of music? ....

36. Did you go to the prom, and if so, with whom? What did that feel like? What did you wear? Did you dance? Describe what that entire experience was like for you.

....

....

....

....

....

....

....

....

37. Describe your first kiss, your first date. Did you go steady?

....

....

....

....

38. At what age did you have your first sexual encounter?

....

a. Did you feel pressured, either from within or from others, to engage in physical intimacy? ....

b. What do you remember about the experience?

....

....

....

c. Has it affected the way you view sex as an adult?

....

....

39. What was the most embarrassing event around your physical maturation? Explain.

40. Describe your favorite teacher, your most memorable class.

41. What were your dreams about the person you were going to be when you grew up?

42. When you were at your happiest, what did that look like? What do you need to do to get yourself in that state again?

43. **What role did sports play in your life as a child/teenager?**

a. Was it something you liked or was it forced on you?

b. What are the best and worst memories you have about playing sports?

44. **What activities did you participate in outside of school? How involved were you?**

45. **What role did religion play in your life as a child/teenager?**

a. Was it something you liked, or was it forced on you?

b. How did it impact the kind of person you were?

46. **Are you part of organized religion today?**

47. What did you do in your youth that you are most proud of? Second-most proud of?

48. What form of recognition did you receive (any awards, trophies, leadership position, etc.) and how was that for you?

49. What role has formal education played in your life, and how do you feel about it?

50. What was the best grade you got, and what was the worst?

51. Which was your best subject, and which one challenged you the most?

52. How did you measure up to your parents' expectations of you? Explain.

53. How much did you worry about the future, getting into college, making a living?

54. Describe your relationship with the first adult you considered a friend.

55. Describe your first car and who taught you how to drive. What did that feel like?

56. Did anyone close to you ever have an accident, a serious injury, or a life-threatening disease? Describe how well you knew them and what happened.

57. If you could give advice to the fourteen-year-old you, what would it be?

58. How would you describe yourself as you were in your youth?

59. What is a positive memory that stands out from your childhood?

....

....

....

....

60. What is a negative memory that stands out from your childhood? What has it taught you about yourself?

....

....

....

....

REFLECTIONS

It is said that every grown-up has a child hidden inside him/her. The childhood we lived and experienced still lies inside us in the form of memories. For some of us, these are fond memories; for others, they are bittersweet.

What was your childhood like? Was that child inside you happy, sad, adventurous, timid, brave, frightened, extroverted, or introverted? Observe in which ways your adult behavior is a reflection of your inner child.

The inner child is often described as the artistic, creative, imaginative, and dreamer part of us. It is the fun-loving, playful, wonder-seeking entity that resides within us.

Growing up can be both the best of times and the worst of times, and who we are as teenagers is rarely the same as who we become as adults. And yet, subconsciously, our behavior keeps reverting back to when we were children.

Why does the inner child still reside within even after we are all grown up? Why does it still clamor for our attention? There could be many reasons. Some of us had to grow up very fast, and the child part of us never got enough time to catch up. In some cases, the small child had to play the roles of mom or dad. It never did get to be the child that it really wanted to be. Some children were abused, and consequently their hurt was never healed. So many reasons are possible.

If the inner child is not healed properly, one faces negative consequences. We start taking life too seriously; play, fun, and laughter become alien to us. We may even find it difficult to enjoy our own children. Life becomes a chore. Sometimes, those who were abused in childhood take out their frustration on their children and may themselves become abusers. Therefore, healing the inner child is crucial to the health of an individual.

For this "Reflection":

1. Think back to the person you were when younger—five, ten, fifteen years old. Then think back to when you graduated from high school. If possible, go back in time and read over the comments from those who signed your yearbook.

Journal your answers to the following questions:

a. How close are you today to the person you were when you were about five, ten, and fifteen years old? When you were in high school?: ....

....

....

....

b. How does who you are now compare to what people thought of you back then?: ....

....

....

....

c. Overall, do you feel that you exceeded or fell short of others' expectations of you since high school?: ....

....

....

2. Reach out to those who knew you well in high school and ask them what you were like. What did you find out?

3. Write a letter to yourself as a teen. What advice would you offer your younger self? What would you have done differently if you could turn back the clock? What reassurance can you offer? What do you want to say to him or her about the future?

4. Who were the teacher(s) or person(s) who made an impression—positive or negative—on you, who motivated you when you were young? Were you encouraged by their support, or did their adverse attitude motivate you to prove them wrong?

a. Write a letter to this person describing how he or she affected you and how your life has changed today as a result of his or her attitude and your interaction with him or her.

....

....

....

....

....

....

....

....

....

....

b. What do you think this individual would say if he or she could see you now? ....

....

....

....

5. **Escape loneliness and reach out to others.** Have you ever suddenly realized that someone you once knew well hasn't been in touch for a while? What did you do? Did you feel rejected, did you worry if the person was okay, or did you call or text to check up? Often we take another person's lack of communication to mean that the person doesn't care instead of stopping to consider what might be going on in his or her life. This week, do one thing that connects you to others such as the following:

   a. Go to places where you're likely to meet people—a park, library, meet-up group.
   b. Accept invitations or offers of help.

c. Make or arrange to meet up with an old friend face-to-face instead of communicating via phone, text, or social media.
d. Volunteer for a cause that brings you in touch with people.

6. **Surround yourself with positive people.** Your happiness level is very much affected by the company you keep. When you surround yourself with people who "fill your cup" rather than drain it, you are much more likely to feel positive and happy. This week, surround yourself with some positive power.

a. List the names of three people in your life who lift you up, whose company you really enjoy, and who make you feel happy. ....

....

....

b. What is it that they do to make your feel this way? Are they supportive, nurturing, complimentary, or energetic? What is it about their approach and attitude? ....

....

....

c. How can you introduce the same positive characteristics and attitude into your own life so you, too can be that for someone else? ....

....

....

AFFIRMATIONS

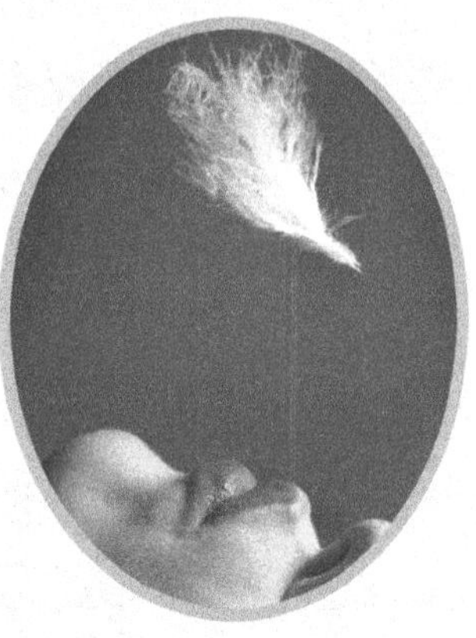

Speak the following affirmations to your inner child. Choose one affirmation for each day, focusing on areas of your life or aspects of your personality that you want to improve. Add feeling. It's important to believe in your affirmation as if it's already 100 percent true.

1. _______________, (your name) I am proud of you and all that you are.
2. _______________, (your name) I love you, I care about you, and I accept you as you are.
3. ____________________, (your name) you are beautiful/handsome and attractive. Everybody loves you.
4. ____________________, (your name) you are free to make your own choices. Live your own life.
5. The child in me is very much alive. It is a happy, joyous, and fun-loving child.
6. My wounds are now healed. I look forward to a rich and fulfilling life.
7. Life is full of joy. I release the past and live only in the present.
8. All is well. The present is great and the future is bright.
9. Today is the best day of my life, and every day is a new day.
10. I am the center of my universe. Everybody loves and appreciates me, and I reciprocate.
11. I have forgotten the sad past. I live in the happy present and know that a happier future awaits me.
12. I release my wounds with forgiveness.
13. I forgive myself for not always being strong.
14. I trust myself to manage whatever life brings me.
15. I am a child of nature. We are forever connected.
16. I forgive myself for my anger and sadness.
17. I release any resistance to what I feel.
18. I know that love opens all doors.
19. The child in me and I are one. We love, care for, and appreciate each other and will always belong together.
20. I choose to see with eyes of love.

FOOD FOR THOUGHT: *Kintsugi and the Precious Vase*

I love flowers. They bring so much joy to my life.

There's a Ming vase with beautiful gold veins running through it that I use to hold my floral arrangements. This vase was once shattered and then mended using the kintsugi method. Every time I feast my eyes on my favorite treasure, I'm reminded how far I have come on my own life journey.

For most of my life, I told myself I was not good enough, that I wasn't worthy. Even though I received so many awards and accolades for my many accomplishments, there was always a part of me that felt I was undeserving. This continuous inner chatter sapped so much of my energy that I often found myself sabotaging my own success.

Perhaps you, too can relate.

Have you ever paused to listen to your internal dialogue? What are you saying to yourself? About yourself?

Perhaps, like me, you've been criticizing yourself for years and didn't even realize it. Isn't it time to start approving of yourself and see what happens?

Many of us wish we had another chance to right our wrongs or an opportunity to do it all over again, whether it's in our relationships, career, health, finances, or lifestyle. Believe it or not, we sabotage our own success and relationships because of what we say to ourselves.

Many people are lying in their graves whose business still remains unfinished. They never got around to living their lives on their terms or bringing closure on certain issues that haunted them while alive. Regrets, disappointments, and heartaches were their norm because they never felt deserving or worthy enough.

Don't let that be you.

We measure ourselves and our self-worth by standards that are not even real. We are indeed our own worst critics. It's our own perspective, our own internal dialogue, our own thinking . . . It's simply us.

But *why*, you ask. *Why are we so hard on ourselves?*

Those limiting beliefs are inevitably rooted in our deep subconscious, planted when we were young. They could have been innocent remarks a teacher made or some things you heard from the elders in your life possibly said in jest or in frustration at something you had done. Perhaps those people didn't even mean what they said, or they were just having a bad day and didn't realize that you would take their words to heart and keep them in your memory forever. Regardless, you believed them to be true.

So, what happens when you believe those labels to be true? You waste your whole life believing those lies and trying to prove yourself to the world. You hunger for approval from others so you can feel better about yourself and your place in society and the tribe you struggle to belong to.

It's certainly good and commendable to set high standards for ourselves, to strive hard and dream big. But when our own self-imposed, high expectations cause us to turn on ourselves with nasty, self-deprecating words, it is then that we become our very own worst critics.

We critique ourselves in so many ways that our entire world exists within this bubble we've created for ourselves. We hold ourselves to an unrealistic standard of perfection, and when we fail to meet that standard, we replay the same words over and over again in our mind, words like, *I'm not good enough, how could I be so dumb?, I never get it right.* These were words that perhaps you heard from elders as you were growing up that had the power to tear you down and make you believe the lies, that stripped away at your self-worth, that became these beliefs that sabotaged your progress and hindered your growth.

When your self-image is rooted in shame, you fear being exposed as flawed, insufficient, or a failure. You believe that your disappointments and failures are the logical outcomes of who you "really are." And because your belief system has been around for a long while, it is self-enforcing. The constant self-critiquing and hateful self-talk slowly kills your self-confidence and your self-esteem. It robs you of joy as you become blinded from seeing anything good and worthy in yourself.

Others may see your successes, and their words and actions may even imply how much they admire you and envy your accomplishments. But you are not likely to believe your successes are anything other than mere accidents. You give credit to others, not convinced that you are the one who made it all happen and that you ought to be patting yourself on the back and give credit where credit is due. Yes, *you* did it!

What we value in ourselves and what others valued when we were growing up can make a difference in how we are living our lives today. The labels we give ourselves when depressed often emerge from a shame-based self-image, which not surprisingly originated from the environment we grew up in.

Be gentle on yourself and treat yourself with the kindness that you would extend to your best friend. Send healing love to yourself, stay calm, and give yourself grace for the moment.

Breaking this habit requires grace. Grace enables us to move on to being more whole, one step at a time. Grace is saying to yourself, *I'm trying my best, it's okay.*

Be more loving and compassionate as you go on this journey to becoming whole. Pick up all the pieces that have been scattered as far back as from the time you were a little child through all those years up until now. Pick them all up and piece them together, and using the kintsugi method, fill the cracks with gold to illuminate your beauty to become this beautiful treasure that makes you proud.

I did it, and so can you. From broken to beautiful, you too can now feast your eyes on your treasure like I do mine and admire its beauty. You can use it to display the most beautiful work of art, your creativity, which reflects your present moment, and see your life transformed right before your eyes.

You are beautiful. You are precious. You are enough.

"Everything in the universe is within you. Ask all from yourself."

—Rumi

WHAT I WANT TO REMEMBER FROM THIS CHAPTER

DATE: ....

KEY POINTS: ....

....

....

....

....

....

....

....

....

....

....

TAKEAWAYS: ....

....

....

....

....

....

....

....

....

....

....

CHAPTER FOUR

The Agony of Growing Up

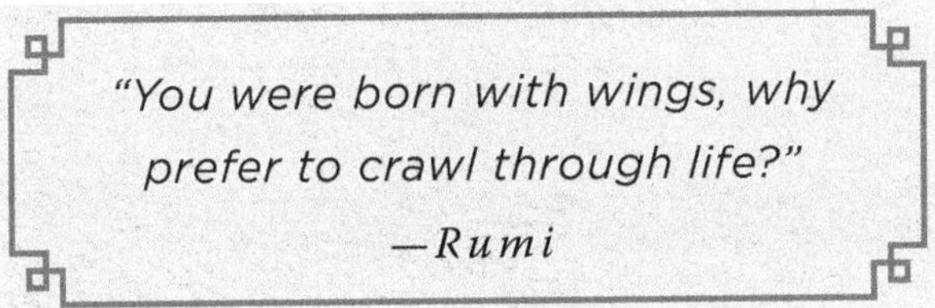

I can remember the agony of growing up.

I went through a period of identity crisis and struggled through "imposter syndrome"—the sinking feeling that you're a fake and a fraud—and a heap of self-doubt; as a result, I overextended myself to compensate for my insecurities. My eroding self-trust translated to many areas of my life, especially in my relationships with family and friends, and I felt like the shell of the person I was.

Unhelpful thoughts and emotions took up most of my energy, distracting me from living and enjoying my life. I knew there had to be more to life but couldn't put my finger on what exactly that was until years later when I realized that it was the boundary I didn't know I was missing, setting personal limits that complemented my needs and desires to strengthen my self-confidence and my self-worth. I never knew I had that choice because everyone around me wanted to control my thoughts and actions.

Boundaries are necessary to protect our inner worlds. Physical and logistical boundaries fail unless they're fortified by strong internal boundaries and a foundation of self-trust. A *boundary* defines a limit, and *personal boundaries* outline our desires, needs, and preferences that serve as invisible walls that nurture self-trust and identity.

Perhaps your journey wasn't as compelling as mine, nor your circumstances as drastic and traumatic. But one thing I'm sure we can agree on: When you and others respect your boundaries, you fulfill your core human needs for safety and belonging. You feel validated; you are able to communicate effectively and with confidence; you become responsible and in control of your thoughts, emotions, and behavior. You trust your ability to make decisions, are not afraid to take risks, and don't get emotionally hijacked by negative people or events. Having healthy boundaries is crucial to healthy living.

The trouble begins when you start negotiating your boundaries, when you turn to the outside world for approval, whether it's in the form of money, status, or chasing someone else's version of success—and in today's world, on how many "likes" you get on social media.

Maybe you never learned how to set boundaries, especially if your parents or family had so-called leaky boundaries. If that was you, then you might recreate the same dynamics with your friends, partners, coworkers, and bosses. Each time you say *yes* when you mean *no* or hold back from speaking up, doubt, indecision, and fear creep in and you lose a bit more self-trust and even credibility with yourself.

You may have faced some boundary issues when you were a young adult and were facing major decisions about your future. You may have had to repeatedly modify your plans around your academic, career, and financial goals based on the influence and opinions of the elders in your life. Perhaps you had to adjust your ideas and aspirations and dream new dreams to please everyone. You may have started to explore possibilities about work and love, and perhaps some limitations were placed on your desires.

On the other hand, you may have had a perfect childhood, parents who were supportive, loving friends and family and no major traumas to overcome. Even so, we all have voices in our heads that are less than helpful. Maybe the voices tell you you're good enough until a certain point, but perhaps not for certain big things—a challenging job, relationship, goal, or health issue. You can't blame your parents—in fact, you should be grateful—you can't blame your childhood because it was pretty good, so you think there's no work to be done.

Your history does not need to be worse than it was to be bad enough to cause challenges for you. It could well be that you were self-assured and self-confident enough to go after your own dreams and follow your own path. But there are still voices in your head that persist somehow.

Freeing yourself from old emotions, pains, and limiting beliefs requires that you know where those beliefs came from. Awareness is key. Whatever you went through, today you have the chance to correct, modify, and empower yourself.

How did your decisions as a young adult shape your life as it is today? Answer the following questions:

1. What was your dream job when you were in high school? ....

2. What did you do right after high school?

....

....

3. Describe your fondest memories of where you went and what you studied as you pursued higher education, training, or the military. What was the value of the experience then and now?

4. What was your highest academic achievement? What did you have to go through to achieve that?

5. Name three teachers, mentors, or authority figures most influential in whom you've become today.

   1. ……
   2. ……
   3. ……

6. What do you wish your teachers and mentors who influenced you had taught you in school that they didn't?

7. Did you learn about money management, social skills, and work ethics in school? Which of these lessons came easily?

....

....

....

....

8. What have you learned in the school of hard knocks?

....

....

....

....

9. How do you feel about competition?

....

....

....

....

10. How do you deal with authority? Is it easy or difficult for you?

....

....

....

11. Were you a procrastinator? How about now?

....

....

12. Did you put off a menial task such as cleaning, home repairs, mowing the lawn, and the like, and waited, hoping perhaps, it'll get done by itself? Explain.

....

....

a. Did the task get done? ....
b. Who had to do it? ....
c. What lesson did you learn? ....

....

13. Were you ever afraid to move to a different geographical location? If yes, why?

....

....

....

14. Did you easily become bored? What was boring, the tasks at hand, your relationships, or something else?

....

....

....

15. Did you ever use lack of sleep or fatigue as an excuse for not taking care of things? What was the reason?

....

....

....

....

16. Did you ever get sick when faced with a disquieting or troublesome task? Describe what happened.

....

....

....

....

17. Were you ever critical of someone else's behavior? Explain.

....

....

....

a. Are you by nature a critic? ....

b. If yes, what do you get out of it? ....

....

18. Describe your first real job.

....

....

....

a. What year was that? ....

b. What kind of employee were you? ....

....

c. What did it teach you about your strengths and weaknesses? ....

....

19. How much were you paid in your first, full-time job?

....

a. Do you believe you were paid what you were worth? If not, why? ....

....

b. What *were* you worth? ....

20. **What was your career decision based on?**

a. the desire to please your family
b. the desire for a higher income
c. a natural talent
d. a strong, intellectual interest
e. a wish to help and contribute to society

21. **Have you stayed in a job that you felt stuck in and unable to grow?** ....

a. What was the reason you stayed? ....

....

b. What did that feel like? ....

....

22. **At what age did you leave your parental home?** ....

a. How far away did you move? ....
b. How did it make you feel? ....

....

c. Describe your neighborhood, your living pad.

....

....

23. **Describe the dreams you had for your future. Did you have to modify them? If so, what was the reason?**

a. academic
b. financial
c. family's or others' opinions
d. How did this affect you?

....

....

....

....

....

24. Name three things you did that you regret.

1. ....
2. ....
3. ....

25. Name three things you are thankful that you did.

1. ....
2. ....
3. ....

26. Describe an incident, good or bad, that has stayed in your memory from your young-adult days.

....

....

....

....

....

....

....

27. What was the first vehicle that you purchased?

....

28. Have you ever experienced road rage or a temper tantrum? ....

a. Describe what happened. ....

b. How did you feel before? ....

c. How did you feel afterward? ....

29. **What is the biggest risk—financial, emotional, or otherwise—you ever took, and what was the outcome?**

....

30. **What is a belief you acquired then and are still holding onto? How is it serving/limiting you now?**

....

31. **Name a piece of music that makes you nostalgic for a certain event you experienced or a certain person you met. Describe what it reminds you of.**

....

32. Have you ever bounced a check, spent money superfluously, or missed important commitments because of negligence? Explain.

33. What is the craziest, wildest party you ever attended, threw, or got kicked out of?

34. What is the biggest mistake you made, and what did you learn from it?

35. What opportunity for love, money, or fame did you pass up? Did you feel relieved or did you regret it?

36. What's the most thrilling adventure you've taken part in?

a. How did it feel?

b. Was it planned/unplanned?

37. Were you comfortable making new friends in social gatherings?

38. How did you go about making connections with friends and lovers as a young adult?

39. How many lovers did you have before you developed a serious relationship with someone?

a. What was not right about them?

b. What were you looking for?

40. Were you ever afraid to take the initiative with someone you were fond of? Why?

41. **Describe your first significant other. What first attracted you to him/her?**

42. **Did you ever hang onto a relationship that had gone sour, hoping it would get better?**

    a. Did your staying on improve the relationship?
    b. If not, why not?
    c. What did you learn from this?

43. **Have you avoided a confrontation with someone, such as an authority figure, a friend, a lover, or a service provider even when you knew the individual was wrong? Explain.**

    a. Did that improve your relationship?
    b. Did that improve the situation?

c. What do you feel now was the right thing to do?

....

44. Who were you with when these historic events took place and what was it like for you? What was it like for your family?

a. the moon landing ....

....

....

b. the JFK assassination ....

....

....

c. the Vietnam War ....

....

....

d. the collapse of the Soviet Union ....

....

....

e. the attack on the Twin Towers in New York City

....

....

....

f. Princess Diana's death ....

....

....

45. What did you learn about the value of money?

....

....

....

....

46. Looking back, what is something that took place that you are most grateful for now? Explain.

47. Describe a day that was especially enjoyable. What made the day so good?

48. What is something you're still holding onto and are nostalgic about because of some loving past memories attached to it?

49. If you could erase one memory from the past, what would it be?

50. What was your greatest strength? Describe a time this strength served you well.

51. What was your greatest weakness? Describe a time this weakness held you back.

52. Were you prone to a "lack mentality," living your life for others and always putting off your own happiness? Are you still that way?

53. If you could turn back the clock and reenact three moments from that time of your life, what would they be? What would you do differently?

a.

b.

c.

54. Name a person who was exceptionally kind to you. What happened?

55. Name a person who made you miserable for the longest time. What happened?

56. What is one failure you experienced that you've turned into your greatest lesson?

57. What is something constantly on your mind that happened that you are afraid/embarrassed to share?

58. Name a person who betrayed you. What happened? Did you eventually make peace with him/her?

59. Name three words you would use to describe yourself as you were growing up.

60. To your best recollection and knowledge, how did other people perceive you?

REFLECTIONS

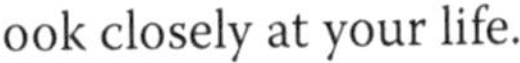

Look closely at your life.

Are you living your life to the fullest?

What would you be doing instead if you had not much time to live?

Stop postponing life. Begin that letter or write that book; take that job, that vacation; tell someone you love him or her; ask yourself, *what's the worst thing that could happen if I did what I'm putting off right now?*

Think of yourself as too significant to live with anxiety about the things you would love to do, to have, to be. Next time you know you're uncomfortable because of "postponement anxiety," remember that people who love themselves don't hurt themselves that way.

Look carefully at your present and what you're avoiding. Begin to tackle the fear of living effectively. You have come a long way from the young adult you were. Time has flown by as you must realize by now. How have you changed? What have you learned?

Take action now. It's not too late. The only thing holding you back is you and the neurotic choices you may have made because you didn't believe you're as strong as you really are. Start using your mind creatively in what were previously boring circumstances. You have a choice. Be courageous about undertaking an activity that you've been avoiding.

I think it's a terrible thing in life to wait until you're absolutely ready and everything is perfectly aligned. I've seen from my own experience that actually no one is ever ready to do anything; there is no such thing as *being ready* or *absolute perfect timing.* The time is never right, perfection does not exist, so stop waiting by telling yourself you must perform well. Remind yourself that taking action and just doing it is far more important.

Rabindranath Tagore, British Indian writer and song composer, said, "Spring has passed. Summer has gone. Winter is here . . . and the song that I meant to sing remains unsung. For I have spent my days stringing and unstringing my instrument."

Don't let your music die with you. Take the chance today and live your dreams. Eliminate the words, *hope, wish,* and *maybe* from your vocabulary. They are an excuse to procrastinate. Substitute these words when you see them creeping into your conversation: Change, *"I hope things will work out"* to *"I will make it happen";* Change, *"I wish things were better"* to *"I'm going to do whatever it takes to ensure that I feel better"*; Change, *"Maybe it will work out"* to *"I will make it work."*

Do the following exercises:

1. Even if you don't think you can draw well, spontaneously create a self-portrait without being too serious.

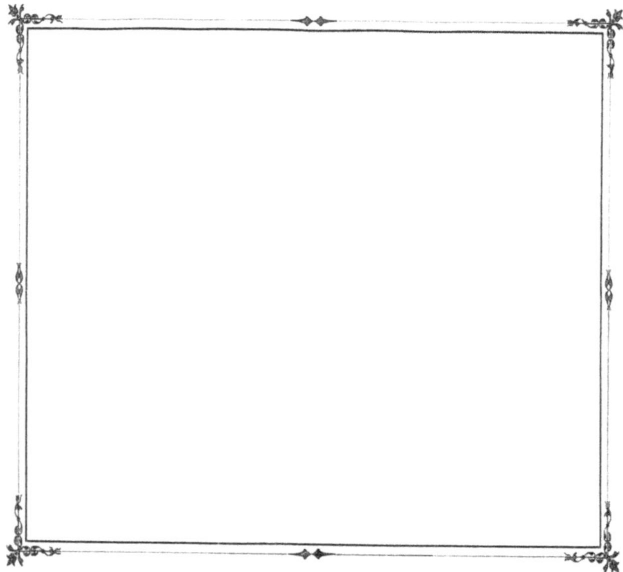

2. Write down ten things you wish you could change about your life.

1. ....
2. ....
3. ....
4. ....
5. ....
6. ....
7. ....
8. ....
9. ....
10. ....

3. List twenty things, big or small, that you've done right. Include your successes, challenges, kind acts, and good deeds.

1. ....
2. ....
3. ....
4. ....
5. ....
6. ....
7. ....
8. ....
9. ....
10. ....
11. ....
12. ....
13. ....
14. ....
15. ....
16. ....

17. ....
18. ....
19. ....
20. ....

4. **Keep a journal of your own complaining and critical behavior.** Write into this every day. You'll soon see the frequency, patterns, events, and people that you routinely criticize. You'll also notice how your critical behavior is really affecting your attitude. And you'll soon become more mindful to avoid this behavior because it'll become such a pain to have to write in the journal!

5. **Stop Procrastinating.** Procrastination is the thief of time and a major enemy of happiness. It can steal your life and rob your confidence, riddle you with guilt, and hinder you from producing your best work. Procrastinators never learn to prioritize their time and dread deadlines. They tend to miss out on the best things life can offer. Disrupt your tendency to delay. Take action by doing the following:

   a. Schedule your tasks by having a well-thought-out action plan. Draw it, create it in Excel, or map it out in such a way that it becomes a visual reminder of what actions to take every moment of every day. Give yourself some room for actual deadlines in case of emergencies. Highlight your start and finish dates in bright, contrasting colors. Discover the joy of completing tasks on time. Your belief in yourself will slowly change, and you will notice how happy that makes you feel!
   b. Look around your home or your workplace and make a list of unfinished projects and create a realistic time line with achievable start and finish

dates. Start with one thing at a time, and plan a project in stages so you don't become too overwhelmed. If you need help finishing certain tasks, ask for help or hire outside help so you can meet your schedule and deliver on time. Continue to follow the plan until it becomes a habit. Your life will visibly improve, and you'll soon begin to notice how much time you have left to enjoy the pleasures of daily living.

6. **See the funny side of life.** The ability to look on the funny side of life is truly a gift. Do you remember what it feels like to be overcome with giggles or shake with uncontrollable laughter, to feel the joy of a single moment shared with someone you care about? It probably happened frequently when you were growing up but became less common as you got older. Genuine laughter transforms the body's energy. It wipes away tension in a single breath and turns a frowning face into a beautiful one. Did you know it takes more muscles to frown than to smile? So try to find the lighter side of life by doing the following this week:

   a. Make time to meet up or connect with someone you can really let your hair down with, someone who makes you laugh. Recalling old times and chuckling about new ones is a wonderful shortcut to happiness.
   b. Treat yourself to a comedy night or watch a funny film. Allow yourself to remember what it feels like to laugh just for the sake of it.
   c. Read your favorite cartoon, tell a silly joke, or listen to a happy song. Look for the absurd in every situation.

AFFIRMATIONS

If you want your world to change, rather than complain about it, speak words of empowerment into your life. Use your present moments to affirm the following:

1. I am blessed with the right gifts, personality, and the ability to fulfill my life purpose.
2. I am making a decision to celebrate each day, to live it to the fullest, and to enjoy the people in my life.
3. It is safe for me to play in this life.
4. When I release my resentment, I see a world of magic.
5. My flexibility allows me to respond with grace to what life brings.
6. I choose to put my attention on the blessings in my life.
7. I forgive everyone for every negative thought and action that has ever occurred.
8. I choose to live in my present experience.
9. Every hardship is an opportunity to let go.
10. Every act of letting go brings a greater experience of freedom.
11. I realize I've been blessed with great people in my life, wonderful opportunities, and I am making great memories.
12. I am flexible and willing to change in order to embrace what's new.
13. I am open to new ideas; I see new possibilities and expect great things in my future.
14. I am gaining more confidence and growing stronger each day.
15. I am faithful to the talent, time, and opportunity that I have been blessed with, knowing that as I make the most of my gifts, more is given to me.
16. I am bold and courageous, taking steps of faith, and making the most of every God-given opportunity.
17. I have the talent, wisdom, and strength to fulfill my destiny.
18. I choose to magnify the good in my life and focus on what I have, not what I don't.
19. I am dreaming a new dream as I now let go of all negativity, disappointment, failures, and setbacks.
20. I stay in faith knowing that the challenges and difficulties I face are ultimately working for my good.

FOOD FOR THOUGHT:
Kintsugi and Your Words

Words matter . . .

There was a young boy who had a really bad temper. He would lash out with his words every time someone said something to him. One day, the boy's father gave him a bag of nails and told him that every time he lost his temper and said mean things, he was to hammer a nail into their beautiful, white picket fence.

The very first day the young boy made the deal with his father, he drove ten nails into the fence. As weeks passed, he learned to control his temper, and the number of nails he was nailing into the fence drastically decreased. Finally, the day came when the boy didn't lose his temper at all.

Feeling proud of himself, he went to his father and handed him the hammer and the box of nails and told him of his accomplishment. The father put his arm around his son and walked him to the fence. He told the boy to remove one nail for each day that he didn't lose his temper.

Several weeks went by, and finally the day came when the young boy removed the last nail. He ran to tell his father.

Proud of his little boy, the father hugged him and then said, "You've done so well at keeping your temper in check, and I'm really proud of you, but I want you to see something."

Hand in hand, father and son walked over to the fence. "See all the holes in the beautiful fence?" asked the father. The little boy nodded.

"Our fence will never be the same again," the father said. "When you say things in anger, those words leave scars just like the nail holes in the fence. You can pull the nails out, but the marks they leave are deep and permanent. The same goes for our words. No matter how many times you say you're sorry, you can never take back the words, and the scars will always be there. They may fade over time, but they never go away."

The boy's eyes filled with tears as he looked at the beautiful fence now riddled with holes and said, "Please forgive me, Father for the holes I put in you."

The father hugged his son and said with a smile, "Of course I do, Son, of course I do. From now on, let's think before we speak, and always speak so our words won't hurt someone else."

The words we speak can have deep and lasting effects on our relationships. We can create or destroy with our words. That's how much power our words have.

Have you ever said something you regret? Uttered words that you immediately wish you could take back? Relationships are precious and need to be handled carefully. Love must be learned, and learned again. Your words have the power to cause your loved ones to build walls around their hearts, walls that will change the foundations of your relationships forever.

It's time to mend the holes your words may have created in your relationships. Make amends and let your loved ones know how much you value their presence in your life. Although the scars will still be visible in some shape or form, like a kintsugi master, you have a choice to fill the nail holes in your picket fence with gold and transform it into something beautiful.

Handle your relationships with care. Choose your words carefully, and before you speak, make sure your words build, not destroy, your relationships.

"Raise your words,
not your voice.

It is rain that
grows flowers,
not thunder."

—Rumi

WHAT I WANT TO REMEMBER FROM THIS CHAPTER

DATE: ....

KEY POINTS: ....

TAKEAWAYS: ....

PART II

CLARIFYING YOUR PATH

PART II

INTRODUCTION

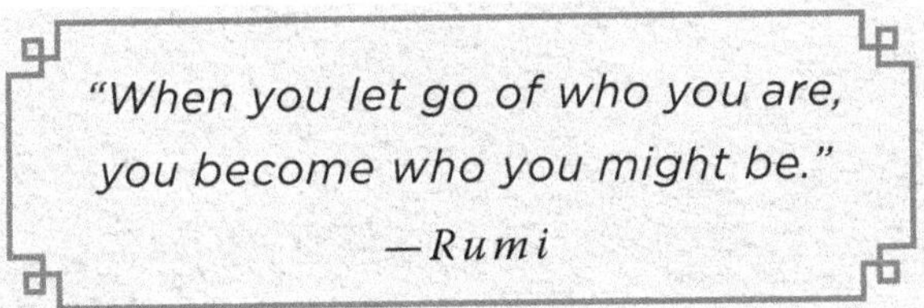

"When you let go of who you are, you become who you might be."
—Rumi

Hopefully, you've gleaned some insights by now and seen some patterns that you have carried over from your childhood to whom you are today.

Part II is about clarifying your path by acknowledging your beliefs, reviewing them, and then asking yourself: *Does this belief serve me? Is this really what I want to continue to believe?*

By challenging your beliefs, you may even learn something new. Verbalizing what you believe can open you up to face the truth of how you've been living until now, to learn about your expectations, and change what has conditioned you thus far. It may afford you a new lens to see old problems. You may find you're ready to open up to new possibilities and a new way of thinking.

Have you ever wondered, *what if I had it all wrong? What if new possibilities are birthed from letting go of old beliefs, by letting go of the things that no longer serve me?*

What do you want more from life? Are your beliefs hindering your progress? Is fear of change holding you back? Change always feels vulnerable and uncomfortable. Change can riddle you with doubt: *What if I don't have the skills or the support I need?* What needs and fears are lurking in your resolution to launch into change?

Yes, you want more joy, connection, and courage to move forward in life. But are you willing to invest the time and effort to make that happen? Are you ready to do the work, learn something new, to challenge your old stories?

It's your choice.

Yes, you *always* have a choice. You can reach out to someone or a group of people who are also choosing to be brave and make the shift. Or you can remain where you are . . . waiting . . . hoping . . . .

Dare to wade into discomfort and vulnerability and face the truth about your stories—choose courage over comfort, accountability over blame and shame. Your current beliefs are the stories you've been telling yourself; they are the rock you've been hiding under, and it's time to get out from underneath. Nobody said it was going to be easy; all I'm saying is it will be well worth it.

It's time, time to make decisions about your life that align with your values, needs, and what brings you joy. You are responsible for your life. No one else is coming to your rescue. You are your own rescue. It's your choice.

What will you choose?

Give yourself permission to be imperfect, and at the same time, believe you are enough.

Because you are.

"Love itself describes its own Perfection. Be speechless and listen."

—Rumi

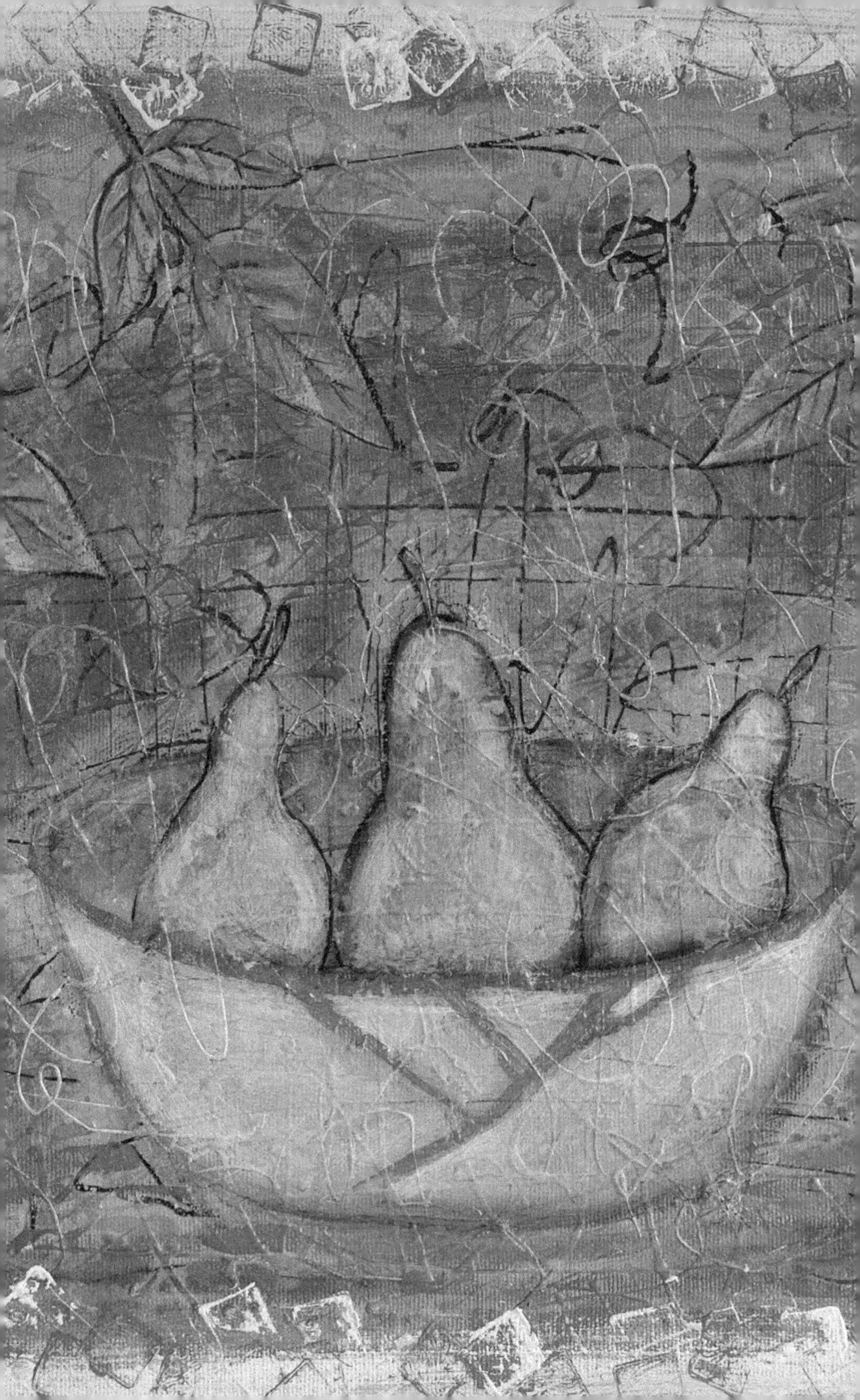

CHAPTER FIVE

Your Personal Life Is a Priceless Treasure

> *"You are searching the world for treasures but the real treasure is yourself."*
>
> —*Rumi*

What are you not seeing that might be right in front of you?

I read a story about a woman who lived in a tiny apartment. She died at the ripe old age of ninety-two in extreme poverty. At one point, she had even been homeless living on the streets. The woman never had any notable victories or successes to speak of and generally kept to herself.

After her funeral, some family members went to clear out her belongings at her little, run-down apartment. Among the knickknacks and things they gathered was a painting. They decided to sell the painting at a garage sale hoping to cover some of the funeral expenses.

The man who purchased the painting took it to a local art gallery for appraisal and was shocked to discover that it was painted by a famous artist in the early 1800s and was extremely valuable. The painting was ultimately auctioned for several million dollars! Imagine how the old woman's life might have changed had she known the value of what she possessed! She was a multimillionaire and didn't even know it.

Just like the poor old woman, so many people are living with a priceless treasure they are holding inside that they are not even aware of. What treasure are you holding? What is hidden deep inside you that you have forgotten about? Wouldn't you like to go deep within and find this hidden treasure so you can understand and know your own value? Sometimes, we have to appraise what's on the inside of us to really understand what we have.

In this chapter, you are invited to go on a journey to discover your own treasures, some that you never realized you had all along. As you record details of your life—your personal habits; your personal image and style; your physical reality; friends you've had; places you've seen and lived in; work you've done; and significant, historic events in your life up to this moment—you will create and clarify a clear snapshot of a typical day in your life and be pleasantly surprised what you end up learning about yourself.

Write freely. Do not edit. Do not second-guess. Document your wildest episodes, your innermost secrets. These are what make you interesting and what will provide value to your journey. It's the only way you will get to know yourself. Walk into your story and own your truth even if it's a story about disappointment or failure. Your brain is hardwired to protect you, and that often means wanting you to run or fight. Don't. Stick to the work. This is no time to hide out, rationalize, or blame others.

It's the small, everyday conflicts and disappointments, the physical and emotional intolerance for discomfort that hold us back from ever truly owning our story. We tend to disengage to self-protect. But this is not the time or the place. You must be fully engaged as you answer the questions in this chapter.

Embrace your own version of the life you have lived. Be spontaneous.

1. Who are you?

...

...

...

...

2. Do you love yourself? Why or Why not?

...

...

...

...

3. What is your ideal physical look? What do you need to do to achieve this look?

...

...

...

...

4. What is your ideal diet? What do you need to do to achieve this diet? Did you ever put off going on a diet even though you knew it would improve your health? Why?

...

...

...

...

...

...

5. **What is your ideal home like? What do you need to do to achieve this home?**

....

....

....

....

....

....

6. **What is your ideal life? What can you do to start living this life?**

....

....

....

....

....

....

7. **Do you like shopping? Or do you:**

   a. shop only for necessities?
   b. browse for pleasure and inspiration?
   c. shop sales for bargains?
   d. impulse buy and regret it later?

8. **What is your shopping style? Do you prefer:**

   a. window shopping?
   b. discount store shopping?
   c. department store shopping?
   d. shopping in boutiques?
   e. thrift shopping?
   f. shopping in flea markets?

g. shopping at yard sales?
h. going to auctions?
i. shopping online or by mail order?
j. shopping by other ways (explain)? ....

....

9. Describe your signature style.

....

....

....

....

10. What do your refrigerator and pantry hold?

....

....

....

....

a. What does that say about your health?

....

....

b. What does that say about your eating habits?

....

....

11. Magnets, reminder notes, and sticky notes on the refrigerator paint a picture of one's daily life. What's on your refrigerator and why?

....

....

....

12. What is your inner dialogue like?

....

....

....

....

13. Do you ever wish you were born into a different

   a. race? ....

   b. religion? ....

   c. sex? ....

14. When was the last time you cried uncontrollably? What happened?

....

....

....

....

15. How do you behave when you are angry? When was the last time you were very angry? What happened to make you so angry?

....

....

....

....

....

....

....

16. When in physical or emotional pain, what are some of the best things you do for yourself?

17. What good habits do you want to cultivate? What bad habits do you want to break?

18. What are some things you've participated in or done that most other people have not?

19. What kind of music do you enjoy listening to most?

    a. List your top-five favorite songs of all time.

b. List five songs you don't really care for.

c. Name your five favorite singers or bands.

d. If you had a theme song, what would it be?

20. **Do you like to dance?**

a. How often do you get the opportunity to dance?

b. How would you describe your dance style?

c. What music do you like to dance to?

d. What was your most memorable dance?

e. At a party, would you sit out the slow dances or the fast ones?

f. Do you ever dance by yourself? At a party? In the privacy of your home?

21. Can you take a compliment? If not, why? How do you respond to negative comments?

....

....

....

....

22. How do you feel about your personality type?

....

....

....

....

23. What are your personal gifts?

....

....

....

....

24. How important are your looks to you? How physically attractive/handsome do you consider yourself to be? What do you consider your best/worst physical feature? Why? Who said so?

....

....

....

....

....

....

....

25. What drains your energy? How can you remove it from your life or protect yourself from its negative effect?

....

....

....

....

26. How do you feel about the pace of your life? Is it:

a. too fast? ....

b. too slow? ....

c. just about right? ....

27. On a scale of 1-10, where are you when it comes to being calm and centered in challenging situations? What are your triggers and pet peeves?

....

....

....

....

28. What do you need to do to have more peace in your life?

....

....

....

....

29. How are you censoring what you really think or feel? What holds you back from being more authentic?

....

....

....

....

30. What does it mean to be your highest self?

....

....

....

....

31. What are the unhealthy habits in your life?

....

....

....

a. Why do you have them?

....

....

b. What do you intend to do about them?

....

....

32. Are you an emotional eater?

....

a. Do you find yourself eating unconsciously? ....

b. Do you eat out of physical hunger alone? ....

33. What struggle points do you have in your relationships?

....

....

....

a. Why? ....

b. Have you communicated these to anyone? ....

34. Are you happy/content with your life? ....

a. If yes, what is bringing that happiness/contentment? ....

b. If no, why not? ....

35. How much personal time do you need each week to function well and feel happy? How would you spend that time? What would you be doing?

....

36. Write down some of the things that are holding you back, for example:

a. I should stop: ....

b. I would be better off without: ....

....

....

c. I need more: ....

....

....

d. I need less: ....

....

....

e. I should spend more time with: ....

....

....

f. It's about time I: ....

....

....

g. I need to give myself: ....

....

....

h. I need to get started on: ....

....

....

37. **How do you sabotage yourself?**

....

....

....

38. **How much do you trust yourself? Do you tend to listen more to others than yourself?**

....

....

....

39. What is something that is true for you no matter what?

40. How do you feel about getting quiet, listening deeply and patiently to your inner wisdom?

41. Do you hold back from asking the big questions? The difficult questions? If so, what scares you? How do you hold back or refuse to take action on what your heart tells you to do?

42. In what ways is your self-acceptance conditional, dependent on specific accomplishments or the validation of others?

43. **Are you physically, emotionally, mentally, and spiritually healthy? In what ways are you healthy or unhealthy in each of the following categories?**

a. Physically:

b. Emotionally:

c. Mentally:

d. Spiritually:

44. **Do you feel comfortable expressing yourself?**

45. **Do you feel seen, heard, understood, and valued? What important needs do you have that aren't getting met?**

46. What does your inner critic tell you? How does it stop you from moving forward?

47. What are your messes and incompletes, things that need your attention (maintaining the car, fixing the roof, painting the house, fixing the garage door, cleaning out the closet)?

48. How do your "shoulds" influence your choices rather than your own wishes and dreams?

49. What makes you feel most authentic? Why?

50. Have you ever failed at something even after you gave it everything you had and could?

   a. What was it?

   b. Under what circumstances would you try again?

51. Are you more positive or negative in your speech?

52. What, in your opinion, are the qualities of a good listener? Do you have these qualities?

53. Are you a reliable person? Are you a good friend? Explain.

....

....

54. Are you a giver or a taker?

....

55. What are your opinions about the following:

a. being prompt: ....

....

b. drinking: ....

....

c. smoking: ....

....

d. dessert: ....

....

e. housekeeping: ....

....

f. your exercise routine: ....

....

g. correct grammar: ....

....

h. war: ....

....

i. terrorism: ....

....

56. What's stopping you from showing up the way you would like to? How does this fit into the vision you have for your life?

....

....

57. What do you need to give yourself permission to do?

58. What would happen if you forgave yourself even though you've done something you shouldn't have? How would that make you feel?

59. How does your imagined behavior compare with how you are actually living your life today? What can you do now to live your life in ways that would feel congruent with your innermost nature?

60. How can you have more fun in life?

REFLECTIONS

I love Maya Angelou's quote: "I've learned that people will forget what you said, people will forget what you did, but people will never forget how you made them feel."

Be a role model and an inspiration to those around you. People may not hear your words, but they are observing your life and tapping into how you make them feel.

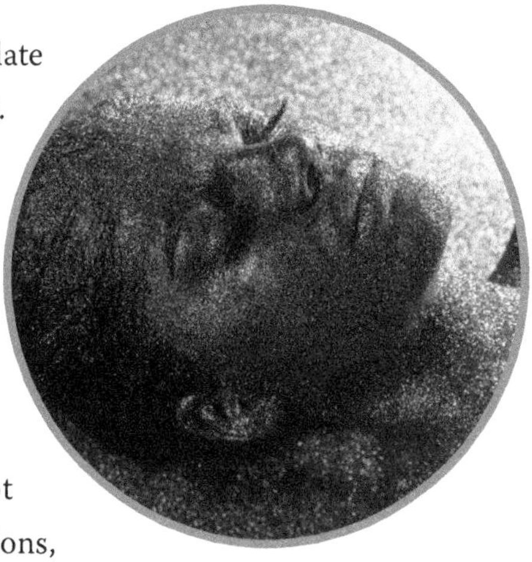

Notice how children often emulate what they see their parents doing. They model their lifestyles and their relationships. Everything seen and experienced growing up is registered in the child's memory. Paint a picture you are proud of, one those looking at you will be proud to frame. Lay stepping-stones not stumbling blocks for future generations, and create the vision and purpose in your home and the environment you live in that others would want to emulate. You are building a legacy. You add value to the world around you.

Speak words of encouragement and invest in those around you. You can have a positive influence in the lives of your family, your friends, and those you cross paths with, even if it's for a passing moment. You may never know what can happen when you touch just one life. Your life is significant. It paints a picture for others to see. Regardless of what you do or who you are, don't ever underestimate your value.

1. Ask someone who sees you often and knows you well to tell you honestly, without bias, what your strengths and weaknesses are. Who did you ask and what did you learn about yourself?

....

....

....

....

....

....

2. Get clear about what you want, what nurtures and nourishes your soul. One of the ways you can gain clarity is to start noticing daily what makes you feel good, happy, and valued. What gives you joy? Write these down. Add to the list every day and keep it where it's visible. Refer back to this list on days when you feel depressed, when your energy is low, and you need a boost of happiness. It's guaranteed to lift your spirits.

....

....

....

....

....

....

....

....

....

....

....

3. **Look at the list of some common limiting beliefs on the checklist below** and ask yourself, on a scale of 1-10, 10 being the most accurate, how true is each belief for me? Note your reaction to each limiting belief and try to recall where that belief originated from. It could be a shared belief that's based on your family, culture, or religion. List the source. Now go back and ask yourself, how true is that belief *really?*

a. I'm worthless. ....

b. I'm a failure. ....

c. I'm not lovable. ....

d. I'm not good enough. ....

e. I'm a victim. ....

f. I'm powerless. ....

g. I'm inferior. ....

h. I'm a sinner. ....

i. I'm all alone. ....

j. I'm a burden. ....

k. I'm dumb. ....

l. I'm unattractive. ....

m. I'm unproductive. ....

....

n. I'm incapable. ....

....

o. I'm guilty. ....

....

p. I'm incompetent. ....

....

q. I'm trapped. ....

....

r. People always abandon me. ....

....

s. The world is a dangerous place. ....

....

t. I don't deserve ....

....(fill in the blank).

Feel free to add any other beliefs that are limiting you. Check in often to see if any of the beliefs have changed; if they have, then replace them with new ones that more accurately resonate with you.

4. When you're not fulfilling your everyday role of spouse, parent, friend, boss, employee, and other, who are you? Answer this question, *who am I?*

Answer it at least thirty times until you've exhausted all of the roles you normally play.

1. ....
2. ....
3. ....
4. ....

5. ....
6. ....
7. ....
8. ....
9. ....
10. ....
11. ....
12. ....
13. ....
14. ....
15. ....
16. ....
17. ....
18. ....
19. ....
20. ....
21. ....
22. ....
23. ....
24. ....
25. ....
26. ....
27. ....
28. ....
29. ....
30. ....

5. Take time to savor your achievements and be kind to yourself by remembering and reminding yourself of all that you've done right, big and small, including anything that was challenging, kind, successful, and good. Now list twenty-five of these accomplishments. This exercise will help boost your self-confidence, give you much joy while being fun at the same time, and grease your path to success.

1. ....
2. ....
3. ....
4. ....
5. ....
6. ....
7. ....
8. ....
9. ....
10. ....
11. ....
12. ....
13. ....
14. ....
15. ....
16. ....
17. ....
18. ....
19. ....
20. ....
21. ....

22. ....

23. ....

24. ....

25. ....

6. **This week make out your usual to-do lists**, one consisting of meal plans, grocery shopping, and so on, another of goals you might be working toward, yet another one of purchases, gifts, and so on. Make several lists that indicate your daily habits and give a clear snapshot of your daily life. What did you notice? Which of these are limiting you, and what would you like to change?

AFFIRMATIONS

Self-love affirmations are an amazing tool for feeling better about yourself and your place in the universe. Maintaining a healthy sense of self-love is crucial to your overall well-being. The more you accept, understand, and appreciate yourself, the more you will thrive in your personal daily life.

To increase your self-love, affirm the following every day:

1. I am worthy of love.
2. My life is a gift. I use this gift with confidence, joy, and exuberance.
3. I acknowledge my own self-worth. My confidence is soaring.
4. I am worthy of all the joys and riches in the Universe.
5. I send love to my fears and let go of what does not serve me.
6. I approve of myself and love myself deeply and completely.
7. My inner peace and harmony match my outer well-being.
8. My imperfections make me unique and special.
9. I love my body and all that it does for me.
10. My body is my temple. I take care and feed it with healthy, nutritious foods.
11. My mind is alert. My heart is at peace. My soul is tranquil.
12. I appreciate my life and satisfaction comes to me with ease.
13. I am growing and learning each day.
14. I surround myself with positive people who help bring out the best in me.
15. I forgive myself for any hurts I may have caused myself or others.
16. I am loving and I am loved.
17. I stay balanced even when others behave in an unbalanced manner.
18. I release all negative thoughts and negative self-talk.
19. I embrace positivity and optimism.
20. I am overflowing with joy, vitality, and energy—I am unstoppable!

Now, go through the following exercises to affirm self-love. A pleasant transformation will take place. You'll feel more love for yourself and an increase in self-acceptance and self-worth.

1. **Do the following mirror exercise to increase self-love.** Do this at least once a day for forty days. *If you happen to miss even one day, then start all over again. It takes the subconscious mind forty days to validate a truth.* Make this the last thing you do before going to sleep each night:
   - Stand in front of a full-length mirror (if possible without any clothes on).
   - Look directly into the mirror. Look deeply into your eyes and say to your reflection: "I LOVE YOU, (your name). I LOVE YOU VERY MUCH. I really, really, really LOVE you."
   - Then scan your body and thank each and every part of your body starting with the top of your head to the sole of your feet. Say, "Thank you, eyes, for the gift of sight, "Thank you, ears for the gift of hearing, "Thank you . . ." (continue until you've thanked every part of your body).

2 **Fill in the blanks of the following gratitude statements.** Give five different endings to each statement that resonate with how your day went. Do not repeat any of the endings. This may be challenging at first, but as you get into this exercise, you will find that you can dig deeper and deeper, find new things to be proud of, to forgive yourself for, and to commit to:

I am so proud of you ....(your name here) that you ....

....

(five things)

I forgive you ....(your name here) for

....

....

(five things)

I commit to you ....(your name here) that I wil ....

....

(five things)

Now affirm: **I am beautiful. I am bold. I am brilliant. I am worthy. I love and accept myself. I am enough.**

FOOD FOR THOUGHT:
Shed Excess Baggage

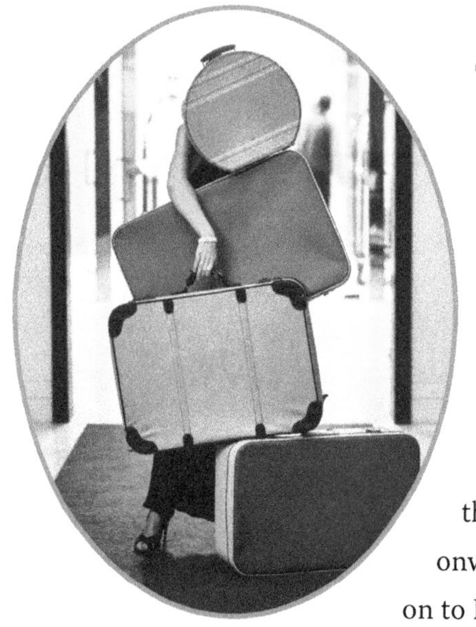

Travel light—let go of excess baggage.

Have you ever travelled to a place where you filled your bags to the max just because you thought you *might* need everything? I have. On a recent trip to Saint Petersburg, Russia, I packed my two bags to the maximum weight that the airline allowed. I was going onward to Milan from there, and then on to Paris by train.

It was one of the most challenging trips I've ever taken. Getting to Saint Petersburg was a breeze, but as soon as I got to Milan, the trouble started because I had not factored in the weight allowed on domestic flights and trains. Hauling those bags was a chore, and I ended up paying enormous fees to the airlines because of the one-bag rule. Honestly, I could have done just as well with one-fourth of what I packed because I never did use or need everything.

I learned a very important lesson: The less stuff you carry around, the lighter you feel, and the more likely your life will be more enjoyable.

What difference can an additional 10 lbs. of baggage make to you? Nothing! If you're a strong person, you might shrug it off with a laugh. But other people or organizations do mind. The airline that carries your baggage is one of those. They will charge you for excess baggage. Excess baggage adds to the load of a plane. Even if it doesn't plunge the plane to the ground, it consumes more fuel and potentially slows down a flight.

So does your journey of life. Excess baggage doesn't make much difference until it affects your health. Baggage comes in all forms and shapes. It includes ego, distractions, fear, and worries. Stress, anxiety, blame, and many other problems creep in, and as you allow them to add up, you're in trouble.

Excess baggage slows down the speed you can travel. It clips your wings and hinders your progress, prevents you from flying and scaling the heights you are meant to soar.

Do what the airlines do. Regularly monitor the weight of the baggage you're carrying and keep it to the minimum. When you find you are lugging around any excess, let it go so that you can live a life of ease. The less baggage you carry, the freer you will be, the more likely that you'll perform your best, and the more you'll find life to be enjoyable.

"Carry your baggage towards silence when you seek the signs of the way."

—Rumi

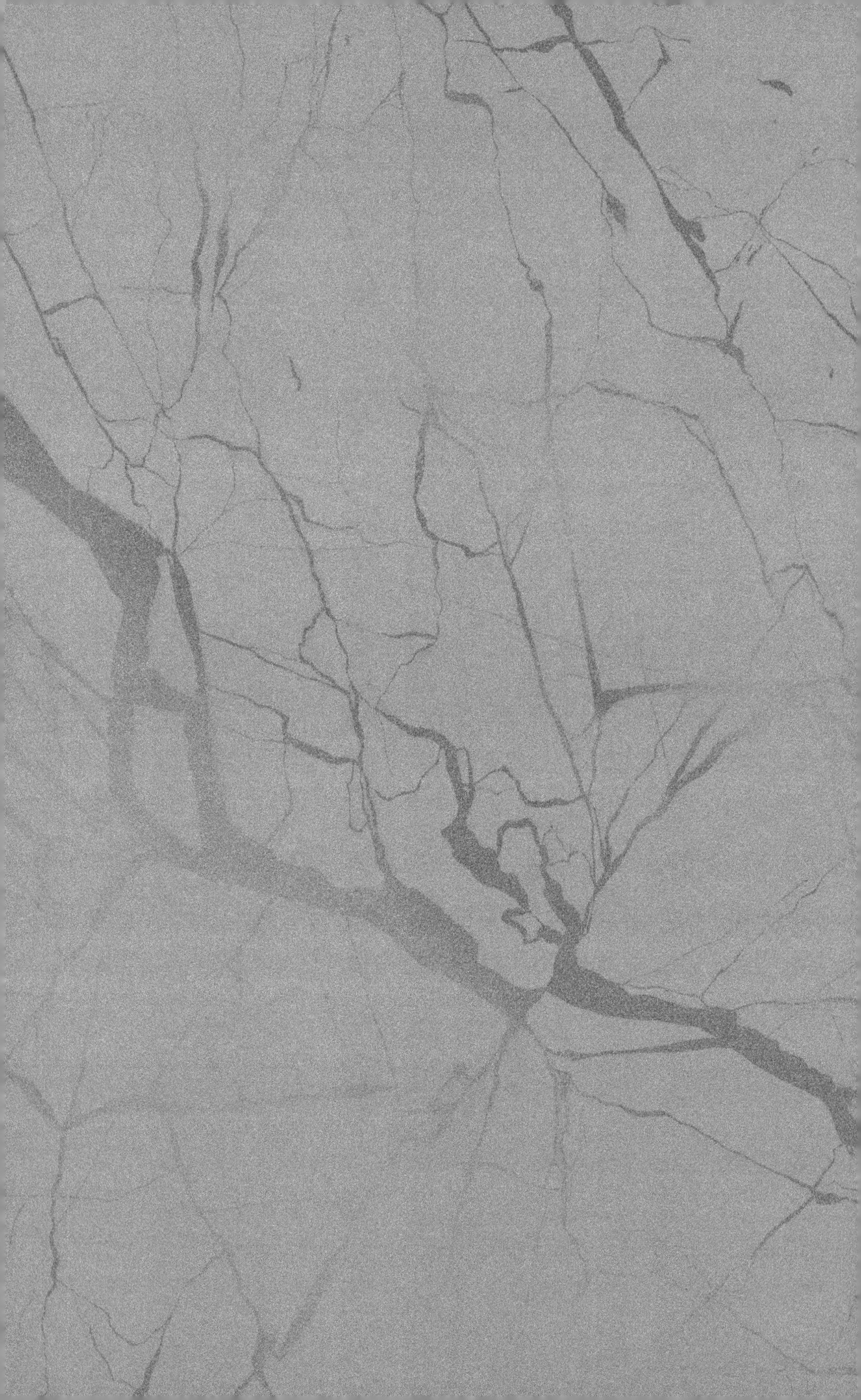

WHAT I WANT TO REMEMBER FROM THIS CHAPTER

DATE: ....

KEY POINTS: ....

TAKEAWAYS: ....

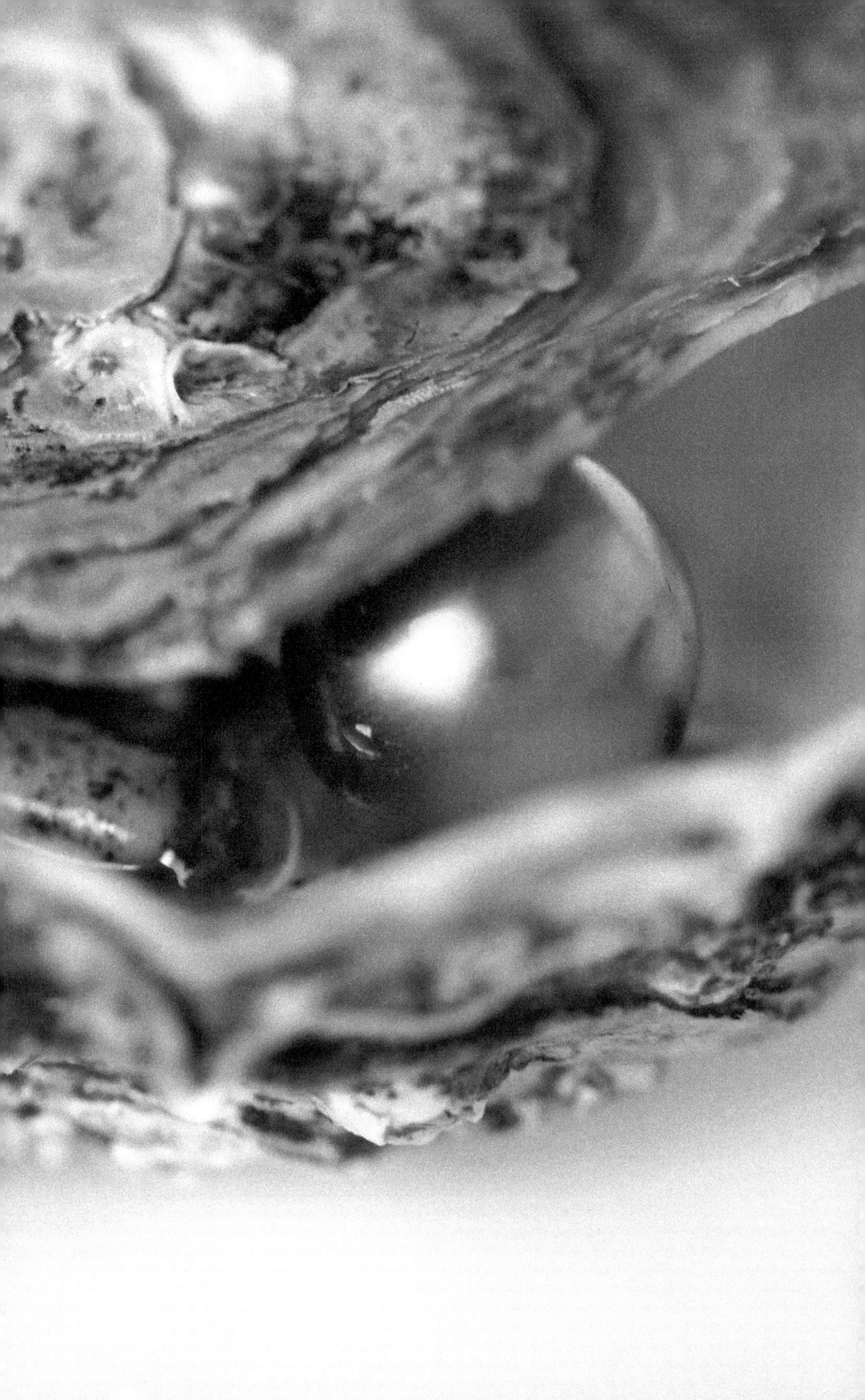

CHAPTER SIX

Your Relationships Are Like Pearls

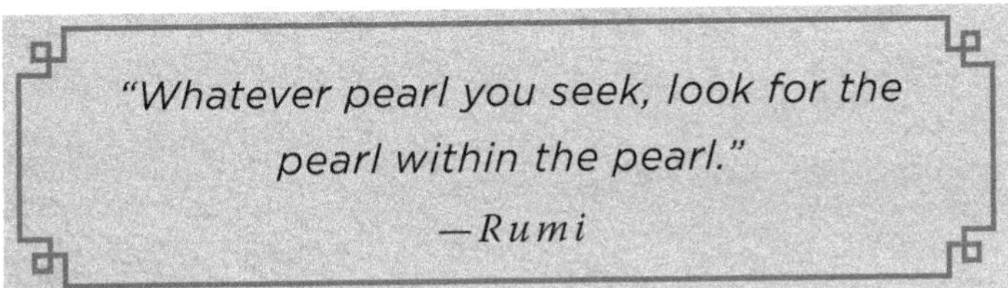

"Whatever pearl you seek, look for the pearl within the pearl."

—*Rumi*

Most people know that a pearl comes from an oyster. But what many don't realize is the amount of work the oyster has to do and the hardship it must endure during the making of that pearl.

A pearl forms when a single grain of sand or a foreign particle finds its way in between the mantle and the shell of an oyster causing it much pain and irritation. To protect itself, what does the oyster do? It secretes a lacquer-like substance called *nacre* that functions as a coating. The oyster carefully turns the grain over and over, coating it layer by layer with nacre as a means to protect itself and eventually succeeds in sealing away the irritation while continuing to smooth the edges, resulting in a beautiful, shiny surface that one day becomes this precious and beautiful pearl so many women enjoy wearing.

Isn't it fabulous what an oyster can do with a morsel of sand?

In many ways, a pearl symbolizes the precious bond in the different relationships of our lives—between mother and child, husband and wife, and even two special friends. In every relationship, there are ups and downs, or "irritations": a child being naughty, a husband or wife taking his or her stress out on one another, or a friend who forgets your birthday. If the bond is strong enough, the offended person will just forgive and add another layer of love to the relationship.

Offenses are just like grains of sand that need to be polished and perfected. What couldn't we do if, like the oyster, we, too learned to deal with the offenses that irritate us? How can we look for the pearl within the pearl? Inevitably in life, unfair things will happen—people *will* let us down, our feelings *will* be hurt, and we will not always be treated the way we think we should. If we allow these offenses to take root in our hearts, they will turn us into bitter human beings and steal our joy and enthusiasm for life.

In relationships, sometimes ego takes over and pride rules. Instead of living with pride and thinking we're always right and everyone else is wrong, we miss out on the best part of life—*living*. Pride only hurts; it never helps.

Relationships can be challenging if we let them. This is especially true in romantic relationships and when we're faced with hard times in life, when we feel broken. Our relationships have the potential to be both our greatest source of joy and our greatest sorrow, our greatest source of comfort and support or our greatest source of undermining and oppression. In even the most precious and vulnerable relationships, we rarely meet the other person as he or she really is or reveal our truest self. More often than not, we show up unconsciously in our default roles and patterns without truly seeing the other person or allowing our true self to come to the surface. Each wears a mask and is overwhelmed with expectations of the other that blinds us to the many possibilities available to grow the relationship into a loving, lasting friendship.

Many people look outward to someone to make them happy. They feel incomplete. In any relationship in which two incomplete people become one, the end result is two half-people. You must bring your *whole* self to any relationship.

I believe it's possible to experience and have fulfilling relationships without jumping through hoops and becoming stressed as long as you bring your whole self to that relationship. Realize that so many challenges around relationships are self-inflicted by reactive patterns that become painful and damaging. The solution, then is to excavate the negative patterns as they play out, recognize them, and inject and inoculate them with positive energy that is kind and caring. Ask yourself often, *where am I placing my energy in this relationship?* Focus on your *vibrational frequency* to make sure you resonate with each other.

The health of your relationships can clearly reflect the condition of your self-esteem. Relationships can affect how you see and perceive yourself and the reality around you. In unhealthy relationships, people have a tendency to make poor judgments, and more often than not, invite toxic people into their lives. Those with low self-worth have difficulty setting limits and establishing healthy boundaries and may even become dependent on the will of another person. Or they have the irrational need to have "perfect" relationships. There is no such thing as a *perfect* relationship. There is only a relationship that is perfect *for you.*

Beware of relationships that drain you. Learn to set limits on people who are toxic, irreverent, and disrespectful. How many people have you known who have sought consistently—under the mask of seeking to help—to tear you apart as a person and reduce your future, hopes, and goals and the very energy of your life? Sometimes, we mistake kindness for submissiveness. Now you can be more vigilant and aware so you can avoid such individuals, set healthy boundaries, and overcome the damage their toxicity can cause to your confidence, success, and well-being.

Remember, the first relationship to improve is the relationship with your self. If you're looking for more love, then you need to love yourself more. This means *no* criticism, *no* complaining, *no* blaming, *no* whining, and choosing *not* to feel lonely. It means being content with yourself in the present moment and choosing to think thoughts that make you feel good.

You may have the tendency to inject your values onto others' lives and try to make them live according to your values. Attempting to be who you are not or to make other people who they are not is futile. Ultimately, if you search and search for *perfect* love, you will miss the love you're living. And that love must begin with the love of self.

If you carry around resentment inside of you about anything or anyone—the person who was abusive, the person who walked out on you, the person who never paid you back, all the things you feel you have a right to be resentful about—it will end up harming you and creating in you a sense of despair, perhaps even causing you to remove yourself completely from social contact just to protect yourself from any further pain.

What I find so interesting about the oyster is that it doesn't let much time pass, nor does it allow the sand to linger before it begins to cover the grain with nacre. There is a very good lesson here. If we allow offenses to fester, they will cause damage that can become irreversible. And that can be devastating. Offenses can be like seeds that take root and begin to grow. If we allow offenses to linger and grow, before long they will become big issues that strain and weaken our relationships to the point of permanent destruction.

This chapter invites you to look at your relationships and provides a place for introspection, revelation, imagination, and declaration. Here you may share secrets, fantasize, boast, complain, and set down your memories. There are no right or wrong answers. Your answers are merely a road map revealing much about who you are while bringing clarity and insight as to why you think the way you do about each relationship you have today.

Answer the following questions.

1. **What type of people do you enjoy spending time with (e.g., intelligent, outgoing, reflective, funny, etc.)?**

....

....

   a. Why do you enjoy these specific qualities in people? ....

   ....

   b. Do you seek people similar to you or different from you? Why?? ....

   ....

2. **How easy is it for you to trust someone? Do you trust your intuition when it comes to relationships? Are you open-minded or judgmental about other people?**

....

....

....

....

3. **If you ever had your heart broken, what was the situation surrounding that occurrence? How did it affect your life?**

....

....

....

....

4. What five life-changing events have impacted your relationships the most?

   1. ....
   2. ....
   3. ....
   4. ....
   5. ....

5. Are you able to stay in long-term relationships, or do you get bored quickly?

....

....

6. If a relationship makes you unhappy, do you choose to stay or leave?

....

....

7. What's the one lie you repeatedly tell yourself about the relationships in your life?

....

....

8. Which quality about people do you hate the most? Why? Which do you love the most? Why?

....

....

....

....

9. In general, do people annoy you? How do you think you annoy other people?

....

....

....

....

10. Do you generally get upset when others don't do as you tell them to do?

....

....

11. What is your biggest problem in relationships that keeps popping up?

....

....

....

....

12. Have you ever been cheated or betrayed by a friend, a lover, or a family member? If so, describe what happened. Have you ever cheated or betrayed anyone? If so, explain.

....

....

....

....

....

....

....

....

13. Has anyone stood by you or helped you when you needed it? Describe.

14. What is your definition of love? What are your primary beliefs about love (e.g., it's easy, scary, short-lived, etc.)?

15. Describe your best overall and worst-ever romantic experiences.

16. In your opinion, sex is:

17. Do you love yourself? Why or Why not? How can you love yourself more today?

18. What is/was your greatest fear about marriage? About having children?

19. Do people generally like you? Why?

20. **Are you afraid of letting others get close to you? Why?**

....

....

....

....

21. **Do you see your relationships as successful? Why or why not?**

....

....

....

....

22. **Describe any relationships you may have lost through divorce, death, or other circumstances and what that felt like.**

....

....

....

....

   a. Have you recovered from those losses? ....

   ....

   b. If not, what can you do now to reconcile and move past grieving? ....

   ....

23. **Do you believe it's possible to be in love with more than one person at a time?**

....

....

24. **What are three traits you look for in a life partner?**

1. ....
2. ....
3. ....

25. **How important is it that your lover or life partner be**

a. rich? ....
b. intelligent? ....
c. physically attractive? In what way? ....

....

d. kind? ....
e. helpful? ....
f. generous? ....
g. spiritual? ....
h. humorous? ....
i. a good communicater? ....

(add whatever else you feel is important to you)

26. **How many times have you been in love? Describe.**

....

....

....

....

....

....

27. **How would you feel if you never had a life partner? Why?**

....

....

....

....

28. **Name your two closest friends and one trait you admire in each as well as one trait you wish each of them could change.**

    a. ....

    ....

    b. ....

    ....

29. **Name a friend you've known for the longest time.**

....

    a. Is this person a close friend? ....
    b. Why or why not? ....

    ....

    c. When is the last time you saw this friend?

    ....

    d. When do you think you will see this friend again?

    ....

30. **Name someone who genuinely makes or has made you very happy.**

....

....

31. **Describe your first romantic date.**

....

....

....

....

32. **Describe your first serious relationship.**

....

a. What attracted you to him/her?

b. What interests, values, and characteristics deepened that relationship?

c. When and why did you consider yourself ready to make a commitment to the relationship?

33. Name a friend with whom you can share anything and from whom you can ask advice.

34. Name a friend who is most like you. How?

35. Name a friend you've lost for a reason other than death.

a. What happened?

b. Would you like to see this friend again?

c. If you were to cross paths with this friend, would you be affected? How?

36. Who is a person you don't like yet you spend time with?

37. Name a person/persons who were close to you who has/have done something terrible to you but whom you've forgiven.

a. Describe what you've forgiven. In other words, what did he/she/they do/did?

b. Are they still in your life?

c. Would you like to have them back in your life? If no, why not?

38. Name a friend who does or believes in something you cannot respect or agree with.

a. What is it that you cannot respect?

b. Have you shared your feelings about this?

39. **Name a friend who makes you feel insecure, unworthy, depleted.** ....

a. Have you shared how you feel? ....

....

b. If this feeling continues to persist, how do you feel about ending the relationship? ....

....

40. **Name a friend to whom you have something important to say but have not had the courage to say it.**

....

a. What would you like to say to this person? ....

....

b. What's holding you back? ....

....

41. **What three best qualities do your friends describe you as possessing?**

1. ....
2. ....
3. ....

42. **Have you ever acted selfishly, been egotistical, or ruthless?** ....

a. What pushed you to that point? ....

....

b. Who was involved? ....

....

c. How did that make you feel? ....

....

d. Did you ever apologize for your action(s)? ....

....

43. What do you say or ask when you really want to get to know someone?

....

....

....

44. What, in your opinion, are three things that are least/most appealing about women?

Least Appealing	Most Appealing
1.	1.
2.	2.
3.	3.

45. What, in your opinion, are three things least/most appealing about men?

Least Appealing	Most Appealing
1.	1.
2.	2.
3.	3.

46. Do you truly believe it's possible to be with one person for the rest of your life?

47. Did you choose to marry more than once? Why or why not?

48. What is your spouse like?

49. If you have children, what are you most proud about each child? Describe the most challenging aspects of parenting each of your children.

50. If you don't have children, what are your feelings surrounding having or adopting children?

....

....

....

....

51. In your relationships, do you make most of the decisions?

....

52. If currently in a relationship/marriage, are you happy? Why or why not?

....

....

....

....

a. In what ways would you like your partner to change? ....

....

b. Why is that important to you? ....

....

c. Could you be happy if he/she didn't change? Why or why not? ....

....

....

d. What did you appreciate about this person when you first met? ....

....

e. What do you appreciate about this person now? Why are those qualities important to you?

....

....

....

f. What is the single, biggest attitudinal change you could make that would enhance this relationship? ....

....

g. What one issue do you find you and your partner argue about most? ....

....

53. **What do you enjoy most about a committed relationship? What do you dislike most?**

....

....

....

....

54. **Describe your most recent selfless act and how it made you feel.**

....

....

....

....

55. **Assuming you just met a stranger at a place you frequent. He/she tells you a bit about his/her life. Are you listening intently? Or are you waiting for an opening to talk about yourself? Describe how this meeting made you feel.**

....

....

....

....

56. To show someone you love him or her, are you likely to use words, actions, or another method?

....

....

57. What are the best words to describe your current relationship?

....

....

58. You partner is not providing you with what you need. Do you tell him or her or suffer in silence?

....

....

59. True or False: "All is fair in love and war." Explain your answer in the context of your life.

....

....

....

....

60. You just received wonderful/bad news. Whom do you tell first?

a. your partner
b. your best friend
c. a stranger/the first person you see
d. share on social media

REFLECTIONS

One of the best things about growing older is the ability to look back at your life as a mature adult and take stock of the kind of person you've become, how you see yourself, how you interact with others, and the relationships you seek.

Take a step back today and look at what you've invested in your relationships. What's the value of the time, energy, heart, and commitment you've invested? Perhaps you're facing some difficult times but consider all the challenges you've come through so far, and rather than focusing on the problems, choose instead to focus on the treasure of the relationship.

In any relationship, it's important to be best friends first. Friendship is one of the most important ingredients for happiness. Friends bear witness to our lives; they help us form and fulfill our dreams, laugh with us, comfort us, and celebrate with us. They lift us up when we're down and remind us of who we are when we lose our way. But friendships, like gardens, need to be tended and cared for in order to grow.

How are you nurturing your friendships? Are you paying attention to them, or do you take your friends for granted? Do you let the people you love know how you feel about them? I often hear people say that it is actions not words that matter. Personally, I believe *both* matter. A simple "I love you" or "I'm thinking of you" when spoken sincerely goes a long way. It lets the person know that you care, that he or she is missed and loved.

Life always mirrors back to us what we give out. Give love and you will receive love.

What about romantic relationships? What do you bring to them? Do you think "we" or just "me"? A relationship between any two humans is a dynamic thing. One cannot expect a relationship to thrive if both persons take each other for granted or do nothing to nurture it.

Choosing fresh ways of responding and interacting with each other even when it feels awkward and uncomfortable is like trying to learn the steps to a new dance in the middle of a crowded dance floor. And yet for all the discomfort, there's also a freedom and a new freshness and sense of intimacy that allows old patterns to fall away so you can meet each other as you are with your whole and naked selves. Part of kintsugi living is choosing the especially discomforting and challenging times to heal our brokenness, to shed the usual patterns, and meet each other again for the very first time without our default patterns in place.

True love can only thrive when it is open and unguarded. True love is not about spending every waking moment gazing into each other's eyes but rather casting our gaze in the same direction. True love means caring and sharing and starts with you and how you take care of yourself so that you may give to another from your overflow.

And if you are single, don't let that deter you from treating yourself as well as you believe your partner would. If you don't have anyone to buy you roses on Valentine's Day, buy them for yourself. If you don't have anyone to celebrate your birthday with, treat yourself to dinner and buy yourself some birthday cake. When you invest in yourself and see yourself as valuable, then others will recognize your worth, too. Remember, how we treat ourselves sets the example for how others treat us. As you develop your inner sense of love and romance, you become like a magnet, and you will attract the right person into your life.

There isn't just one way to experience love. We all experience love in different ways. For some to really experience love, they need to *feel* love through being hugged and touched. Some need to *hear* the words *I love you.* Others need to *see* a demonstration of love, like a gift or flowers. It's important to really study and know the people you allow into your life. Their actions speak louder than their words, and their needs are revealed by their actions.

Two interconnected humans—be they parent and child, husband and wife, brother and sister, lovers, or simply two friends—have to interact positively for the relationship to form, be maintained, and flourish. For this to happen, each must be mentally tuned into the other.

If you are single today, take the time to watch a person's life before you give him or her your heart. If you're considering a business partnership, take time to learn the character of the person you're dealing with before you make that commitment. Also, don't ignore the red flags that may show up. When questionable issues show up repeatedly, pay attention and ask yourself, *what is this telling me?* Take the time to study the people you allow into your close circle. When you know and understand the people you're in relationships with, you can better adapt to them in the future.

If you're a parent, maybe you feel you have failed or weren't as good a parent as you should have been. Perhaps you were too busy trying to make a living, keeping your head above water and the household running and consequently you were not as present in your children's lives as you would have liked to be. You may be feeling guilty and think, *if only I had spent more time with my children and made them a higher priority.*

We've all missed such good chances, but it's still not too late to look for creative ways to communicate with the people in your life. Take time to be present and get to know them, find out what they want, encourage them, be considerate of their feelings and their needs, and then do your best to provide them.

By listening to your children and giving them your undivided attention, you help build their confidence and make them feel valued and loved. Allow them to have their thoughts and feelings even if they are completely contrary to yours. Let them find their own solutions. It's okay to let the solution be the other person's idea. When someone takes ownership of an idea, that person is more likely to get behind it. *Remember, it's not about who's right, it's about what's right.* Ultimately, you'll never fail at your relationships unless you quit.

I know some people who have a tendency to approach relationships with an "I'm-going-to-fix-you" attitude. They believe they are on this earth to impart wisdom and to straighten others out. But that never works because most people we're in relationships with already know the areas they need to work on and don't need anyone else to point out their shortcomings. When we start "fixing" everyone around us, what we're really saying is you're not good enough the way you are, and we miss the true riches we would otherwise gain from those relationships. People need to know that they are loved unconditionally, accepted just as they are, and be allowed to be who they are. Just relax and enjoy your relationships.

Have realistic expectations and give the people in your life the room to be human. Accept the fact that nobody is perfect and that even the best people will fail us at times. Don't hold mistakes and failures against your loved ones when they disappoint you. It's not up to anyone else to keep you happy and content. That is your own responsibility. Too often, we expect our partners to cheer us up when we're down and to always be loving and kind, our friends to always be there for us, and for our bosses to recognize our hard work. But those are unrealistic expectations. The perfect spouse doesn't exist, neither does the perfect boss nor the perfect friend.

Oftentimes, the people who are closest to you may not always be sensitive to your needs and may not even realize that they've hurt you. Help the people around you understand you better by communicating your needs. The people in your life can't read your mind, and consequently you can't always expect them to know exactly what you want or need, what you like and dislike, what helps you and what bothers you.

Give people room to be human and have realistic expectations of them. Accept them as they are, and save yourself the heartache and disappointment by simply understanding that no matter how much you love people, or how much they love you, at some point they will not live up to your expectations. One of the most freeing experiences for those in relationships is to recognize that they are two different people who see things differently and who can still love each other and stay connected. You don't have to see eye to eye to walk hand in hand.

Relationships are all about learning and getting to know one another. In marriage, you're learning to become one; in families, you're learning to get along; in friendships, you're learning to make allowances for one another; and in business, you're learning to work together. To learn about each other, you must become a good listener, be fully engaged and present. Life is a learning process.

Keep no record of wrongs, ignore other people's shortcomings, and instead find something in them that you love and that exceeds your expectations. Focus on the positive so your relationships will not only survive but thrive.

A good relationship is ultimately just a decision you make to believe in each other, respect each other's opinions, support each other, and move through life together, always connected.

Reflect on this chapter and take some time to answer the following questions:

1. What kind of a person are you today? What do you think others think of you?

2. If you could change anything about yourself, what would it be?

3. We usually rely on our sense of smell, touch or taste, sight and sound, to remember things so they stay fresh indefinitely. Write about a memory that links to an emotional state where you experienced profound loss. Include as much sensory detail as possible. How long ago did this event take place? How have you healed since?

4. Make a list of people who negatively affect you, who make you feel small, and in whose presence you feel anxious and irritated. Next to each name, write what it is that they do or say that irks you. Now step back and read those words and ask yourself, *is this true?* More often than not, you'll realize that what they say or how they feel about you is really not about you at all but a reflection of their own beliefs about themselves and their own insecurities.

....

....

....

....

....

....

....

....

Every day for twenty-one consecutive days, pray for them and send blessings their way. You will notice a shift: Either the relationship will change, or your attitude toward these persons will change. If things haven't improved much, continue the process, and in the meanwhile, avoid spending more time than you have to in their company. But if you can't avoid spending time with them, then shield yourself with a bubble of white light that their negativity cannot penetrate.

5. Think of the positive people in your life and how they lift you up and are good for you. Name three people whose company you enjoy:

1. ....
2. ....
3. ....

a. What effect do they have on you (e.g., are they supportive, nurturing, energizing, etc.)?

b. What do you like about their behavior, their approach, and their attitude toward life?

c. How can you introduce some of what you love about them into your own life? Explain.

6. **Something fabulous occurs when you put your complaints on paper.** Paying attention to your complaints is one of the best ways to get clear about what you want. List what bothers you, things you wish would change in your relationships in Column A. Now in Column B, rephrase each negative statement with its opposite. Be specific (e.g., change, *I hate that my partner is always too busy for me* to *I love that my partner makes time to be with me*). Column A feels negative while Column B implies beauty. After you've finished with your list, draw a big black X through Column A and start taking small but immediate steps toward making Column B your reality.

Column A (What I Hate)	Column B (What I Want)
....	....
....	....
....	....
....	....
....	....
....	....
....	....
....	....
....	....
....	....
....	....
....	....
....	....
....	....
....	....
....	....
....	....
....	....

AFFIRMATIONS

When you think joyous thoughts, you are a happier person; everyone is drawn to you. When you're happy, then all of your relationships improve. A happy person is very attractive to others. Happiness is contagious.

Affirm the following daily to cultivate more love in your life. Watch as your love for yourself and others grows, attracting more and more love to you. Affirm:

1. Today I choose to give love.
2. I use my words to compliment and encourage others.
3. I realize how much weight my words carry and seize every opportunity to paint positive pictures on the hearts of those I love.
4. I attract only healthy and loving relationships.
5. I am safe in all my relationships.
6. I show my love through acts of kindness, always mindful that no act of kindness is ever too small or wasted.
7. I speak faith into my family and compliment them every chance I get.
8. I look for ways to find common ground with the people in my life and focus on what we agree on rather than allowing disagreements to separate us.
9. I choose to see the best in those I am in relationship with and give them the grace to make mistakes and the freedom not to be perfect.
10. I make time for those I love and every effort to stay connected.
11. I take full responsibility for my own happiness and realize it's not up to anyone else to keep me happy and content.
12. I love myself more and share that love with all those around me.
13. I'm comfortable looking at my reflection in the mirror daily and saying to myself, I love you, I really love you.

14. I am beautiful and everybody loves me. Love greets me wherever I go.
15. I let go of all the offenses and wrongs done to me and send love and blessings to the people in my life.
16. I choose my words carefully knowing that my words can build bridges to the hearts of those I love.
17. I treat the people in my life as I want to be treated.
18. I am very thankful for all the love in my life.
19. I love and accept myself just as I am.
20. I know that love opens all doors.

FOOD FOR THOUGHT:

Be Present and Smile!

A smile is contagious—pass it on!

Did you know it takes more face muscles to frown than it does to smile?

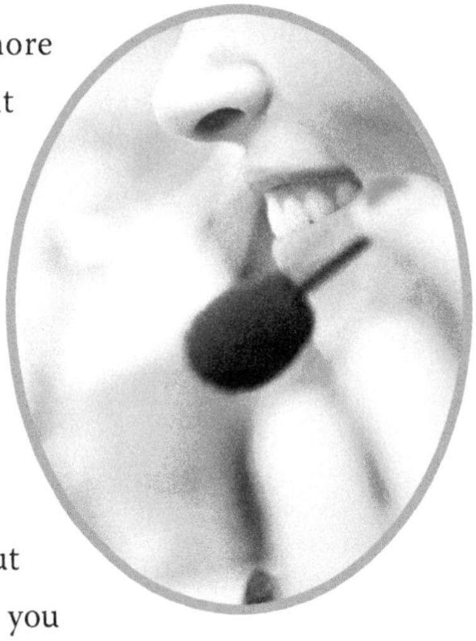

Have you ever noticed that when you smile, people are automatically drawn to you? Your positive attitude is like a magnet that attracts others and makes them want to be in your company. Try it.

When you smile at someone, you make them feel welcome, feel good about themselves, feel as if they matter, and that you see them.

Your attitude is contagious. Bring a good attitude, a smile, and your whole self to your relationships. Pay attention when you are in the company of others; listen consciously to what they are saying without interrupting so they may finish sharing their thoughts; be fully engaged and communicate consciously.

As the saying goes: "We have two ears and one mouth so that we can listen twice as much as we speak."

When we feel heard, acknowledged, and understood we feel more loved, connected, and supported. We feel more compassionate and are more likely to extend that compassion and our presence to others. This is the greatest gift that you can share. It is a gift of positive intention.

One person's happiness can lighten the mood of a whole roomful of people.

I encourage you to get up every day and put on a fresh new attitude. Don't reminisce on the good old days. Remember *these are* the good old days. Make the most of every moment and keep the right perspective. And smile.

This week, pay attention to how you act when you are with others. Communicate with very few words but with genuine engagement and a positive attitude. You will notice a big shift in how people relate to you and great improvement in even the most challenging relationships.

Be fully present; talk less and listen more; communicate with your eyes; engage with interest; pay undivided attention to what is being said; show enthusiasm; be sincere; turn off your smartphone; simply listen; and smile.

Conscious communication is a relationship builder. Try it, with a smile.

"Whatever happens just keep smiling and lose yourself in Love."

—Rumi

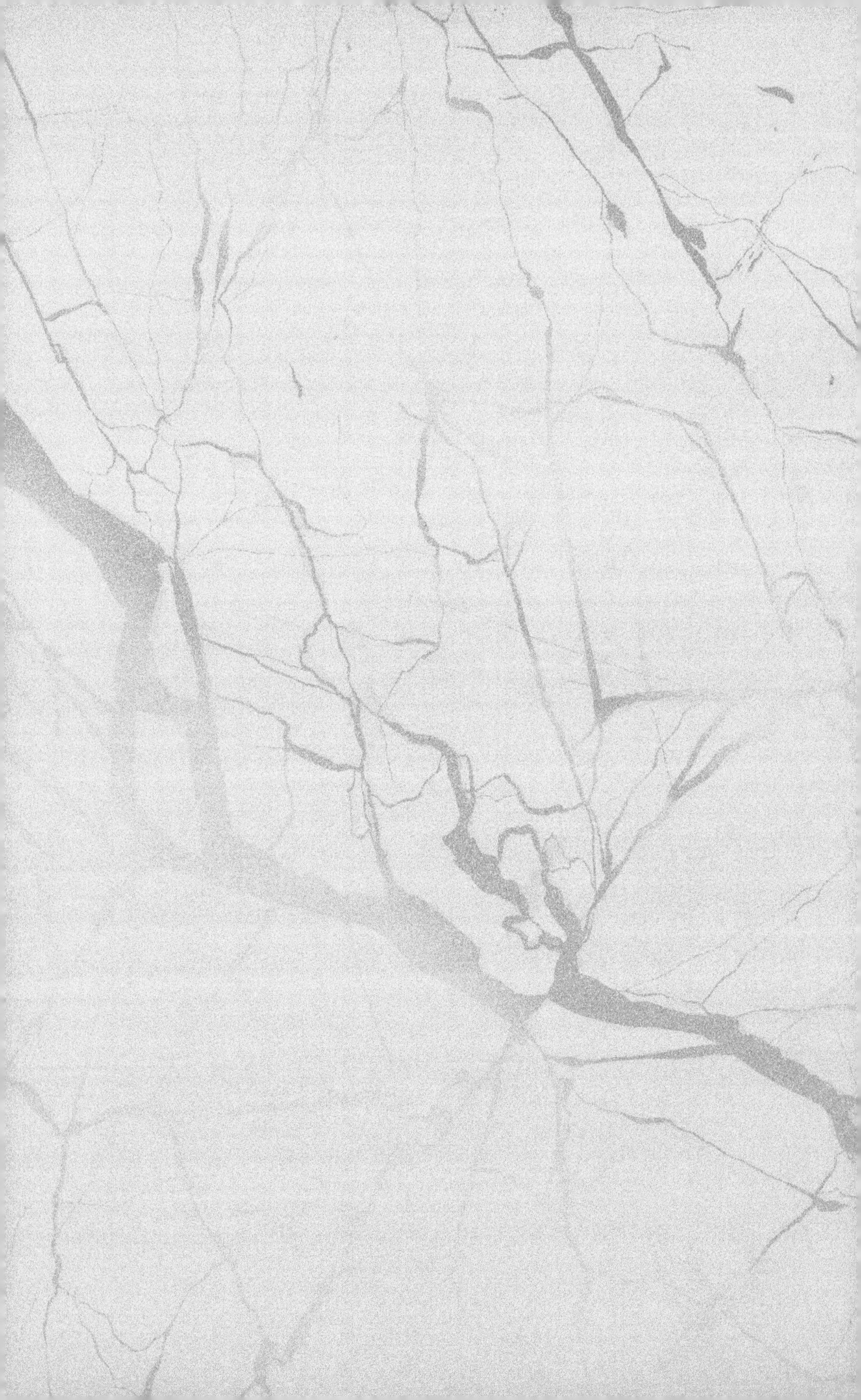

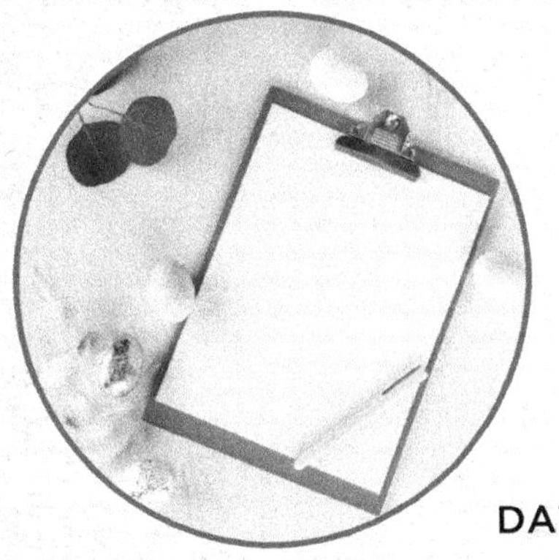

WHAT I WANT TO REMEMBER FROM THIS CHAPTER

DATE: ....

KEY POINTS: ....

TAKEAWAYS: ....

CHAPTER SEVEN

Finding Your Life Purpose

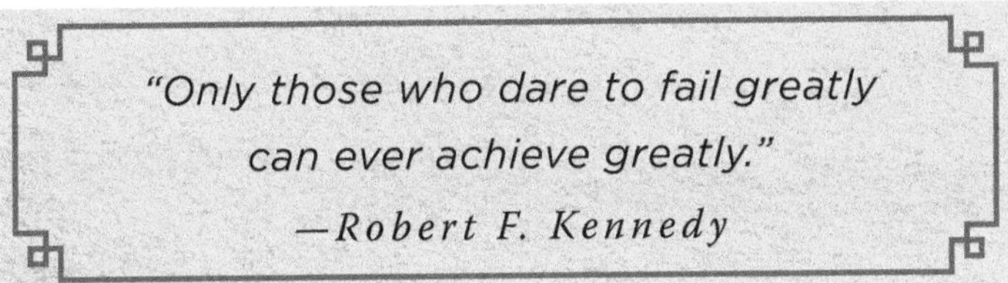

I was reading about the world-famous boxer Muhammad Ali and how, just before every boxing match, his trainer Angelo Dundee would write a number on a small slip of paper and place it inside Ali's glove. The number Dundee wrote was the round he predicted Ali would knock out his opponent. Although a strange thing to do, Dundee was so confident in Ali's ability to win—not *whether or not* he would win, but *when* he would win—and Ali knew it. The confidence Dundee showed and the positive effect this action had on Ali helped give him a champion's mentality.

Most of us do not have an Angelo Dundee in our lives to help instill the self-confidence we need to go out into the world and face our opponents. Fear can hold us back from stepping into our greatness to create the success we desire. Do you think fear was ever a factor as he stepped into the ring to trade blows with his opponents? Do you think that Muhammad Ali was ever afraid? My guess would be that he was. But that little slip of paper in his glove reminded him that the person who knew him best believed in him, and that gave him the courage to face his fears.

Surround yourself today with those who believe in you and your dreams, who genuinely care for you and wish to see you succeed, those who support your passion and are your cheerleaders. Push past your fears and uncertainties with confidence and move into your destiny.

What dreams do you have for your professional life? What's holding you back?

Do you love what you do, or is it simply a means to an end? Is there a balance in your life between the time you spend working and your leisure time, or is it a seamless continuation where one blurs into the other? Does your work fire you up with enthusiasm, or does it drain your energy? Are you living your dream? Have you set goals around your dream and achieved your goals? Or, has life gotten in the way and steered you on a different path? Are you suffering from the shiny-object syndrome and distracted by too many ideas and choices?

Some of the reasons so many become dissatisfied with their work but don't take any steps to follow their dreams and their life purpose are the following: fear of failure, fear of losing their identity, and fear of losing their status. So we play it safe. We feel so much has been invested in our current roles, we're good at what we do, and it's comfortable and predictable, so why change?

Besides, we are creatures of habit and not comfortable or at ease with our capacity to adapt, change, live our own dream, and rebuild ourselves by creating the circumstances we want. Our habits provide us with apparent safety; our routines are an anchor in the middle of a sea of uncertainty. At times, we become determined to ignore the alarm signals that our brain sends telling us that change needs to happen.

Our fear of the unknown holds us back. Breaking the barrier of fear is difficult, so taking action becomes an uncomfortable compromise, one which we're not willing to take.

Ultimately, we become innately dissatisfied with life, detached and resentful, and distracted. Distraction takes us away from our focus. It draws attention away from our center and leads us through unnecessary and costly detours. We create movies in our mind telling stories of an imagined failure, a terrifying future, so we slam the brakes on what could have become an amazing journey to success.

Keep it simple and stay focused on your goals and on the end result. Don't let the external noise distract you from realizing your dreams. Take one small step at a time and avoid becoming overwhelmed. You can be your own cheerleader without the need of an Angelo Dundee in your life. Develop your own championship mentality and success will be yours.

Finding the one thing that gives you joy, trusting your heart, and embracing a new path is the first step toward living a life of your dreams. This is followed by an action plan that will get you from where you are to where you want to be.

The key to getting the career you want is first to focus on the one you already have and to do it to the best of your ability while you plan action steps toward your new goal. Readjust and recalibrate your journey constantly to avoid major shifts. Transform your dream into bite-sized projects that are realistic and manageable. Don't get swayed by too many shiny objects as this Tao master teaches his disciple, because ultimately they distract you from your life purpose.

The new disciple is excited upon seeing the master for the first time and curiously asks, "How do you practice Tao, Sir?"

"When you are hungry, eat," thoughtfully says the master, "When you are tired, sleep."

The answer is astonishingly simple to the disciple as he is expecting something sagacious and profound. "Isn't that what everyone does anyway, Master?"

"No," says the master matter-of-factly, "Most people feed themselves with thousands of desires when they eat, and dream of thousands of designs when they sleep."

Pondering deep, the disciple nods his head and is happy with the new insight.

The Tao master is sharing what it means to suffer from the shiny-object syndrome.

No wonder so many people cannot excel or succeed at one single task; they're overflowing with too many distractions and are unable to concentrate on what matters most to them. They lose focus.

Remove distractions and there are no longer multitudes of desires when you eat or thousands of designs keeping you awake. When you are focused, you can be present. When you are present and fully aware, you can take solid steps toward your goals. You sleep better and eat better. Focusing allows you to get results from the things you do BY DOING LESS.

Rather than investing in an outcome that you can't possibly fully control, focus instead on achievement. Take small steps daily recognizing that each step is an achievement in its own right, and each marks progress on your way to reaching the ultimate goal you desire. When you do not have clarity, you cannot reach your goal; your dream cannot come true. Once you've made up your mind what your goal is, take the first step, however small that step is.

Try it. Don't underestimate the impact. Eventually, you'll understand the power of "non-doing," the art of accomplishing more by doing less.

Action is necessary to realize your goals. Without action, there is no momentum. Transform your desire into objectives, create an action plan, work-think-work, readjust, make decisions, and then decide whether what you're doing is viable or not. Taking the first step no matter how small can be difficult. It involves risks, learning new skills, getting to know new people, and making sure you are moving in the right direction. Take these steps and soon your dream will turn into a beautiful reality.

As you go on your journey to fulfilling your dream, one of the most valuable lessons you can learn is to never identify yourself with what you've accomplished in the past and the material items you've acquired. Thinking like this will stop you from fulfilling your passion, your dream, and your goal. These past actions don't make you who you really are now. They are merely labels that show your ego at work.

On the road to success, you will encounter many people who will be more than happy to share their opinions on the path you're following. By all means, listen to their ideas and advice, assess them, but examine them carefully before incorporating them. Trust yourself and your capabilities. Trust your gut instinct. What is your inner voice telling you? Pay attention. Build your dream little by little and take your time. There's no need to rush things. It's better to be safe than sorry, to do things slowly and mindfully rather than quickly and badly. Whatever you do, you don't want to regret your actions.

Your experiences and your life purpose are what make you, *you.* They help shape your life, develop your leadership traits, and help you perceive how good leaders should be as well as influence the kind of leadership you aspire to in both work and life.

Different situations at work, home, in politics, and in any and every endeavor often require different styles of leadership. Mentors, coaches, mastermind groups, self-reflections, and affirmations can help any person stretch into the leadership behaviors needed to become an effective leader.

When you are able to remove the roadblocks keeping you stuck, you are able to be inspired and creative, to achieve success in life and in your career. Your inspired creativity demands that you break through your preexisting conditions, beliefs, and paradigms. Your life choices are determined by your past conditioning, unless you actively and purposely change your perceptions.

The following questions will help you gain clarity on the root cause of some of your roadblocks. Your answers will help you tap into your purpose, to create an efficient and effective pathway to fulfill your highest values and achieve the success you deserve.

1. **What is your definition of success? Do you think you are successful? Why or why not?**

....

....

....

....

....

2. **What acquired skills and accomplishments are you proud of? What are your five greatest strengths?**

....

....

....

....

....

....

....

....

3. **Are you currently doing the type of work you love to do?** ....

a. If not, what type of work would you rather do?

....

....

b. What has stopped you from pursuing this type of work? ....

....

c. What can you do to change that? ....

....

4. At your dream job, what would be:

a. the ideal environment? ....

....

b. your ideal work team? ....

....

c. the ideal number of hours you would work per week? ....

....

d. the ideal pay? ....

....

5. Describe your current place of work:

a. Where do you work? ....

....

b. How far is it from where you live? ....

....

c. How long is your commute? ....

....

d. Do you like the environment of your workplace? Why? Why not? ....

....

6. **What does money represent to you (e.g., security, peace of mind, freedom, etc.)? Does thinking about money make you peaceful or anxious? Why?**

7. **How much money do you believe you deserve to be making annually? Why?**

   a. What would it mean to you if you made more or less than this amount?

   b. Why?

8. **What is the one award/trophy/distinction you would be honored to earn?**

9. **Do you have an easier time doing business with men or women? Why?**

10. **Describe one of your most driven moments.**

....

....

....

11. **How confident are you in your abilities to make decisions for yourself?**

....

....

12. **What is your biggest self-limiting belief regarding your career?**

....

....

....

....

13. **Would you consider yourself hard working or lazy?**

....

....

   a. How do you view hard-working people? ....

   ....

   b. How do you justify your drive or lack of work ethic? ....

   ....

14. **Are you comfortable making tough decisions, or would you rather play it safe to not offend anyone?**

....

....

15. Do you think you would make a leader worth following? Or are you more a loyal follower? What is your evidence for either choice?

....

....

....

....

16. Who is your greatest role model? Why?

....

....

....

....

17. What is one failure that you've turned into your greatest lesson?

....

....

....

18. What three lessons have you learned the hard way?

....

....

....

19. What is your ideal career or dream job? How can you start creating your ideal career starting today?

....

....

....

....

....

20. **What empowering beliefs can you take on to help you achieve your goals?**

....

....

....

....

....

21. **Who are your mentors in life?**

....

....

22. **Who are the creative and courageous people who inspire you?**

....

....

a. What about their approaches and ideas resonate with you? ....

....

....

b. How can you be like them? ....

....

....

23. **Think of a time when you felt brave at work. What did you do?**

....

....

....

a. How did others respond? ....

....

....

b. What did you learn from the experience? ....

....

....

24. **Do you have opportunities at work to interact with people whose experiences and opinions are very different from yours? Explain.**

....

....

....

....

....

25. **Do you lean into a challenge or away from it?**

....

....

26. **What would you absolutely do if you had the talent or the opportunity?**

....

....

....

....

....

27. **How has your intuition helped you in the workplace?**

....

....

....

....

....

28. **Describe a time you were given a challenge you weren't sure you could complete.**

....

....

....

....

....

a. How did the situation make you feel? ....

....

....

b. Did you see it to fruition? ....

....

....

29. **How do you feel after you've done something you've been meaning to do for ages?**

....

....

30. **What's the one thing you wish you could learn with the snap of your fingers?**

....

....

31. **Imagine you're in a room with a group of people who all share the same opinion on a certain topic. Do you go with the flow or argue the counterpoint?**

....

....

32. **Imagine a group of people having a conversation on a topic you know nothing about, and one of them turns to you and asks your opinion. Do you admit ignorance or bluff your way out?**

33. **Imagine you are on a team of people creating an iconic building. Which job do you offer to help with? Why did you pick that job?**

    a. managing the project
    b. designing the building
    c. ensuring its safety
    d. planning the interior

34. **Let's say you've just started working at a new job and one of your colleagues is mean/unkind to you. How do you handle the situation?**

35. **Given a choice to work at a job you love for very little pay or work at a job you hate for a luxurious salary, which would you take? Why?**

36. What is your meaningful work? Does it align with your gainful employment?

37. What hobby are you passionate about that could very well be your full-time job, if only it paid?

38. What would it look like to integrate play into your professional life? Describe.

39. What is your hope for your work and career?

40. **Someone gives you a complex task you're not sure how to accomplish. Do you:**

....

....

a. make a plan?
b. ask someone for help?
c. research how others have done similar projects in the past?
d. read a book on the topic?
e. What does your choice tell you about your learning style?

41. **You have an important task to do. Do you do it now or procrastinate?** ....

42. **At work you:**

a. make most of the decisions
b. don't make most of the decisions

43. **If you didn't have commitments to others, what would you do?**

....

....

44. **Your to-do list this week is overwhelming. Do you ask for help or give up sleep to do it yourself?**

....

45. **Describe one of your plans or projects you worry might fail.**

....

....

46. **How has a feeling of scarcity affected your work experience?**

....

....

....

....

....

47. **Have you ever been hurt by putting your work out in the world? How did you react to the criticism?**

....

....

....

....

....

48. **Have you ever been embarrassed about your work? Why?**

....

....

....

....

....

49. **Do you seek perfectionism in your work?** ....

   a. How has that worked for you? ....

   ....

   ....

   b. Has perfectionism hindered your success? ....

   ....

   ....

50. Have you ever not pursued a dream job for fear of failing? ....

a. Do you regret not taking the leap? ....

b. If you had to do it all over again, would you take the chance? ....

51. What is the most fulfilling job you've ever had? Which one did you hate the most?

....

....

....

....

....

52. What sort of work do you do currently (includes stay-at-home mom)? ....

a. What do you like about what you do? ....

....

....

b. What do you dislike about what you do? ....

....

....

c. How good are you at it? ....

....

....

53. What are the shortcomings of your work?

....

....

....

54. **Did you ever quit your job? If yes, under what circumstances? Have you ever been fired? What was the reason?**

....

....

....

....

....

55. **Do you overcommit and:**

a. work when you should stay home to rest?
b. are reluctant to go on vacation?
c. fill your weekends with projects and errands?
d. have sleepless nights worrying about pending projects?
e. never take a leave of absence?

56. **What do you think about retirement?**

....

....

a. What in your opinion is the ideal age for retirement? ....

b. At what age do you plan to retire? ....

57. **How good are you at delegating tasks? Why?**

....

....

....

58. **What is your most important goal right now?**

....

....

....

59. **Imagine today is your first day at your dream job. You're so excited you can barely contain yourself. When you arrive at work, you take a minute to look around and appreciate the moment. You can't believe you actually got this job.**

a. Where are you? ....

....

....

b. Why do you value this job so much? ....

....

....

60. **Create a newspaper headline you would like to read about yourself and your accomplishments.**

....

....

REFLECTIONS

Life has put you in front of a mirror so you can take a good look at yourself and the choices you've made and continue to make.

What do you see?

Are you one of those people who wiles away the hours and does the bare minimum required of you? Do you spend your days feeling bitter and hate having to get up to do what is necessary to make a living? Do you hate your job, your career, your lifestyle?

Hopefully, this chapter has helped you gain clarity and acknowledge about what has worked and what hasn't, what inspires and motivates you and what doesn't so that you now know what you want, what you feel called to do, be, and have, and ultimately tune in to your life purpose.

Without a purpose in life, one can wander and drift aimlessly, accomplishing little with no clear destination in mind. But with a purpose, everything in life seems to fall in place—people, resources, and opportunities naturally gravitate toward you.

When you perceive yourself as fulfilling your purpose, your self-worth and self-confidence grow exponentially. Your purpose is more of a journey rather than a destination. It is expressed by your state of being, doing, and having. Your accomplished goals are merely stepping-stones along the path of your life's purpose.

Learn from your past and what you've gone through. Close the dark chapters of your life and open new ones. If you're not happy where you are, with what you're doing, leave and take the chance to follow your passion. The unknown can be scary, and leaping into the void without a safety net can make one panic. I've been there so I know the road well. All I can say is you'll be surprised and relieved once a decision is made, however painful that decision may be.

It's the decisions we *don't* make that actually end up hurting us more.

These are times that require additional effort on your part. Action is required. But action without planning is a useless investment in unfocused energy that leads nowhere. You must dedicate more time and energy to your goal and have proper and realistic expectations, and above all, dissociate your self-esteem from your professional achievements. Remember, you are more than your successes.

This is not the time to look back and blame yourself for your mistakes. Neither should you reject them or settle into them. This is the time to analyze so you can transform your negative emotions such as shame, resentment, and self-pity into constructive criticism and instructive lessons. Learn from your mistakes and avoid repeating them. Keep your feet on the ground and be realistic in your expectations. Pick up your broken soul and shattered past, repair your life and your dreams, and fill the cracks with gold to create the beautiful jewel that is worthy of you.

Perhaps after reflecting, you'll realize you're actually satisfied and even passionate about what you're doing now. If that's the case, then amplify it! Do you realize what a huge favor life has bestowed upon you? Take advantage of this favor by going after your dreams. Life is waiting for you. Don't waste it.

Are you clear now about your WHY? About what drives you?

1. **Write down your life purpose statement.** Here's an exercise that will help you create a compelling statement of your life purpose:

   a. List two of your unique personal qualities, such as *creativity* and *enthusiasm*. ....

   b. List one or two ways you enjoy expressing those qualities when interacting with others, such as to *inspire* and to *support*.

   ....

   ....

   c. Assume the world is perfect right now. What does it look like? How are people interacting with each other? What does it feel like? Write down a statement in the present tense describing an ideal, perfect world as you see it and feel it. Remember, a perfect place is a fun place to be, one that brings peace and joy.

   ....

   ....

   ....

   ....

   ....

   ....

   d. Now combine the three previous answers (a, b, and c) into a single statement. Example: *My purpose is using my creativity and enthusiasm to support and inspire others as I freely express my talents in harmony, love, and joy.*

   ....

   ....

   ....

Make sure the statement includes a balance of giving (doing) and getting (having). Maximizing your self-worth and elevating your state of being can only be achieved when you maintain a fair and equitable exchange with others.

Read your life purpose preferably twice a day, first thing in the morning and at night before you go to sleep. Inject feeling and passion into your statement. Backing your thoughts with your feelings enables you to reach new heights to attract and impact everything that resonates with a similar vibration. Always end with gratitude. Then make sure to go forth into the world and **act as if** everything you desire has already come true for you.

Visiting your life purpose statement daily will act as a constant reminder and keep you focused. Add clarity by engaging all five senses—sight, hearing, taste, smell, and touch—to your thoughts and feelings. Visualize what you would love, and in your mind's eye see it as if it's already come to pass. Make sure that your vision, goal, and values align with your life purpose. Then take daily action steps that will move you closer to fulfilling your purpose.

As you begin living your purpose, you'll feel inspired and motivated. As you are inspired and motivated, your enthusiasm will rub off on those around you. Your actions inspire others to dream more, learn more, do more, and become more. Suddenly, you become a success magnet, a leader others want to follow. People start paying attention to you and want what you have, and you begin to win the respect of those you interact with.

Remember, you cannot lead or help others achieve what they would love without helping yourself achieve what you love first.

2. **Do you have what it takes to be a leader?** Take a few moments to reflect on the following:

   a. Do you value others and their contributions? If so, how? ....

   b. Do you demonstrate your approval and gratitude with action (e.g., a personal note, a bonus check, or public recognition)? ....

   c. Do you make an effort to study what motivates the individuals in your organization?

   ....

   d. Do your best employees/associates/team members appreciate your curiosity? Are they more engaged with their work as a result of your engagement? ....

   e. Do you help those around you find meaning in their work? ....

   f. Are your vision, the organization's mission, and your core values aligned?..

3. **Recall the best and worst bosses you've ever had**, as well as leaders, officers, and politicians you may have voted for in past and present elections, and then describe the leadership qualities he/she either demonstrated or failed to demonstrate.

....

....

....

....

....

   a. What do you wish they had done differently or better? ....

   ....

b. Do you see some of their traits in yourself? If so, what are you going to do about it?

4. **Make a list of the three most important goals you've been working on** or that you've dreamed of and want to achieve. What actions have you taken/will you take toward these goals?

5. **Describe one thing that if you were to change about yourself** would create enough momentum to make you do what you need, to have what you want. Write convincingly how not having this thing is holding you back and what you can do to get it and achieve what you want as a result.

6. **Determine the top-five emotions that are unique to you.** Those who end up having great careers in life that they enjoy are those who learn how to add their top-five emotions to the everyday part of their careers. Once you learn how to do that, your career not only becomes more rewarding, it fulfills your calling and brings out the best in you. Start your list now.

1. ....
2. ....
3. ....
4. ....
5. ....

AFFIRMATIONS

We are constantly evolving in our life's journey. Declaring that you are capable of certain leadership traits and of achieving your goals can subconsciously help you put forth higher levels of focus, energy, and intent toward achieving them.

Affirm what you love. Saying affirmations on a daily basis can help you move toward your purpose and live "on purpose" with less resistance. Researchers say it takes three weeks to make or break a habit, so repeat these affirmations for twenty-one consecutive days with no break in between to catapult you to achieve the success you long for:

1 I am using my unique skills and abilities to manifest my perfect career.

2 I am living my full potential, earning a wonderful living doing work that is important to me.

3 I am committed to providing excellent service and value in everything I do.

4 The more I give, the more I receive.

5 I make decisions quickly, and I keep my methods flexible.

6 I am a good communicator. I communicate to achieve a desired result rather than simply to deliver information.

7 Every moment holds an opportunity for me to expand.

8 I am empowered by my soul's urge for creative expression.

9 I value the agreements I make with myself and follow through with grace and ease.

10 I choose to be intentional when I make agreements with others.

11 I use my words with care.

12 I am a people person and have excellent relationships with everyone who works for and with me.

13 I am blessed to be working with creative, supportive, and loving people.

14 I attract wonderful employees and business partners who believe in me and who assist me in my career.

15. I am willing to make the sacrifices necessary to accomplish the results I want.
16. I am grateful for and continue to improve my skills and talents.
17. I think and act according to my moral compass and am passionate about helping others live their full potential.
18. I dream bigger than others think is practical and expect more than others think is possible.
19. I am proactive and have clarity about my career path and my life purpose.
20. I maintain a positive outlook on life.

FOOD FOR THOUGHT:
Dare to Fail

The secret of never failing lies in the way you perceive the situation. You may ask then, "*What is the usefulness of a fall*?"

If you see falling as a failure, then it is a failure, and the usefulness of the fall is typically associated with failure. You can view failure as a stigma, and this can of course be dismaying. But if you see the fall as one of a series of steps along the journey to fulfilling your dream and a stepping-stone toward your success, then it is no longer perceived as a failure. It becomes a part of success rather than failure.

Fear keeps us from trying. It encourages us to stay put; it's the voice that whispers in our ear, *it's not worth the risk*, that *it's better not to try than to fail.*

Thomas Edison's teachers said he was "too stupid to learn anything." He was fired from his first two jobs for being "nonproductive." As an inventor, Edison made one thousand unsuccessful attempts at inventing the lightbulb. When a reporter asked, "How did it feel to fail one thousand times?" Edison replied, "I didn't fail one thousand times. The lightbulb was an invention with one thousand steps."

There are times in life when we need to risk all to follow our dreams and let go of the aspects of life that feel comfortable and familiar. Otherwise, we risk the danger of forfeiting an opportunity and living a life filled with regrets.

What are you afraid of? Is it something real or imaginary? Remember, our minds cannot differentiate between the two.

What's holding you back? What if you took the leap? Would it lead you toward or away from further happiness?

Fear is the body's way of protecting us from real or perceived threats but has no root in reality. Instead, live from a state of constant curiosity and see every failure as a stepping-stone to success. If you viewed every act of failing as something useful, one that leads to success rather than failure, you will never fail! Each failure in the conventional sense then becomes something like Edison's one thousand attempts to create a lightbulb—a necessary stepping-stone to achieving your dreams—and an element of success.

Michael Jordan dared to fail, and that is why he became successful.

"I've missed more than 9000 shots in my career.

I've lost almost 300 games.

26 times, I've been trusted to take the game-winning shot . . . and missed.

I've failed over and over and over again in my life.

And that is why I succeed."

—Michael Jordan

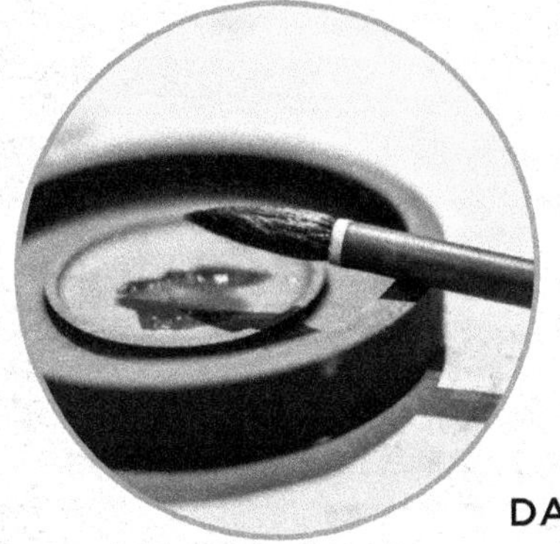

WHAT I WANT TO REMEMBER FROM THIS CHAPTER

DATE: ....

KEY POINTS: ....

....
....
....
....
....
....
....
....
....
....

TAKEAWAYS: ....

....
....
....
....
....
....
....
....
....
....

CHAPTER EIGHT

Shift Your Life Perceptions

> *"There are only two ways to live your life. One is as though nothing is a miracle. The other is as though everything is a miracle."*
>
> —*Albert Einstein*

Everything we see and experience in life can be seen from two perspectives: the first is how things *appear* to be; the second is what they *actually are*. Our perceptions can change at the blink of an eye, and they all stem from awareness.

A teapot is a teapot because it looks like a teapot, but it doesn't *need* to be a teapot. It can be turned into a sugar container or displayed as a piece of art.

The same goes for failure. If you've ever failed in life, you'll understand. That you did indeed fail is a fact. What you decide to do with that knowledge is your choice. It all depends on how you perceive the situation. It's all about perception.

As you go through life, pay attention to how you perceive every incident. Your life perceptions determine your success as well as your failure. Keep your perceptions in line with how you wish to live and your eye on the end result. A failure can be perceived as a miracle. If you hadn't failed, you might not have tried to do things differently and hence not been able to create the success that was waiting for you.

How do you perceive your life? What lessons has life taught you?

A young man, desperately seeking answers to why he continues to fail at everything he does, takes great pains to trek to the mountains in Northern China to visit a revered Tao master. People from far and wide come to visit this master to seek his advice.

Weary and tired, the man finally arrives at the master's humble abode and pays his respects.

"How can I be successful, Master?" humbly asks the man eagerly awaiting an answer.

Instead of giving an answer, the master asks, "What's the shape of water?"

The man is puzzled. "The shape of water? Why! Water has no shape!"

The master takes out a cup and fills it with water.

"Oh, I know the answer now. Water is in the shape of a cup!"

The master shakes his head and silently pours the water into a vase.

"Now I see; water is in the shape of a vase!" exclaims the man.

Silently the master pours the water to the ground. The ground is sandy and the water vanishes into the sand in no time. "The man ponders and says, "So . . . water has no shape, and yet it can be in any shape."

The master nods his head and leads the man to a corner outside his house. Pointing to a rock on the ground, he asks, "What do you see?"

"There's a hole in a rock formed by drips from the roof," says the man.

"There you are! If you want to deal with the ever-changing world, be as pliable and yielding as water," says the master. "Stay close to reality. Be as focused and consistent as water so that you can penetrate a rock," says the master.

Awestruck, the man thanks the master for the insight that changes his life.

Water can be in any shape. It stays close to reality, focused and consistent, strong enough to destroy the resistance of a rock.

Similarly, your success in life depends on your life perceptions and the meaning you give to all that is happening around you. Be soft, pliable, and yielding like water so you can learn life's lessons and yet stay so focused that you can penetrate even a rock, and be consistent in your beliefs so you may forge the path toward your success.

Be comfortable and at peace with every situation. Simply reassess the circumstance and go within to look for answers. Your inner world reflects your outer world. Knowing this, why add more clutter in your inner world that the outer becomes unnecessarily complex? Why not embrace simplicity instead?

Answer the following questions:

1. What is the best age to be in your opinion? Why?

....

....

....

2. How do you feel about getting older?

....

....

....

3. What did you wonder about when you were younger? Do you still wonder about those things now?

....

....

....

4. What did you do when you were younger that you feel you can't do now? Conversely, what can you do now that you're older that you couldn't do in your younger years?

....

....

....

....

....

5. What do you wonder about now that you're older? Do you believe it will matter ten to twenty years from now?

....

....

....

6. What do you regret not having done in your younger days? Fill in this sentence:

If only ....

I would've been ....

7. What was the best year in your life? What happened? What was the worst year of your life and why?

....

....

....

....

....

....

....

....

....

8. How and when do you expect to die? What makes you believe that?

....

....

....

....

....

9. What are the ten things you wish to see, do, have, and accomplish before you die?

1. ....
2. ....
3. ....
4. ....
5. ....
6. ....
7. ....
8. ....
9. ....
10. ....

10. What was your first experience dealing with death (grandparent, parent, pet, other)?

....

11. If you only had six months to live, how would you spend your time?

....

....

....

....

....

12. What do you believe about death and life after death? What do you think will happen after you die?

13. Do you believe in heaven, hell, or reincarnation?

14. If reincarnation does exist, what would you like to come back as?

15. How do you react to tough times?

16. Do you believe your destiny is predetermined or in your hands to shape however you wish?

17. What do you believe is the meaning of life?

18. What are the biggest lessons you've learned in life to date?

....

....

....

....

19. What do you believe about God/ Source/ your Higher Self?

....

....

....

....

20. How has your childhood affected your beliefs about God/Source or lack thereof?

....

....

....

....

21. What characteristics do you believe God/Source possesses? Why do you believe that?

....

....

....

....

22. What is your relationship with God/Source? Is it the relationship you want? Why or why not?

....

....

....

....

23. Has God/ your Higher Self spoken to you, and if yes, what was said?

....

....

....

....

24. If you could ask God/Source one question, what would it be?

....

25. Describe your most spiritual moment.

....

....

....

....

26. What in all Creation do you feel most awed about?

....

....

....

27. Do you believe that most wars are started because of religious conflicts? ....

28. Do you believe everything happens for a reason? ....

29. Do you read your horoscope? ....

30. If you had unlimited funds, what would you be doing? If you had millions of dollars, how would you spend it?

....

....

....

....

31. Name three charities or people to whom you would donate money. Why did you choose these?

1. ....
2. ....
3. ....

....

32. Name a crime or natural disaster you fear.

....

33. What are you most afraid of?

a. failure
b. success
c. crowds
d. spiders
e. knives
f. guns
g. sirens
h. injections
i. hair loss
j. other (name) ....

34. What has been your most fearful moment?

35. What does life want from you?

36. What are the best words that would describe your life now?

37. What are your biggest obstacles in life right now?

38. What's the most important thing in life for you?

39. What's the one piece of wisdom you would pass onto a child?

40. What traits of your parents do you appreciate now that you're older?

....

....

41. Did you at some point switch roles to become the caretaker of your parents? ....

a. How? ....

....

b. What happened? ....

....

....

c. How did you feel? ....

....

42. How comfortable are you with your own mortality?

....

....

43. Do you believe money is the root of all evil?

....

....

44. How do you view rich people? How do you think you arrived at these views?

....

....

....

....

45. **How do you view poor people? How do you think you arrived at these views?**

....

....

....

....

46. **Which form of economy do you prefer the most?**

a. Capitalism (an economic system in which a country's trade and industry are controlled by private owners for profit rather than the government)

b. Socialism (a system in which wealth and income are shared more equally among people)

c. Communism (a system in which no private ownership of property is allowed)

47. **What issues about current world affairs mean the most to you (e.g., abortion, equal rights for LGBT, illegal immigrants, gun control, etc.)?**

....

....

48. **If you could change one law, what would that be?**

....

....

49. **On behalf of the issues that mean the most to you, have you donated time/money?**

....

50. What do you think is the difference between treating people fairly vs. treating them equally?

51. Do you think world peace can exist? Why? Why not? What is currently happening to make you feel or see "the situation" this way?

52. What in your opinion is the worst crime against humanity?

53. Do you believe a person is defined by what they do for a living? If yes, why?

54. How do your mind, body, and soul feel?

55. Do you feel you must please some people in your life all the time? Who are these people?

56. What do you think would happen if you stopped saying yes to those you love?

57. Do you have boundaries in place? If not, what would you like them to look like?

58. When did you last say no to someone and how did this make you feel?

59. Do you plan time for yourself and stick to the plan?

60. **Do you/have you volunteered time or money to a community, religious, or political group?** ....

a. What have you done? ....

....

b. If you have not, will you volunteer? ....

c. What will you do? ....

....

REFLECTIONS

Upon reflection, you may have noticed that some of your perceptions are flawed.

How you perceive your life, the people and events around you, lies precisely in your beliefs, in what *you* believe to be true. Beliefs stem from meanings you infer, imagine, and interpret. We interpret other people's attitudes, imagine their behaviors, and infer meaning behind their actions based on our own beliefs rather than on what is actually taking place.

Most perceptions are ingrained in our past, in what was told us as we were growing up. My advice is to ignore the opinions of others and stop letting their judgments of you be the cause of your suffering. Review what you think others believe and put their judgments in the context of their own partial and inferred information about you. Be selective and choose whose opinions you will value and ignore the rest.

For every current belief that does not serve you, go to the origin of that belief, be as objective as possible, and ask yourself the following:

- *What actually happened (*not what you **think** happened*) to contribute to this current belief?*
- *Why did it happen?*
- *Who was involved?*
- *What was said to make me believe this?*

When you eliminate a belief from your subconscious, your brain activates all cognitive functions and puts them at the service of your mission. When you change your perceptions to ones that empower you, your thinking improves, you become capable of developing skills that you never knew you had, you attract the right relationships into your life, and you are able to live your purpose.

What answers have you gleaned from this exercise? Sometimes the answers are right in front of us, but we make them more complex than they really are.

When your life feels like an uphill battle and things aren't going as planned, remember it's because *you* created this in some way or another. Certainly, it seems like an easy solution to stand around complaining about things and blaming the circumstances or someone else for the way things turned out.

It's time to shift your perception and take 100 percent of the responsibility for your life. Whether you like it or not, everything that's happened in your life was somehow the result of your own actions and reactions. The outcome of any event is dependent on your response to that event. You always have a choice and the power to determine how you respond. The event is what it is, something you cannot change, but how you respond or react to the event determines the outcome. It's really up to you.

If you have the power to create an outcome, it's correct to believe that you also have the power to recreate something better. So, walk away from the stories you've been telling yourself and reframe them. Change the perceptions that don't contribute to your best life. Tell a new story, one that will empower you and help create a better, brighter world.

Past conditioning and your life perceptions have a role to play in how you move beyond your limiting beliefs. Until you go within and change how you perceive the world, the people in your life, your surroundings, your career, finances, even politics, and shift your thinking, your world cannot change.

Ultimately, if you search and search for a perfect world, you will miss the one you're living in. So, adopt a healthy outlook on life. Take 100 percent responsibility. Shift your life perceptions.

Now reflect on the following:

1. When you were a child, you probably had tons of questions. You asked why often and without abandon. Invent a series of questions (at least fifty) without censoring yourself. Invent and write down every silly, deep, provocative, commonplace, or outrageous question you can think of. Be your own interviewer and answer as sincerely as possible. You will be surprised at your answers and the insights that your subconscious mind reveals. Don't hold back.

....

....

....

....

2. **What are you grateful for?** Write these down in a journal. Noting big and small things that happen in your daily life and journaling them kick-starts an attraction for even greater abundance. Take time to look around you now. Notice and appreciate the present moment. Doing so will help you experience life more fully. Name twenty things that you are grateful for and the reasons why. Add more as you're inspired to do so.

3. **Investigate your personal definitions of common words. What is YOUR specific definition of the following words?** Define precisely and specifically the way *you* think and feel about these words and what's true for *you*. You will find that their meanings, even though not drastically different from the dictionary's, will start to have more impact on your life once you define them.

   - myself ....
     ....
   - truth ....
     ....
   - honesty ....
     ....
   - love ....
     ....
   - happiness ....
     ....
   - success ....
     ....

- responsibility ....
....
- acceptance ....
....
- trust ....
....
- guilt ....
....
- anger ....
....
- appreciation ....
....
- belief ....
....
- inner ....
....
- knowing ....
....
- peace ....
....
- soul ....
....
- fear ....
....
- joy ....
....
- intention ....
....
- friend ....
....
- mistake ....

....

- judgment ....

  ....

- reality ....

  ....

4. **Check your laughter meter.** When was the last time you had a good, healthy belly laugh? How do you perceive yourself? When was the last time you laughed at yourself? When was the last time someone else had a laugh at your expense? Did you take it personally? Do you need to lighten up a bit so you can enjoy life? This week, make a conscious effort to find something to laugh about every day if you can. Perhaps meet up with someone who makes you laugh and whom you can let loose with. Consider treating yourself to a self-styled comedy night. Tell a silly joke. Read a favorite cartoon. Watch a funny movie.

5. **Don't feel guilty.** Guilt and shame are emotions that serve no purpose. They are rooted in your past, and regardless of how you may wish to, you cannot undo what was already done.

   a. Write down five things that were said that you are still living with today, things you cannot seem to be able to shake, things that still bring up feelings of guilt and shame. What was it that was said? Who said it? Why was it said? What happened? What story have you been telling yourself?

      ....

      ....

      ....

      ....

      ....

b. Now turn that story around to one that empowers you. Check your inner dialogue and affirm the new story as true; keep repeating it to yourself until you actually start believing it. Give your new story a touch of optimism, lots of feeling, and above all, self-respect. Make sure the story is one that inspires and motivates you. Remember, you are still the same person you always were but under some new circumstances. You think differently, and your life perceptions have shifted to ones of empowerment. Don't worry about what people might say about the new and improved you. The people who understand you will get it; all others don't really matter.

6. **Change your attitude.** Sometimes, we're so attached to a particular view of ourselves that we don't realize how it's limiting our potential and holding us back. Have the courage to let go of the person you think you are right now and be brave enough to live life to the fullest. Get out of your comfort zone of familiarity and safety; do something unfamiliar no matter how daunting that is. Change your perceptions of life. A very safe life can become an anxious life, one that is lived within self-limiting boundaries. Feel the fear and do it anyway. This week, decide on a new challenge and choose to behave in a way that's opposite to your usual behavior:

a. Join the Toastmaster Club or visit a local library or school; ask if you can speak on their stage for ten minutes. Pick a subject that you're passionate about, one that is relevant to your audience. Public speaking is one of the greatest fears most people shy away from. How did you feel?
b. Say *no* to something or someone about something you always felt obligated to do but that never really gave you joy. Most of us go around saying yes when we really would rather say no to things that steal our time and effort and go against our nature. When you say no to something, you're opening yourself up to saying yes to things that really matter to you.

AFFIRMATIONS

Life can be wrought with challenges and tense moments. When we're tense, we become very serious. Turning things around in our minds can be a great way to change our moods and help us tap into the lighter sides of life.

Asking for Higher Guidance by using affirmations helps us get to a place of lightness and joy. Affirmations work only as long as they don't conflict with a more tightly held dogma or with our subconscious beliefs. Your imagination and beliefs are the most powerful tools you have to create your best life. If you cannot imagine it, you cannot create it.

Affirm the following:

1. I am free to love and be loved.
2. I am in wonderful health.
3. I am at peace with myself.
4. I am open and receptive to everything the Universe has to offer me without limits, restrictions, judgment, or criticism.
5. I give myself permission to say no when I am asked to do something I really don't want to do, and I refuse to feel guilty about speaking up for myself.
6. I give myself permission to rest and heal without guilt.
7. I am able to see each day as an opportunity to heal myself of

   ____

   (fill in your health concerns).
8. I relinquish my anger, let go of impatience, and accept peace and joy into my heart.
9. I forgive so I can be free.
10. I surrender to the flow of the Universe and accept positive changes through all areas of my life.
11. I see myself as healthy and happy.
12. I feel the ways I resist my life and I now let go of these ways.

13. My energy and attention are extremely valuable.
14. All the energy I need is available to me.
15. I accept myself for who I am without judgment or criticism.
16. I accept myself for who I am without fear of rejection from others.
17. I own my own power and take responsibility for the choices and decisions I make every day.
18. I respect myself.
19. I see each day as an opportunity to make things better.
20. Everything is perfect.

FOOD FOR THOUGHT:
Trust in the Divine

A frail and weak, old seer, living with his young son in Northern China, loses his prized horse to nomads who raid his farm in the middle of the night. His neighbors come around to comfort him, but he is unfazed and says to them, "What makes you so sure this is not a blessing?"

Months later the horse returns, bringing with it a handsome nomad stallion.

Everyone congratulates the seer but are perplexed when he says, "What makes you so sure this is not a disaster?"

The family is now richer by adding the fine horse. The seer's young son loves to ride. Unfortunately, one day the boy falls from the horse and breaks his hip. Neighbors are concerned and come around to comfort him, and still the man says, "Perhaps this is a blessing that we don't yet comprehend."

A year later, nomads cross the border to attack the country. Every able-bodied man has to take his sword and fight in the battle. Nine out of ten on the frontier are killed. Because the seer's son is lame, he was rejected by the army and thus did not fight in the battle. Upon hearing the devastating news, the father, now almost blind, is sad but also grateful to God that his son was spared.

Sometimes, we don't understand why disasters strike and fortunes are lost. We wonder when all our misfortune will end. We blame God, the Universe, and anyone and everyone we can think of.

It's always hard to comprehend why things happen, why challenges are thrown our way. When we are in the thick of calamities, it's difficult to see the good that will come out of our sadness and failures. But if we would just keep the faith, we may learn over time the lesson and the ultimate good that is meant for us.

Don't abandon your faith. Trust that there is a Higher Plan, and Divine timing is perfect.

"There is a voice that doesn't use words, listen.

—Rumi

WHAT I WANT TO REMEMBER FROM THIS CHAPTER

DATE: ....

KEY POINTS: ....

....

....

....

....

....

....

....

....

....

....

TAKEAWAYS: ....

....

....

....

....

....

....

....

....

....

....

PART III

WHERE THE MAGIC HAPPENS

PART III

Introduction

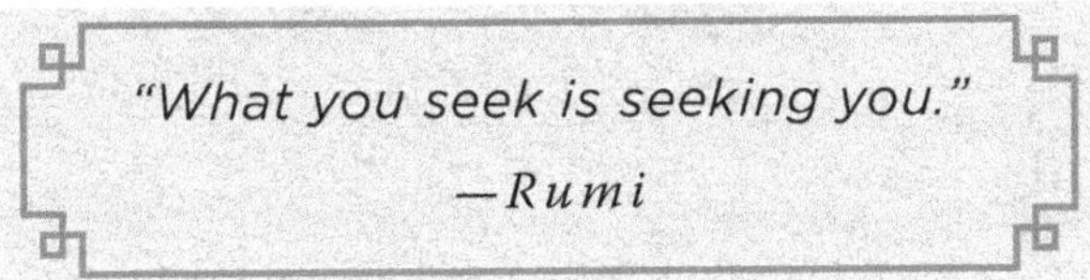

The magic begins with you. Your life is your signature creation. Your life's mission is to express yourself boldly, to live true to yourself, to create what you love and love what you create.

But you must first make a commitment, a firm decision that you want to have a better life, better relationships, to love again intensely and with authenticity, to be happy and at peace with your life.

Learn from your past experiences but leave the ghosts behind.

There is no need to rush things. First, become strong in yourself, and then look for what exactly is lacking in your life. At every turn, ask yourself, *is this decision, this action, this situation, empowering or draining my energy?* Your intuition will never lie. But you must pay attention by going within and asking the right questions. Nobody has the exact answers you need but you. No one has walked in your shoes and knows *exactly* how *you* feel. Only you.

To tap into the right answer and move forward effectively, analyze how you interpret what has happened in your life, especially your negative experiences and behaviors. Now is the time to learn and relearn by first identifying the persons that were involved and the situations that took place with a false positive—in other words, in error—so you can draw a better conclusion.

No matter how difficult it is to become aware of *all* that has gone wrong in different areas of your life, without awareness you cannot move forward and emerge whole. Come to terms with the fact that you probably have been distorting reality to suit your interests. Yes, indeed, it is sad but true. This acknowledgment and acceptance about yourself is the only thing that will stop you from repeating the same patterns and mistakes.

To know where you want to be, you must take a step back and answer some questions no matter how uncomfortable they may be, questions such as the following:

1. Do I feel helpless?
2. Am I living with self-delusion?
3. Do I still experience pain around certain people and situations?
4. How can I be self-efficient?

Think differently. It's possible you've tried different strategies to heal yourself. Did they work? Did your efforts have even the slightest effect on the source of your problems? If not, then it's time to stop fiddling around and focus instead on treating the symptoms from the root. And that root cause is embedded in your past. Know yourself, and you will find the answers you are seeking.

Your brokenness has no doubt left scars, and some things may still reverberate on occasion. But you have survived, and that is an honor nobody can take away from you. Don't feel ashamed of your scars. There is no need to cover them up or hide them. Wear them proudly and show off their beauty because your scars are the best proof of your strength. The kintsugi masters never hide the scars on the works they repair. In fact, they take pride in highlighting them and decorate them with gold and silver. No matter how fragile a broken ceramic piece is, it is living proof of its hidden value, and the master treats it with respect through careful reconstruction so it can emerge even more beautiful than before.

Your scars have afforded you the necessary strength to build a new reality, to rebuild a new life, and have provided you with the energy that characterizes you; your scars have given you the courage to build a better world, one you love and can be proud of. They are proof of your strength.

You are a shining example of survival. Your hurts have allowed you to be more sensitive and better understand others who have also been hurt. Just as you broke and were able to rebuild yourself, be the rock and share your strength with those who need it. Transform your pain into education and help lift others so they, too may rise in their strength.

You have come far on this journey, recorded the rudiments of your family history, given expression to your inner voice, shared your life and your aspirations, and hopefully had some enlightening moments along the way.

To be sure of where you want to be, open yourself to your subconscious mind's suggestions. Be open and willing to change past conditioning and allow new thoughts and fresh ideas to take root.

Empty yourself to allow the good to come in.

Have you emptied your cup today?

A scholar widely known for his keen intellect visits a Tao master at his humble abode.

The master graciously serves him tea just as he does to every visiting guest.

While the master is pouring tea, the scholar talks about Tao.

The master continues pouring even when the cup is filled to the brim. The cup soon overflows, and the scholar can no longer pretend not to see it.

"The cup is overfull, Master!" he exclaims. "No more tea will go in!"

"You are like this cup," says the master. "How can I show you Tao unless you first empty your cup?"

Are you aware that you could unknowingly be doing what the scholar did? For example, do you remember to empty your mind every day before the next day begins? Or before you contemplate a new project? If you don't, how can you make room for anything fresh to enter your mind?

One of the most effective ways to let go of the day is to journal at the end of each day. This way, you're emptying your mind of the day's thoughts and events and making room for the new to come into your life.

Journaling is a tool for change, and many claim to have coaxed more abundance and transformative shifts and synchronicities into their lives because of journaling. Going through this process clears your head and forces you to drag reality out for inspection.

You will begin to feel lighter physically and mentally. It's almost as if a burden is being literally lifted. You start feeling more positive and hopeful about your life situations, more aware that solutions, results, and prosperity *are* possible. You feel a confidence that you didn't have before. Many of these signs will appear even *before* you manifest any outer tangible results.

Memories trigger memories, questions provoke questions, and you may well find that you suddenly know what you really want and have a lot more to say. The more you examine your personal history and your deepest thoughts and beliefs, the more meaningful and life changing this process can become. It's the inner that produces the outer. Your "inner world" is preparing you for outer results.

You are like a scientist performing a life-changing experiment in the laboratory of your mind. You are "brewing" a new consciousness.

It's important to have just the proper amount of ingredients and equally important not to allow contaminants to enter your laboratory or your mental brew. You are on your way to brilliant success for you have the greatest power in the Universe as your benefactor.

Now be open. Empty your mind, and let your answers pour out spontaneously.

"Maybe you are searching among the branches, for what only appears in the roots."

—Rumi

CHAPTER NINE

Creating Your Treasure and Legacy

> *"We will be known forever by the tracks we leave."*
> *—Dakota Indian proverb*

When I was a young girl, I was very shy and mostly kept to myself. I was a dreamer with a vivid imagination, and I always felt that there was something big inside of me.

When I was nine years old, I was sent away to a Catholic boarding school in the north of India, and it was there that I met my English teacher, Miss Rundlet. A stern, intimidating, tall British woman, she scared most students away but to me she was my biggest cheerleader, my mentor, someone who constantly tried to push me out of my comfort zone. For the ninth-grade school play, she encouraged me to play the lead role, but because I was so shy, I refused. Looking back, I'm grateful to her for refusing to hear my protests and insisting I step up to the plate, adamant that I had every talent I needed. Because of her belief in me, I started to believe in myself. I was able to fulfill that role beautifully and continued to gain more and more confidence over the years, going on to become the vice-captain, then captain of my school in my senior year.

I learned early on that success is about self-confidence, self-belief, and one's attitude toward life; it's about the choices we make and the actions we take. Have I ever failed? Yes, more times than I care to recall. But each time, I shook off my failures and picked myself up. I took a step forward each day to live my passion, to continue to work toward the legacy I wished to leave behind.

Because of Ms. Rundlett, I gained enough self-confidence to pursue my dreams, to become an award-winning fashion designer; a #1 international best-selling author of several books; a sought-after mentor, coach, and image expert. Just because a stranger believed in me, it was enough to lead me to big stages, platforms, and even speaking engagements on the TED stage.

Do you have someone in *your* life who believes in you, who encourages you?

If not, do you at least believe in and encourage yourself? Are you clear about your passions? What are your life aspirations? What motivates you to get up each morning? Are you going after your dreams and living your purpose? What legacy do *you* want to leave behind?

So often, we sit in the wings of life hoping and wishing we were doing more, believing that we have more in us, waiting for our big moment. Yet when opportunity knocks on our door, we feel we are not ready and find every excuse not to move forward, thinking *I can't do that* or *that's impossible* or *I don't have the finances.* Very soon, those excuses become our truth, and we sabotage our own success.

Don't let that be you. Don't allow yourself to make excuses because if you make them long enough, you may start to believe them.

When I published my very first book, *Your Body, Your Style,* I didn't give myself time to reason it all out in my mind because I knew there was a good chance I would talk myself out of it. Instead of thinking of all the reasons that I couldn't do it, I thought about all the reasons I *could* and why my message was worthy of being shared. Rather than wait to find a publisher, I published my first draft on Kindle. I felt empowered and became more daring and continued to write and publish many more bestsellers. Now I'm only half-scared. The truth is I pressed through and gained ground. The more I did it the easier it became. Now I not only write but also speak all over the world!

I know that if I had wallowed in self-doubt, I would not have written the words you are reading today nor experienced the satisfaction and joy my work gives me.

It's not about how much talent you have, it's about *using* what you have. If you are really believing and expecting big things to happen in your life, you must put action behind your faith and take advantage of every opportunity. It's not always easy to step through a door of opportunity, but sometimes you just have to be bold and go for it. Don't let fear hold you back.

Fear robs us of the will to live fully. With fear running our lives, we're glad to merely survive. But surviving is not living. To live requires doses of emotional strength. One must be bold and brave to make decisions, overcome complacency, and actively go forth to seek development and growth without expectations, and often without support from others. When we live intensely, the world seems full of color, everything is more intense and emotional, and life is full of passion.

Living also means we become more fragile and run risks of falling and failure. But that is a chance we take because we *choose* to live.

Be ready and prepared to live fully. Develop your gifts and talents so when opportunity presents itself, you will have the confidence to meet it.

Open your mind to possibilities and focus on your passion and purpose. After all, your legacy depends on the actions you take today.

Write down your thoughts of the moment. Those that come to mind spontaneously are the most authentic. Don't underestimate the value of what you have to say. Let ideas flow no matter how lofty they may seem. You are creating a treasure for yourself, for your family, and for many generations to come.

Answer the following questions:

1. What do you believe is possible for you?

....

....

....

....

....

2. What's your life purpose?

....

....

....

....

....

3. How confident are you in your abilities to make decisions for yourself?

....

....

4. Is there anything you'd want to change in the world for the better?

....

....

....

5. How do you see yourself making an impact in the world?

6. What are your values?

a. What do you represent?

b. What do you want to embody?

7. Would you rather be a worried genius or a joyful simpleton?

8. What's on your "supposed-to" list?

a. Who says?

b. Why?

9. What can you choose today/this season/this year that will carry you toward maximum satisfaction and minimal regret?

10. What kind of legacy do you want to leave behind?

11. How does your being here in the universe change humanity for the better?

12. If you could have one single wish granted, what would it be?

13. What are you busy with today?

   a. Will this matter one year from now?
   b. three years from now?
   c. five years from now?

14. What opportunities are you looking for? How can you create these opportunities?

15. What would you do if you could not fail, if there were no limitations in money, resources, time, or networks?

....

....

16. What do you want to achieve one year from now?

....

....

a. three years from now? ....

....

b. five years from now? ....

....

c. ten years? ....

....

d. How important are these goals to you? ....

....

17. What do you really and truly want?

....

....

a. Is this REALLY what you want? ....

b. How much do you want this? ....

18. What are your biggest goals and dreams?

....

....

a. What's stopping you from pursuing them? ....

....

b. Why? ....

....

c. How can you see these realized? ....

....

19. Are you putting any parts of your life on hold? Why?

20. What's the top priority in your life at this moment? What are you doing about it?

21. What are the biggest actions you can take now to create the biggest results in your life?

22. Where are you living right now—the past, future, or present?

23. Are you living your life to the fullest right now?
    a. Do you have any regrets about your life so far?
    b. What changes can you make now so you don't continue to live with regrets?

24. What would you like to stop worrying about? What steps can you take to let go of this worry?

25. How can you make your life more meaningful, starting today?

26. What drives you?

27. Recall the times you were most inspired, most motivated, most charged up.

   a. What were you doing?

   b. How can you do more of that starting today?

28. What are the operating principles of your life?

....

....

....

29. What's the one thing you would like to do more of and why? How can you make that happen?

....

....

....

....

....

30. What's the one thing you would like to do less of and why? How can you make that happen?

....

....

....

....

....

31. In what areas of your life are you trading authenticity for safety or what appears to be safety?

....

....

32. What are you currently resisting?

....

....

33. Describe a dream you've had more than once. Describe a dream that later materialized and turned out to be true.

34. Describe a period of time in your life: when you felt safe and protected; when you felt vulnerable, unsafe, and unprotected; when you felt smothered and overprotected.

35. When are you most comfortable?

a. at work
b. in a social setting
c. spending time with someone
d. alone
e. observing others

36. What does your ideal day look and feel like?

37. How can you change someone's life for the better today?

38. What in your life bores you?

39. What would you do even if you knew you might very well fail?

40. How are you getting in your own way?

41. Do you tend to gravitate toward the safest option at the expense of growth?

42. Are you willing to do whatever it takes to get where you want to go?

43. What do you want to learn today? What is the most important lesson you learned recently?

....

....

....

....

....

44. Does what you do spark joy? ....

45. How well have you been able to balance:

a. your work life with your personal life? ....

b. other people's needs with your own? ....

c. self-acceptance with others' evaluation of you? ....

46. What do you stand for today?

....

....

47. What personal beliefs have affected the way you think, act, or understand the world?

....

....

....

48. What's the BEST thing that could happen to you? What's the WORST thing that could happen to you?

....

....

....

....

....

49. Where can you add value today?

50. What are you passionate enough about that you can endure the most disagreeable aspects of it?

51. What's your biggest dream?

52. How would you act differently if you knew that your actions and attitude on this one day were going to be a permanent testament to your life?

53. Are you truly happy with the way you've spent your life today/this week/this month/this year?

54. What unresolved matters would you like to have closure on?

55. **Describe the best day that you wish would, but hasn't, happened yet.**

....

....

....

....

....

56. **Where would you choose to live if you had no personal ties or obligations?**

....

....

57. **If you had the option to disappear for a long period of time, would you?** ....

a. Where would you go? ....

b. What would you do? ....

c. Who would you be? ....

58. **If today were the last day of your life, would you still want to do what you are about to do today?** ....

59. **How do you plan to spend the last years of your life?**

....

....

....

....

....

60. **If a movie were to be made about your life, who would play you?** ....

a. What type of movie would it be? A comedy, a thriller, a tearjerker?

....

b. What music would be in the soundtrack? ....

....

....

c. Who would be cast as your parents, spouse, best friend, boss, significant other? ....

....

....

d. Does your movie have a happy ending? ....

....

e. Would you change the plot? If so, how?

....

....

....

....

....

....

....

....

REFLECTIONS

Have you ever used a GPS navigation system in your car to get you from where you are to where you want to go? The GPS calculates the best route, and along the way if you're distracted and miss the exit, the GPS will instantly recalculate and get you back on track.

In a similar fashion, there's a GPS that is leading you to your destination. Keep your eyes on the road, turn your thoughts toward the present, and keep looking for new opportunities that present themselves along your path to the future.

The GPS is leading you to where you want to go so you may continue to build upon a beautiful legacy, but you must pay attention to the road you're on so you don't encounter too many detours and are able to get to your destination quickly and seamlessly.

Keep your eyes on the bigger picture, on the legacy you are building, but don't miss the beauty of the moment. Be present. Don't look back on the good old days. *These are* the good old days, so make them count.

1. Identify your current cause—the thing that lights you up and drives your day-to-day existence. What makes it the thing you want to wake up to every day? Elaborate on your plans to grow this cause.

....

....

....

....

....

....

....

....

2. Make a list of habits, mind-sets, experiences, and things that you love, hate, and bother you. For example:

   a. What Bothers Me (e.g., lazy people, people who brag, abuse others, etc.) ....

   ....

   ....

   b. What I Love (e.g., animals, beach, traveling, etc.)

   ....

   ....

   ....

   c. What I Hate (e.g., greedy people, failed marriages, financial struggles, etc.) ....

   ....

   ....

   d. What I'm most Afraid of (e.g., failure, ridicule, success, etc.) ....

   ....

   ....

3. Sometimes in life change becomes necessary. And even though we know we must change so that more good can come into our life, fear holds us back. At the slightest thought of change our subconscious rebels. Remember that fear is not real but simply an old paradigm grasping at your old life; remind yourself why you want to change. Write down all the

reasons change is necessary, and every time you feel fear, visit this page to reaffirm and strengthen your beliefs.

....

....

....

....

....

....

4. Write down at least one step you can take today to move closer to your ideal life. For example, I can:

   a. go out and network with others.
   b. take up some hobby/activity that is outside my comfort zone.
   c. have a heart-to-heart conversation about what is bothering me.
   d. travel solo to places I've never been but always dreamed of going to.
   e. be willing to be vulnerable.

....

....

....

5. Using your imagination, write a letter to your child, grandchild, or your great-grandchild about the future and speculate what the planet will be like by then. Talk about your hopes and dreams as well as your fears for future generations, about technological and medical advances that will have been developed.

....

....

6. **Write the obituary or eulogy you'd like to be read at your death.**

   a. How would you like to be remembered?

   b. Now can you live it?

....

....

....

....

....

....

....

....

....

....

....

....

....

AFFIRMATIONS

Speak affirmations that resonate most with what you wish for yourself. Add power and life to them and sing them with energy and conviction.

1. I believe prosperity is possible in every area of my life.
2. I am open to receiving all that is necessary for my success.
3. I love what I do, and I'm doing my best to build a beautiful legacy.
4. I am motivated to meet every challenge and view challenges as opportunities to succeed in life.
5. I have all the answers I need to succeed.
6. I take initiative to bring about change in my life and believe I'm worthy of success.
7. I am determined to succeed and trust that the Universe supports my efforts.
8. I clear away all clutter to make room for success.
9. I appreciate the effort I put into my work and believe I'm worthy of success.
10. I welcome success into my life.
11. I welcome prosperity into my life.
12. I am ready to accept all that is available to me.
13. I open the door to prosperity and believe all things are possible.
14. I am worthy of all good things.
15. I welcome all forms of abundance.
16. I let go of my resistance to wealth and prosperity.
17. I appreciate what the Universe has given me, and I trust my needs will continue to be taken care of.
18. I am open to accepting opportunities for abundance every time they knock on my door.
19. I am open to accepting what is appropriate for me without limits or restrictions.
20. I welcome abundance into my life.

FOOD FOR THOUGHT: *Longevity and Legacy*

To create a worthwhile legacy, it's important to be healthy and alive long enough to build it.

While how long you live depends on several factors that are beyond your control, there are quite a few things you can do. As with everything in life, it all starts with your mind-set. Have a healthy outlook, see the great value of life, treasure the privilege to be alive and the opportunity to perform something useful during your lifetime.

To maximize this potential, learn to allow your body and mind to function at their best. Moderation is key.

"Stretch a bow to the very full, and you will wish you had stopped in time; Temper a sword-edge to its very sharpest, and you will find it soon grows dull," warned Lao Tzu, an ancient Chinese philosopher.

Moderation brings you peace of mind and a state of balance, both essential to a healthy and long life. What can you do to bring about moderation? Lao Tzu says in order to live in moderation, one must learn to let things be; learn to flow like water.

Water is so strong that it can destroy the hardest rock in the world, but it's also ready to accept what is and adapt. Its robustness and vitality derive not from being aggressive and headstrong, but from being soft and yielding despite its tenaciousness.

"Water is fluid, soft, and yielding. But water will wear away rock, which is rigid and cannot yield," says Lao Tzu. "Whatever is fluid, soft, and yielding will overcome whatever is rigid and hard. This is another paradox: What is soft is strong."

Be like water. Accept that things will not always turn out according to what you desire; accept people will not be as perfect as you would like them to be; be ready to listen and see things from others' perspectives. Be grateful and happy with what you have. Find a balance between your desires and reality so that you can stay in your center. This doesn't mean that you should not strive for what is better. It means that you must not strive at the expense of losing your center.

Being able to accept what *is* allows you to open your mind and become more tolerant like water, creating a smooth flow of your life force that allows for an alert and vigorous mind and keeps illness at bay—all important elements in laying a good foundation for a healthy and long life.

A lifelong and healthy-enough life allows you to maximize your full potential and the energy to build your legacy. Have a healthy life perception and live a balanced life.

Look at your life now. Do you feel you are neglecting important areas of your life? Which area do you feel depleted in? Give more attention to that area. Allocate some daily time around it, and make more effort to develop that area.

Strength and balance in the six key areas of your life—spiritual, mental, physical, social, emotional, and financial—are crucial to your well-being. Evaluate your life and check in regularly: *Am I neglecting any essential area*? If you neglect even one area, your entire system suffers.

Much like your diet, if you aren't getting enough of one essential nutrient, even if you're eating healthy and drinking plenty of water, the system still begins to break down.

- If you don't focus on financial growth, bill collectors start to nag at you.

- If you aren't developing yourself mentally, you'll begin to feel stagnant.
- If you aren't nurturing yourself spiritually, you'll begin to feel empty inside.
- If you aren't focusing on the social aspect of your life, you'll begin to feel lonely and isolated.
- If you aren't taking control of your emotions, you become more reactive and feel "out of control."

Nurturing the six areas of your life is like tending to your garden: There are many early warning signals that the leaves are sagging or turning brown. Do you listen to the signals and nurture the vital areas of your life, or do you ignore them and place excessive focus on only one area of your garden?

The key to living your life to the fullest is balance, but if you are lacking in one or more of the six areas, how can you create balance? Perhaps you're successful in your career, but will that matter if your family life is not happy? Perhaps you are brilliant and smart, but if your body is sick, will that matter?

Here are some things you can begin to be mindful about and take actions on:

1. SPIRITUAL

Personally, I feel this is the most important area of your life because it's where your life purpose and meaning come from. *Spirituality* deals with your conscience, values, and principles as well as your relationship with the infinite. However, this doesn't mean that you should focus solely on developing your spirituality because what good is it if you are spiritual but have not bothered to develop the other areas?

2. MENTAL

The mind is a fascinating tool. It has the ability to absorb new skill and knowledge and apply it to any area you focus on. The world is changing at an increasing speed, so it's important for you to feed your intellectual hunger and adopt a constant desire to learn. Find things you're passionate about and role models/people who inspire you and emulate them. Stay hungry for knowledge.

3. PHYSICAL

You act through the vessel of your body. Keeping it healthy and operating from a high level of energy will allow you to accomplish your tasks with enthusiasm and speed. Eat healthy, add a variety of fruits, vegetables, and protein to your diet to make sure you are getting all the essential nutrients and building blocks your body needs. Exercise to keep your body in optimum health.

4. SOCIAL

We are wired for connection. It's in our biology. As infants, our need for connection is about survival. As we grow older, connection means thriving—emotionally, spiritually, and intellectually. Connection is critical because we all have the basic need to belong, to feel accepted, to be valued for who we are. Relationships give meaning to life. The greatest fulfillment doesn't come from your achievements; it comes from your relationships. You can have all the money in the world, but if you don't have a support system, a meaningful connection with family, friends, and loved ones, then life can lose some of its meaning. Remember to reach out and stay connected.

5. EMOTIONAL

To feel love and acceptance from others is a necessary emotional need. When we don't feel this love and acceptance, it's painful.

Rejection doesn't just hurt like a broken heart but can also damage the psyche. Social exclusion activates the same pain. Relationships are very important to our emotional well-being. The power of touch is one of the most important human needs. Small touches like handshakes, pats on the back, holding hands, massages, and especially hugs are incredibly powerful. So hug someone today. A hug, especially a long one, releases a neurotransmitter and hormone oxytocin, which reduces the reactivity of the amygdala. Research shows getting five hugs a day for four weeks increases happiness big time. So do yourself a favor and keep your emotional bucket full.

FINANCIAL

This is where you are able to birth your dreams, follow your passion. It's an area that deals with your career and achievements, with making a living that affords you the ability to create a life in alignment with your desires. Increasing your output in this area leads to productivity and contributes to your self-esteem and self-confidence.

So how do you balance the depleted areas of your life on a daily basis? Simply go down the list and ask yourself, *how do I feel about this area right now?* Then ask, *what can I do to improve in this area of my life?* Set clear, specific, and realistic goals, goals that you can actually take action on without any excuses.

Even if you are insanely busy, setting aside ten minutes to stretch or exercise first thing each morning, nurturing yourself spiritually by listening to an inspirational tape while driving to work, or making quick phone calls to connect with people you love and just to let them know you're thinking of them is far better than not taking any action at all. You don't need to spend the same amount of time in *all* areas of your life (what a relief, isn't it)?

Build your life on developing these key areas and you'll see how your life improves. Remember, *energy flows where focus goes.* It's as simple as that. There are no excuses so stop telling yourself stories about why you aren't doing the work. Tackle each area of your life with clarity.

To gain clarity, feel free to write down your ideas and action steps for each area. I suggest a lovely new notebook in a style that makes you want to happily peruse it. If you are a visual person, then by all means draw, mind map, or create a vision board so you can see your ideas. Read, visualize, and meditate on each area with great joy daily.

Take daily steps, no matter how small, to nurture yourself and work on your goals. Think and work on correcting negative beliefs in each area as well. The key is to develop and create balance in all the previously listed six areas so you can live a fulfilled life.

"We carry inside us the wonders we seek outside us

—Rumi

WHAT I WANT TO REMEMBER FROM THIS CHAPTER

DATE: ....

KEY POINTS: ....

....

....

....

....

....

....

....

....

....

....

TAKEAWAYS: ....

....

....

....

....

....

....

....

....

....

....

CHAPTER TEN

Victory Starts in Your Mind

> *"Whatever the mind of man can conceive and believe, it can achieve."*
>
> —*Napoleon Hill*

Life can throw us curves and roadblocks. It's up to us to navigate around and through them so we can emerge victorious.

My own life journey has not been smooth sailing.

I can still remember how much fear I had to overcome when I started my design house, St. Pucchi, in Dallas, Texas in 1985. I had absolutely no experience designing wedding dresses and never went to school to study fashion design. I was an English major with a passion for fashion.

I had no family or friends who supported me, and not enough capital to start my own company. I really had no business starting something that I knew nothing about. Not only that, but at a time when foreign goods were frowned upon, I was a woman from Thailand introducing fashion made in Thailand. I had so many things to prove to the close-knit bridal industry. Failure was not an option because I had a family to support, children to feed and school, and I had spent every last penny I owned to launch St. Pucchi.

My first collection—which in my opinion was breathtaking—was almost a disaster when I realized that I had not done my homework nor spent time to study the US marketplace. My sixteen-piece bridal collection, all in color, was totally out of place among the sea of white polyester dresses that the American bride expected and accepted in 1985. To my great surprise, this same collection actually launched me as a pioneer in the bridal industry and I was hailed by the fashion press as having single-handedly changed the US wedding industry by introducing color and pure silk in bridal wear.

Words cannot express what a struggle it was in those early days to make ends meet. But because I was passionate and believed in what I was doing, I was driven to succeed in a male-dominated world and in a foreign country doing something I so loved but was clueless about. I spent years filled with anxiety and consumed by thoughts of doubt and defeat.

To the outside world, I was this audaciously bold woman who knew it all, who was polished and confident and fearless. But inside of me, fear was always present and was trying very hard to paralyze me, threatening to keep me from stepping into my new experience and growing to the next level. Years later, a Japanese client would describe what I felt as the cold breath of *Buruburu*, the ghost of fear.

This all-consuming fear tried to influence me to quit and give up on my dreams many times. But as each day passed, I envisioned myself bigger than my fear. I kept telling myself that I was strong, talented, and capable. And as I planted those seeds in my mind, I could feel my confidence growing. I saw myself moving forward, accomplishing my dreams, and stepping over this threshold of fear.

My journey was full of bumps and roadblocks, but I prevailed. I drew my strength from the deep-seated faith that lived inside of me. I knew there was a Higher Power holding me and cheering me on. I've come a long way. I'm still the same person I always was but with a greater sense of conviction. I know now that I'm much more than my circumstances. It does not matter what I am; what matters are the decisions I make and where my priorities lie.

What about you? What are you passionate about? What fears consume you and stop you from living your destiny? What past conditioning are you holding onto? What lessons have you learned?

What do you know for sure?

Your journey need not have been as challenging nor as traumatic as mine. In the years that followed, my children were kidnapped and taken away from me by a husband who was physically, emotionally, and mentally abusive, a person I had been forced to marry against my will, someone who took pleasure in mocking me, who ended up ruining my business not once, but three times, just to spite me. It's not easy to hold your head high and hide behind the tears. You need strength to navigate through the ups and downs of life. If you are fortunate to have a support system, which I did not, then the journey becomes a little more tolerable, a wee bit more comforting.

What I know for sure as I write these words today is that victory starts in your mind. The mind is a very powerful weapon. It's capable of paralyzing you but also instrumental in helping you overcome the paralyzing fears that block your way.

Healing the past and navigating through the journey of self-reflection is a powerful tool for cultivating a fulfilling and meaningful life. When you dig deep enough, you discover what it is you know, what you believe, and how you want to be in the world.

If you've experienced loss in your life—whether it's the loss of a loved one, the loss of a job, or health, or even the loss of a dream—give yourself time to reposition yourself. Stay open and welcome change, let go of yesterday and embrace the future, and discover the grace to move forward.

Now each time I experience a setback, I pick myself up quickly. I'm determined not to stay broken and wounded nor give others the pleasure to see me fallen. I remind myself that as long as I live, there will be accusing voices, fault finders and rock throwers. When the negative voices come, I have a choice: to believe them and stay where I am, or decide to love myself and lift myself up and go on with my life knowing that I deserve, that I am worthy and equipped with everything I need to live a blessed life.

I have a choice, and I choose to pick myself up, dust off the hurts, and move on. And like a kintsugi master, I am constantly repairing my broken pieces, filling my wounds with gold so I can emerge from being shattered to whole and shine in my beauty.

We've all fallen at some time or another and heard the voices trying to tear us down. But we have a choice not to replay the failures. Sadly, many allow fear of failure, and embarrassment over past mistakes, rob their confidence and destiny.

Replay your victories. Replay your accomplishments. Remind yourself of all that is right with your world. Get right back up again and again, keep moving forward toward your dream and fulfill your destiny. Rewrite your story. Tell yourself a new story, a better one, one that empowers you. Never let the negative opinions of others cause you to shrink back or steal your joy and confidence. Focus instead on the times when you succeeded and keep those victories forefront.

If I had allowed people to rob me of my confidence, I would have never known what success felt like, what beauty and talent I have been blessed with, and the sheer joy of the opportunity given me to help so many across the world.

And if I had stayed fallen, you would not be reading this book today.

Now let's go back and revisit some of the key questions, shall we?

Ask yourself each of the following questions **at least ten times**, writing down ten different answers for each one. You will notice that by the tenth answer, the real truth will emerge.

1. WHO AM I?

Exploring this question helps reveal your essence as an energetic being and highlights your potential and possibilities. It reminds us that we're more than our bodies.

2. WHAT IS IT THAT I MOST NEED RIGHT NOW?

In this busy world, we often neglect what we most need to stay happy and healthy. For instance, you may need more rest, a massage, exercise, or sleep. Whatever it is, respond to your need. Asking this question on a regular basis not only addresses your short-term needs but also, by extension, your long-term happiness.

3. WHAT MEANING CAN I DRAW FROM THIS EXPERIENCE?

Contemplate the different things that are going on in your life at this time. Every experience has a purpose and potential lesson. Of course, the lesson may be tough to swallow, but asking the question brings awareness, curiosity, compassion, and resilience and gives you the strength to cope with tough situations.

4. WHAT DO I WANT TO BE, DO, AND HAVE MORE OF IN MY LIFE?

This question will help you explore what you really want and whether what you're currently doing actually reflects that. When you're creating a fulfilling life, it's important to cut out the things that weigh you down and add the things that lift you up.

5. WHAT AM I HOLDING ONTO?

The fear of not being enough or not having something turn out the way you want shows up as resistance or attachment and prevents growth. When you identify what you're holding onto, whether it's an event that caused you grief; a failure or a decision you made in the past that caused you loss; a relationship that went awry; a grudge against someone; fear of something; or lack of self-worth, you can refocus and let it go so you are free to experience life fully. The past is gone, never to come back, so it's useless to waste your energy on something you cannot change. Look forward.

6. WHOM AM I STILL BLAMING?

There is no logic that can explain adversity, tragedy, suffering, or abuse, and no answer that is ever correct. We believe that so-and-so is to blame for how our lives have turned out. Or perhaps we blame ourselves for something we may have done. We seek answers and get frustrated with the voice that keeps rearing its head in our minds. Now that you have made a decision to be at peace with your past and moved on to create a beautiful life, you must let go of the blame and shame. The past does not matter; what matters is your present and future.

7. WHAT ARE MY UNIQUE GIFTS AND HOW CAN I SHARE THEM WITH THE WORLD?

Your gifts might include writing, speaking, playing a musical instrument, creating art, or volunteering your time. Keep your wins forefront. They are a reminder of what you are capable of and reinforce your self-esteem and self-worth while boosting your self-confidence to allow you to take chances and risks so you can move beyond fear. Whatever your gift is, use more of it and share it with the world. Joy is a result of sharing and caring.

8. HOW CAN I CELEBRATE MY LIFE EVERY MOMENT, EVERY DAY?

Look around you. There is abundance everywhere. Every moment is ripe with gratitude and gifts if only you would notice. Ask yourself what is *right* in your world, not what's wrong. Pause to give thanks and mark the moments that uplift you.

9. WHY AM I HERE?

Every experience, every person you meet, and every gift and talent you have exist to support you in accomplishing your life purpose. What is that for you? Why do you think you are here? What do you believe is your calling? What is the legacy you wish to leave behind?

10. WHAT IS THE LESSON I'D LIKE TO LEARN?

Be open and willing to try something new, something that takes you outside your comfort zone. Make a list of things you're passionate about learning, make a plan, and then go out and make it happen. If we're not learning, we're not growing; the more we learn, the richer and deeper our life experience.

11. WHAT BRINGS ME JOY?

Often it is the simple things that bring us the most joy. Make a list of the things that bring you joy, then begin incorporating those things into your life on a daily basis. Don't wait for a special occasion to purposefully make your life joyful. You deserve joy every day.

12. WHAT AM I MOST AFRAID OF?

Fear can be your enemy if you let it. It can keep you from living to your highest potential and paralyze you from moving forward in life. Fear can also be a great teacher and a catalyst for change. Fear is a motivator; it can wake you up to be more creative and diligent and lead you to success. Once you identify what it is you're afraid of, make the decision to overcome your fear. More often than not, fear is more perception than reality.

13. WHAT AM I NOT FORGIVING MYSELF FOR?

It's time to let go of everything that you believe you've caused and stop berating yourself. Don't allow yourself to be angry at what you might have done or how you might have acted in the past. The way you behaved or acted was not because you were bad or broken but was because of an old pattern that was installed as a result of bad experiences in your life. The past is gone forever and will never come back. Put your hand on your heart now and say, *I forgive myself for....* Write down every incident that comes to mind until you have exhausted your list.

14. IS WHAT I AM DOING MAKING ME POWERFUL OR POWERLESS?

Ask yourself this question before you do something or are about to say something. When you do something that makes you feel powerful, you will know immediately. You will feel good, happy, strong, and full of joy. But when you do something or are in a situation that drains your energy, you will feel powerless. It will evoke a feeling of unhappiness, depression, and possibly make you weak. Write down some of the things that make you feel powerful and those that make you feel powerless. And from now on, before you are about to do or say something, pause and ask yourself, *will what I'm about to do make me powerful or powerless?* Choose only actions and words that will make you feel powerful.

15. WHAT IS ONE STEP I CAN TAKE TODAY TO MOVE CLOSER TO MY IDEAL LIFE?

Taking a step toward your dreams will generate excitement for the possibilities available to you. Write a vision of your ideal life and then move toward it one step at a time. Celebrate your steps along the way. Consider that following rules and tradition is not a prerequisite to success. Open your mind to creating your own opportunities; it's what I call "entrepreneurial thinking."

REFLECTIONS

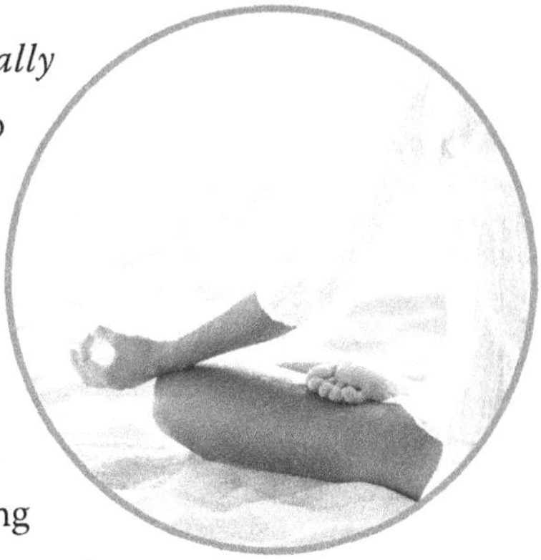

When you know yourself, *really* know yourself, you are able to live according to your values and passions, make a positive contribution to the world, and simply have more joy. Knowing yourself also influences your connection to others. When we get to know ourselves, we are more open and loving toward others because we see their humanity and the gifts that they bring.

On the other hand, we cheat ourselves when we wallow in self-delusion. Conversations with yourself that say, *there was nothing else I could have done, time will fix everything, it's not my problem,* and so on are self-defeating. Self-delusion is a very common strategy to keep us paralyzed and prevents us from taking responsibility and the necessary actions for our growth. It's the voice that convinces you that no matter what you do, it won't make a difference. When you practice self-delusion, you are delegating your future to the hands of chance. You lose control of your own choices.

Now is the time to reconcile with your past and tell yourself a new story, one that empowers you. Albert Einstein was right when he said, "We cannot solve our problems with the same thinking we used when we created them." Change your thoughts, change your story so you can change your life.

Heal your wounds and reconcile with your past. Your beautiful scars give you the necessary strength and courage to build a new reality. In your scars and in the proof of your strength lie the anchoring you'll need when you find yourself in dire circumstances. The masters of kintsugi are aware of this, which is why they respect the main value of a reconstructed piece—its scar. When you value your scars, you'll gain clarity and know your priorities and perspectives; you will be able to make deliberate decisions based on what is important to you and intentionally create a more connected and meaningful life that is true for you.

Take a step of faith today, and even if you feel fear, don't let it paralyze you. Don't allow past mistakes and failures affect your confidence. Consciously open your heart. Never see yourself as a failure, and never allow the fear of failure get in the way of your destiny.

Love yourself and love your life. You don't need to wait for someone else to validate you. You are good enough just as you are. Understand the value of who you are and what you have. Loving your life means being willing to make changes. Invest in yourself and see your life with a fresh new perspective, beyond where you are right now, with the potential to overcome every obstacle that may show up, and celebrate your life. Your past does not define you, nor does it determine your future. It's not what happens *to* you but what happens *in* you that matters most. Leave the past behind and make room to embrace the destiny that lies ahead of you.

Remember, when one door closes, God will open a bigger and better door for you. You don't need to have all the answers; you just need to be open to the possibilities that lie ahead of you. Failure is just a stepping-stone toward success teaching us what we need to let go to make room for something better. It could be that God is trying to stir you out of a situation that is not good for you and preventing you from going in the wrong direction. Have you ever thought of that?

Trust and stay in a state of knowing. Know that this, too shall pass.

AFFIRMATIONS

Your negative chatter can be a tough opponent. Shutting it down can give you a happiness boost, but let's face it, that's not easy because it has been around for a while and is well practiced. Therefore, it's important to divert your attention toward positive affirmations.

Offer the negative chatter and your fears to your Highest Self and ask to have them replaced with peace. Ask to be reconfigured. Ask to have your fear circuitry cleaned up and hauled away. When fear surfaces, don't resist it. Keep breathing deeply into the bowl of your pelvis and forgive yourself.

Affirm the following:

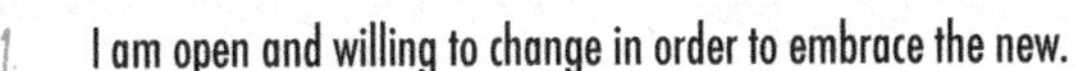

1. **I am open and willing to change in order to embrace the new.**
2. **I see new possibilities and stay in a state of expectations for great things in my future.**
3. **I live my life in faith and know that everything is happening for my highest good.**
4. **I am focused and determined and growing stronger, gaining more confidence each day.**
5. **I allow love and light to permeate, heal, and illuminate me.**
6. **I open myself to receiving.**
7. **I am imperturbable.**
8. **The Divine works through me to find myself in everything.**
9. **I awaken to my true identity.**
10. **I am the One who is experiencing itself as all of creation.**
11. **I trust in the ways of the Universe.**
12. **I choose my Highest Self.**
13. **I know that my victories are still ahead, and I am destined to win.**
14. **I continue to remember my accomplishments and replay my victories and know that success is mine as long as I believe.**

15 I keep stretching, growing, and learning and I keep my focus on the good in my life.

16 I live with a champion's mentality and fill my memory box with only good things.

17 I focus on my good qualities, and rather than wait for others to applaud me, I applaud myself.

18 I live with confidence knowing I am valuable and have something great to offer.

19 I stay positive and hopeful, and even when things look impossible, I know God is looking out for me.

20 I believe I've been equipped with everything I need to live an abundant and fulfilled life.

FOOD FOR THOUGHT:
Be Grateful

Meister Eckhardt wrote, "If the only prayer you ever say in your entire life is 'Thank you,' it will be enough."

What are you grateful for?

Hundreds of things go right for you every day, from the moment you wake up to the moment you put your head on your pillow to sleep at night. Through some magic you don't fully comprehend, and though you've been unconscious for many hours while asleep, you realize that you're still breathing and your heart is still beating.

Your eyes register an array of colors through nerves that you don't control. You can see! You smell, you hear, you move, and you feel, interesting gifts that you don't really pay much attention to but that are there courtesy of a Higher Power.

It's easy to be grateful when life is good, when everything is going your way, when you are surrounded by loving family and friends, when you have good health and abundance all around you. It's also easy to take those things for granted and live from a place where you feel the world owes you.

The challenge is when there is an unexpected disruption in your life because inevitably there will be instances that occur that may trigger you—unforeseen circumstances and upsets that cross your path; health and relationships that challenge you. Can you be grateful for the bad, the good, *and* the small stuff?

You have a choice. You can choose to see what happens to you as a curse or a blessing. You can choose to blame others, or you can choose to see the role you played in bringing about the circumstances. You can live in regret for things that occurred to set you back, or you can see them as blessings in disguise that forced you to look at your life with new eyes and see what an opportunity this is!

You see, you always have a choice.

And if you're not careful, little moments will pass you by that could have been some of the richest experiences of your life.

Wake up . . .

Life is waiting for you to show up.

Take each person and experience that shows up in your life as a guide from beyond because each has something to teach you and help you grow.

And this I know for sure!

"This being human is a guest house.
Every morning a new arrival.

A joy, a depression, a meanness,
some momentary awareness comes
as an unexpected visitor.

Welcome and entertain them all!
Even if they're a crowd of sorrows,
who violently sweep your house
empty of its furniture,
still treat each guest honorably.

He may be clearing you out
for some new delight.

The dark thought, the shame, the malice,
meet them at the door laughing,
and invite them in.

Be grateful for whoever comes,
because each has been sent
as a guide from beyond."

—*Rumi*

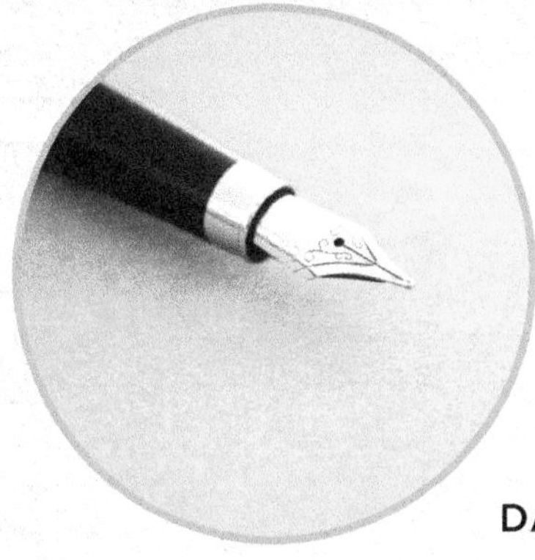

WHAT I WANT TO REMEMBER FROM THIS CHAPTER

DATE: ....

KEY POINTS: ....

TAKEAWAYS: ....

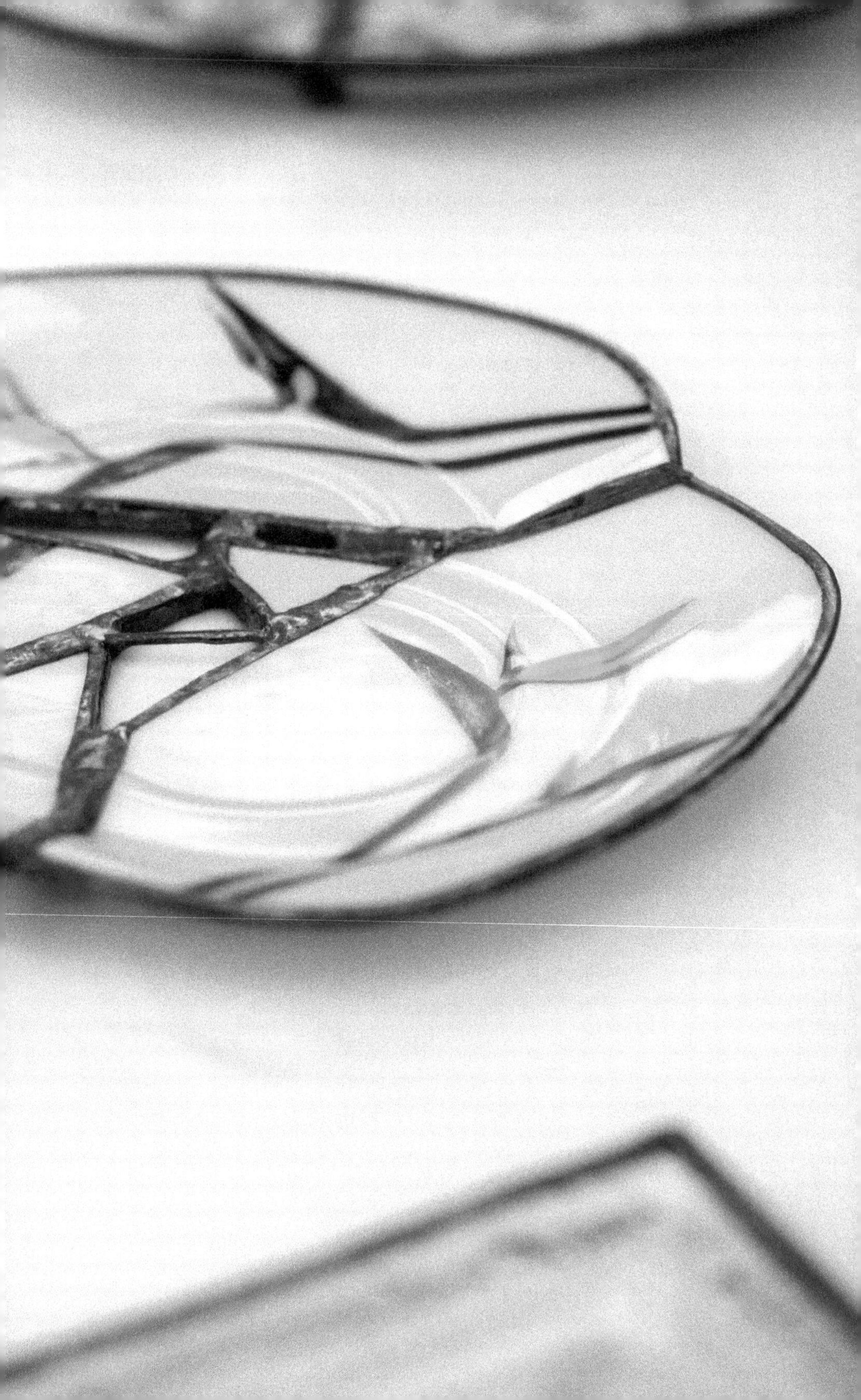

PART IV

THE ART OF REPAIRING AND LETTING GO

PART IV

INTRODUCTION

> *"Every mortal will taste death,*
> *but only some will taste life."*
> —*Rumi*

On a visit to Paris in June of 2016, I had a strange and mystical experience, one that caused a revelation and redirected my perception.

It felt as if a flash of light had come on inside my head—not just an ah-ha moment but a permanent shift—a revelation that had so much significance as to change the way I look at my life and the world around me even today.

I was at Notre Dame in Paris and bravely climbing up the spiral staircase, a total of 387 steps with not a lot of places to rest along the way. The staircase was narrow and fan shaped, and claustrophobic as I am, I was determined to brave this feat. A long line of tourists was following me, and there was no room to back down or rest, no room to look left or right, no room for people to overtake me even if they wanted to. I felt obliged to keep going, and often I felt quite faint as if I were about to collapse. For those who've done this climb, you know how steep and narrow the winding stairs are. As I was navigating my way, my eyes were looking down the whole time making sure that each foot was firmly planted on each step as the stairs got narrower and narrower.

I concentrated intensely so I wouldn't fall. At that moment, my entire reality and everything I could see was only the concrete and the limited amount of land beneath my feet. After climbing for about ten minutes, I had the opportunity to take a break and stepped out onto a narrow balcony. It was just about that time that the clouds parted and the sun shone through. I looked up from the floor, and from where I was standing overlooking the vast expanse, a panoramic view of the whole of Paris came into focus. There was the Eiffel Tower, the Montparnasse in the distance, and the River Seine below; there were tall steeples and tiny buildings and villages and walkways and roads.

How strange it is, I thought, to engage in perceptions that cause one to bend reality. For example, if I'm looking at a cluster of buildings in a particular suburb, I can see all of them from my vantage point, but the people living down there can only see their little suburb, their own street. So in a typical Socratic dialogue, I wondered *who, then has the full understanding of reality? Is it the person sitting at the one café on one street, or is it me who sees all the streets and homes from up here?* This is a classic question about perception. Everything one perceives depends on the position where one is standing.

What you observe, what you believe you see, depends on the level of your perception—the floor of the building you're on, the perspective that you're able to maintain. So as I looked at all these streets and houses, the churches and the tips of the steeples with the gilded spires, the sun was coming out and glistening on the city where moments before there had just been rain. I could smell the fresh air, and I said to myself, *I've got to remember this. I want to remember everything about this. It's so beautiful!* Then I thought, *just a second ago, all I could see was concrete and I was missing all this because I wasn't looking up. All this beauty was there all the time; how could I have missed it?*

I can't communicate how much it struck me that this beautiful view was there all the time! *All the time.* But I had missed seeing it because I wasn't looking up. And it occurred to me how much more I must be missing in life because of the way I was not observing something.

What a revelation! Just as I said, *I want to remember this, every moment about it,* I realized that I could hardly remember most of my life! As I stood there in Paris on that tiny balcony, on who knows which floor of Notre Dame, this *Huge Truth* came to me that asked, *how much of your own life do you remember?* I do remember significant birthdays; I remember the day I graduated; I remember the day my brother died; I remember the birth of my children—all those significant things—when my first book came out; I remember the first day I walked into my husband's home and the horror of it all; I remember all these markers along the way. But if I ask myself, *Rani, where were you on your fortieth birthday?* I have no idea. None. I don't even remember where I was on my fiftieth birthday; I don't remember where I was on New Year's Day in 1995. I have no idea. Zero.

So it seemed that the majority of my life was actually one big, blank page. Who knows where I was! I remembered the stream of it and incidences that stuck out but not the ones that held them together. At that moment they were lost to me.

And this led to another thought. As I stood there I thought to myself, *how important could my life be if I can't even remember it?* Then I thought, *my whole life could end right here, right now, and this view of Paris could be the last thing I see. And what difference would it make because I can't even remember the life that I think is so significant. And it's my own life I'm talking about!*

So what have I been doing, what have I been focusing on, that I have not enough memories? What have I been concentrating on all my life? Have I been looking at stones and concrete? Or have I been looking at magnificent vistas? What exactly have I been casting my attention on that I should have missed so many other beautiful views like this one in my life?

In realizing that I didn't remember a lot of the odds and ends, events that at one time were perhaps quite important to me, it occurred to me that I must have forgotten a whole lot of things that once upon a time upset me to no end, too!

Now *that* realization was a big deal and bears repeating again: There must have been a whole lot of things in my life that I must have been **upset** over, and although I can remember a lot of them, it's funny that I couldn't recall that many as hard as I tried on that beautiful June day on that balcony of Notre Dame.

Now, as I write this, I can sit back and say, *of course I remember that, and I remember that . . .* but in that moment, none of those occurred to me. None at all. They weren't significant. They didn't matter.

What mattered in that incredible moment of realization was, *what do you want to relate to for the rest of your life? Where do you want to cast your attention?* Among these beautiful vistas and on these concrete steps, on the roads and pavements, and stones and cement, *do you want to look down or do you want to look up?*

That moment changed my life. It changed the bearings of my life. Right there in Paris, on the top of Notre Dame, on that narrow balcony, it was as if a light *did* go on inside of me. And I reshaped the way I would live the rest of my life. I amplified the attention that I would give to every day of my life. I upped the choices, the consciousness with which I would make choices of where and how I spend my time, how I listen to people, how I pay attention, what is important to me, why I make the choices I make. Everything went up a notch.

I no longer wanted to ignore life, ignore anything. I didn't want to forget the small details. I wanted to heighten my attention because it dawned on me on those steps at that cathedral that I had ignored so many beautiful moments in my life. And I said to myself, *and now everything is going to occur to me. I'm upping the bar. That was a moment of great revelation where I thought, no more! Now I'm going to amp up my awareness; now I'm going to record everything in my memory.*

What I want to communicate to you is that this experience influenced immediately every relationship in my life because it amplified the importance of every moment that I have. It immediately made everybody in my life, everything about each moment, all that much more important to me, more significant.

Each experience is important; each person I communicate with is important because that's who I am with, that's the person I'm talking to, that's the person I'm having a meal with. And even though I don't believe in mere accidental anecdotes, I believe that things are very well coordinated and choreographed, and even though we might not understand how the Power works, it doesn't matter. Everything in nature, in the Universe, the planets and the stars, everything is somehow arranged. Even in chaos, there is order, and order has chaos in it. Everything is in accordance to the Law of the Universe.

Now everywhere I go, whether it's to the supermarket, a restaurant, or even a cafe, I look around to see who's there. I no longer believe they are there randomly. I see everything through a different lens now.

Obviously, I had been concentrating on the stones and not the vistas. In that moment on the top of Notre Dame, I felt this incredible sensation that that was not going to happen again, that somehow it was time to let go of the trivial things in life and to live more fully, to be more alive, more present, to be in the moment every moment.

What about you?

Is there something that you are holding onto today that's keeping you from living your best life? What are you focusing on? Where is your attention?

Let go and see things from a new perspective. Get a new vision for your life. Lift up your eyes from the ground and look up. Appreciate the beauty that surrounds you. Be open to seeing new vistas.

Let go!

"On a day when
The wind is perfect,
The sail just needs
To open and the world
is full of beauty.
Today is such a day."

—Rumi

CHAPTER ELEVEN

Give Yourself a New Opportunity

> *"It's your road, and yours alone.*
> *Others may walk it with you,*
> *but no one can walk it for you."*
> —*Rumi*

Finally, it's *time.*

Time to let go; time to let go of your self-descriptors, the neat labels you've accumulated over the years, the tags that said, *that's me. I've always been that way. I can't help it. That's my nature.* Every time you use these sentences, you're essentially saying, a*nd I intend to continue being the way I've always been.*

Begin now to unknot all the ropes that link you to your past; eliminate all those self-defeating "I ams" that have kept you chained; let go of the trademarks you've used to identify yourself and open yourself up to new opportunities. Stop negating yourself by identifying with the past limiting beliefs and hindering your own potential for growth. Ask yourself, *what is possible when I let go?*

When you view every challenge in life as an opportunity to let go, a tremendous array of additional opportunities present themselves.

Every act of letting go becomes an opportunity to wake up, to forgive, and to reunite with a fragmented part of yourself.

By letting go, your perspective on life changes; you find new ways to play, to put what you've been learning to the test, and to practice flexibility. This leads you to the desire to reaffirm your values, to level up, to practice going with the flow and using your God-given gifts and talents. You become open to connecting with others, to growing and relinquishing control. You start loving and living your purpose, and the Universe conspires to send you those who will support you on your path. You become lighter, more trusting, and you start to love yourself, which ultimately allows you to become the best version of you.

Some labels you've lived with probably came from the people who surrounded you in your life as you were growing up. They were pinned on you as a child, and you've carried them around to this day. Perhaps you ascribe the reasons you are your labels to your parents or to other significant adults in your childhood such as your teachers, grandparents, and neighbors. By giving them responsibility for your present day, you're giving them a measure of control over your life today. Understand that people *want* to label you, to pigeonhole you into neat little categories. It's easier that way. Don't let them. Declare your independence. Free yourself from the chains that bind you. Remember, you are treated the way you teach others to treat you. Let go.

Other labels might have resulted from your own choices in life, ones you placed on yourself in order to avoid uncomfortable or distasteful activities. These could be, *I'm too old, I'm not smart enough, I'm not really interested,* or *I don't have the time.* Sound familiar? These are relics of the past. If any of them belong to you, you might like to change them. It's time to stop creating excuses and think up some delicious new labels that are not connected to the choices others have made for you or those you made for yourself. Release those old, tiresome labels, the negative self-talk and disempowering behaviors that are keeping you from a great deal of pleasure and excitement that's waiting for you. You deserve to live a rich, fulfilling, and healthy life. Let go.

If you haven't made the changes you well know would benefit your life, there's a reason you're consciously resisting making them. Perhaps you're not yet aware of this resistance, and if so, write down why you aren't doing anything about them. Your answer can be as simple as *I don't know how* or as complex as *If I do things differently, people may laugh at me; my family might become worried.* Being aware of your resistance enables you to release it. Let go.

The next step is to make a decision. Making decisions reduces worry and anxiety. Making decisions includes creating intentions and setting goals. Making decisions changes your perception of the world and leads to finding solutions to your problems. But deciding can be hard. So what kind of decisions should you make? Make a "good-enough" decision and don't sweat it if it's not the absolute 100 percent best decision. We all know being a perfectionist can be stressful. Sometimes good enough *is* good enough. So don't sweat too much. Just decide. Let go.

You may be stuck and holding onto false beliefs about yourself, stuck in your identity, feeling guilty and worried about choices you made in the past. Now you can begin to evaluate their falsity and turn these beliefs into kind and loving affirmations that express your true self. Guilt and worry are useless emotions rooted in the past. No amount of guilt and worry can ever undo anything. In fact, they use up your present moments and keep you immobilized in the present about something in the future—frequently something over which you have no control whatsoever. Let go.

In this section, you will find questions that will push you to make the changes you know deep in your heart are necessary in order to create the beautiful life that's waiting for you. Be specific. The clearer your vision, the more likely you'll reach your goal.

As you answer the following, be fiercely honest with yourself. No one will ever read your personal entries unless you decide to share them, so let what you really think about and feel strongly about come out onto these pages. When you feel stuck, take just a few minutes and contemplate what might be holding you back. Make this a stress-free writing exercise. Be curious and inquisitive and leave all judgment aside. This is a wonderful way to get in tune with your deepest thoughts and feelings about yourself, of your ability and capacity to make lasting changes in your life.

Being aware of negative thoughts, beliefs, and behaviors allows you to replace the self-defeating thoughts with positive affirmations. Make sure your answers are honest and true.

1. What changes do you know you absolutely must make?

....

....

....

....

2. What are your thoughts and feelings about making these changes?

....

....

....

....

3. Why are changing these habits important to you?

....

....

....

....

4. How will creating these new habits improve your life?

....

....

....

....

5. What will making these changes lead to in your future?

....

....

....

....

6. Do you believe that your mind is your own and that you're capable of controlling your own feelings?

....

7. Are you motivated to change from within rather than from without?

....

8. Why are you resisting important changes to your health, happiness, and financial well-being?

....

....

....

9. Are your fears about making these changes real, or are you just afraid of change? ....

10. Are you free from the need for approval and set up your own rules of conduct for yourself? ....

11. Are you treated by others the way you want to be treated? ....

12. Have you eliminated all dependency relationships and grown your own roots? ....

13. Have you eliminated all blame and fault-finding in your life? ....

14. Can you love yourself at all times? ....

15. Can you give and receive love without expectations?

....

16. What are your limiting thoughts (e.g., I'm just not good enough, No one loves me as I am, etc.)?

....

....

....

....

17. What would be your ideal, new positive thoughts (e.g., I'm really fun to be around and everyone loves me).

....

....

....

....

18. Are you free from ever feeling guilty? ....

19. What are your limiting beliefs (e.g., I shouldn't even try because then people will see that I'm not perfect)?

....

....

....

....

20. What are your new positive beliefs (e.g., People really enjoy my company once they know me)?

....

....

....

....

21. What are your new, positive behaviors (e.g., I'm going to socialize more and more because I enjoy spending time meeting new people)?

....

....

....

....

22. Are you able to live in the present and avoid worrying about the future? ....

23. Are you motivated by your potential for growth rather than a need to repair your deficiencies? ....

24. What are your limiting behaviors (e.g., I'm not socializing because people think I'm boring)?

....

....

....

....

25. Do you have unfinished business? What is it and with whom? What steps can you take now to bring resolution?

....

....

....

....

26. What are you ready to let go of?

....

....

27. What are your most important values and how are you living in ways that are not aligned with those values?

....

....

....

28. What are your most important needs and desires? Does your present life fulfill them?

....

....

....

....

29. In what ways do you feel responsible for someone or something?

30. What old facts do you remember that most everyone else doesn't? What do you regret? How can you deal with this?

31. When you think of the future, what do you:

a. fear the most?

b. hope for the most?

32. When people first meet you, what are you afraid they will think about you?

33. What do you truly want to be known for?

34. What is the number one thing on top of your "bucket list"?

35. What are the most important things to you in life?

36. Imagine yourself five years from now. What would this future self advise the person you are now?

37. What's the one thing you wish you could change about your life?

38. What's holding you back from living fully right now? What do you need to do to make this happen?

39. What is something that has been on your mind lately?

40. What stories from your life will you proudly tell your children (or your nieces and nephews) about?

REFLECTIONS

Say yes to life, and life will say yes to you. Opportunities are everywhere, but you must be open to receive, recognize, and seize them. To do so, you must leave a few things behind and change your thinking.

If you're willing to give up the "shoulds" and "ought tos" you've learned throughout your life, then your forward journey becomes that much easier. The choice is yours, and it's up to you to decide if you want to be free or remain chained to the expectations others have of you.

There is only one moment in which you can experience anything and that is now. Don't throw away precious moments by dwelling on past or future experiences. Turning your now into total fulfillment is the touchstone of effective living. It's your choice.

Present-moment living is your choice. Once you master that, you will begin to ask questions that may have never occurred to you before like, *why am I choosing to feel upset now*? and *how can I make more effective use of this moment?* Be committed to your own happiness. No one can make the change for you. It's up to you.

Once you've completed this writing exercise, go back and read what you wrote as if the answers belong to your best girlfriend and she was sharing her thoughts and beliefs with you. What would you say to her? What would you do? What would you think of her? Wouldn't you hug and thank her for being vulnerable, for stepping up and wanting to make an everlasting change? Wouldn't you commend her for her efforts and her honesty? Now extend that kindness to yourself. Send that love to yourself.

We spend so much time beating ourselves up over what has gone wrong. Now it's time to focus on what's right with your life. Make this fun and powerful by looking at yourself as your own best friend. Tell your friend how amazing she is!

Be sure to revisit your entries often, especially when you face an obstacle or a setback. Your written words can give you the motivation you need to move forward no matter what comes your way.

You're doing great!

AFFIRMATIONS

One of the most important factors in taking your life in a positive direction is opening yourself up to new opportunities, new adventures, and all the benefits that come with fresh life experiences.

The following positive affirmations will help naturally transform your mind and give you the ability to effortlessly manifest new opportunities in every area of your life.

1. I open my mind to the endless opportunities that surround me.
2. Every opportunity I pursue expands into even greater possibilities.
3. I am now surrounded with an abundance of opportunities.
4. I effortlessly attract positive opportunities.
5. My world is filled with endless opportunities for expansion.
6. I am an opportunity magnet.
7. Positive opportunities seem to be naturally attracted to me.
8. I focus in the moment so that I can hear when opportunity knocks.
9. Every day is a blank page, and I eagerly fill it up with new possibilities.
10. When I am ready to try, I am ready to fly!
11. I bless my being with limitless opportunities.
12. I am thankful for every opportunity that comes my way.
13. I welcome endless possibilities into my life.
14. I make the most of every opportunity that comes my way.
15. The more opportunities I seek, the more opportunities I find.
16. Defeat is my opportunity. Victory is my opportunity. Every missed opportunity is really my new opportunity.
17. I seize all opportunities with bold determination.
18. I am naturally tuned-in to all the opportunities of life.
19. I am joyfully living the lifestyle I want and deserve.
20. When I open the door for opportunity, I open the door for my dreams.

FOOD FOR THOUGHT:
Declutter Your Life

Messes and incompletes that irritate us, clutter that robs us of the room to breathe and think, things that we hold onto sometimes stop us from allowing the new and good to come into our life.

Part of *letting go* is taking inventory of your environment and shedding things that no longer contribute to your new vision of life.

Holding onto "stuff" gives us a false sense of abundance. Our craving of physical objects is more often than not a sign of discontent of the soul. Inevitably, the hunger for physical pleasures and pursuits is never satisfied because we are in fact empty from the inside.

The cycle is never ending as we try to fill the void by accumulating more and more until it becomes a bottomless pit that never, ever gets filled and satisfies only our ego. Unfortunately, we live in a world where we are judged by what we own and how we dress and come across; where greed overpowers need;, where we are measured not by our values but by the quality and quantity of our possessions.

Collecting items merely for the sake of propping up our ego or declaring our status to the world does not serve us as it still leaves us with a feeling of insecurity and of not being good enough. Clearing the clutter is something I would encourage you to do even though it can feel difficult at first to let go of possessions you have collected for years. However, as you let go of what no longer serves you, you will start to recognize the more meaningful things and people that will fill the needs of your soul.

Decluttering your life includes shedding and letting go of toxic relationships as well—people who may have been holding you back from being the best version of you.

As you release all that does not serve you or nourish your soul, you create space, *inner space,* to move and grow and fill. Now you can acknowledge and give yourself room to grieve all that is past. It is time to heal and find closure.

This process will not happen overnight, so be patient. Just *leaning into it* and *taking action* daily will propel you to achieve your goal, the goal of freedom at last—freedom from worrying about what others think, freedom from the limiting belief that you are not deserving or good enough, freedom to go after your dreams and fulfill your life purpose—to be, do, and have all that you thought was possible for others but never for you.

Now you know differently. Now you have a choice. There is room for new awareness and realization, of what you are really capable of, what your personal choices are, and new perspectives on past events.

It's time to clear all that doesn't serve you and to live an authentic life.

Life is happening. Go forth and live each moment immersed in peace, joy, and contentment. It may seem like a distant dream, but as long as you are moving and taking action, it will be your reality sooner than you think.

"Yesterday I was clever,
So I wanted to change the world.
Today I am wise,
So I am changing myself."

—Rumi

WHAT I WANT TO REMEMBER FROM THIS CHAPTER

DATE: ....

KEY POINTS: ....

....

....

....

....

....

....

....

....

....

....

TAKEAWAYS: ....

....

....

....

....

....

....

....

....

....

....

CHAPTER TWELVE

Create an Action Plan

> *"A good plan implemented today is better than a perfect plan implemented tomorrow."*
>
> —*George Patton*

The time has come to make an action plan for the biggest job you will have in your life. Rebuild your life by setting a firm foundation consisting of strong materials of courage, confidence, and self-esteem so you can be free to achieve what you've worked so hard for.

Looking at your past in depth with an eye toward changing your present and future and repairing your life independently without compromising were the reasons you picked up this book. Do you believe your behavior and your actions have been congruent with that wish?

When we understand the bad things we've experienced, we can overcome them. You have the capacity to overcome. It's time to reprogram your inner dialogue, to replace that old image of yourself from a helpless little puppy with that of a lion full of courage and valor. Change is tough; there's no doubt about it. If you're like most people, every fiber of your being will resist taking on the hard work of eliminating the thoughts that have so far supported your self-forfeiting feelings and behavior.

Being healthy in all areas of your life is your natural state, and the means for achieving it are within your grasp. A mixture of hard work, clear thinking, humor, and self-confidence are the ingredients needed for effective living. If you can cultivate an approach that relies on responsibility for and commitment to yourself, plus an appetite for living and a desire to be all you choose to be at each moment, then this journey will be pleasant indeed.

Commitment is the key. Commit to your own happiness and work on it every day while simultaneously helping others make similar choices.

It's time now to write down your goals and create an action plan. Be very clear what you wish for. Work with a clear objective in mind for you to regain hope. Be specific and make sure your goals are realistic and attainable. Keep all delusional thoughts at bay. Don't rule out the need to seek out a mentor or coach to help you reach your goals and redecorate your life. Feeling joy and living to your highest potential is what you're after, so leave no stone unturned. Taking the first step is the hardest part but take that first step anyway because it will bring nothing but benefits, I assure you!

Choose a deadline so you won't put off starting. Start small so you don't feel overwhelmed or give up shortly after you start. Taking small steps each day toward making a change or developing a new practice will encourage you to keep going. Drastic change never lasts because you can soon begin to feel deprived.

For example, let's say you want to lose 10 pounds; you could start by cutting out sugar for a week, cutting down on your soda intake, then start adding more vegetables to your diet. Pay attention to your food and be mindful when eating. Stop when you feel satisfied. Take baby steps. Slowly but surely, you'll have less cravings and form a healthy habit, a healthier lifestyle that is sustainable and long lasting.

Be excited! You will not be motivated until you are excited about how your actions will improve how you feel, look, or interact with others. Feel the feeling you would feel once you've achieved your goal. Feed your excitement. Excitement will give you the energy you need to overcome sabotaging thoughts and limiting beliefs.

Don't forget to pat yourself on the back for following through! When you acknowledge your successes, you are more motivated to continue on your path.

Do the following now:

1. **Make your intentions clear.** Whether you want to start a business, find true love, or lose 10 pounds and get in shape so you can wear that dress you've been eyeing, you have to decide to take action. Your *want* must be bigger than the *how*. Write down your plan with specific goals and dates. Make a decision and stick with it.

2. **Create an action plan.** Let's say you want to lose 10 pounds. You know you must change your eating habits and exercise regularly. Make a promise to yourself to do one or the other or both for thirty days, no matter what! Track your progress and successes.

3. **Acknowledge your wins.** Unexpected things can come up, and there will be days when you'll have a valid excuse for not following through—your car breaks down, you had a sleepless night, your boss asked you to work late. But you made a decision to stick with your plan, no matter what. So you'll go for a run or bypass that delicious chocolate cake . . . You can do it!

4. **Share your success with others.** Let others know what you're doing and your progress along your journey to taking care of yourself. What you are doing is awesome and worth sharing. You will see that friends, family, and colleagues will cheer you on, and that will serve as emotional and psychological reinforcement of your commitment to success.

Imagine you've reached your desired goal. Write down how you feel. Do you feel more self-confident? Did achieving your goal boost your self-esteem? How about your self-image? Put feelings behind your thoughts and make it real. ACT AS IF!—as if everything you desire has already been achieved. How do you feel? What do you see, hear, taste, and smell?

Remember, it's not enough to want something or even just to set a goal. The difference between those who succeed and those who don't is action. Nothing moves unless you do. Take action today and start working on your personal action plan so you can have the happier, healthier, and richer life you always dreamed of.

MY GOALS

Make a list of your top-five goals to work on in the next thirty days and make a commitment to follow through the action steps you've listed. If possible, find an *accountability partner*. Being held accountable helps you to not fall off the wagon. Reach out to a dear friend or a family member to share this journey with you, someone who understands you, someone you trust to be firm and hold you accountable, someone who'll keep you on track and motivated. And do the same for your friend.

Lao Tzu said it best, *"A journey of a thousand miles begins with a single step."*

All you have to do is start with one step, and then build from there. It's proven that it takes twenty-one days to create a new habit and ninety days to create a lifestyle. So don't stop; just persevere and keep going. You'll soon see how your life will change for the better!

Goal 1: ....

Deadline: ....

Vision: ....

....

Area of Focus: ....

Action Steps: ....

....

....

....

Goal 2: ....

Deadline: ....

Vision: ....

....

Area of Focus: ....

Action Steps: ....

....

....

....

Goal 3: ....

Deadline: ....

Vision: ....

....

Area of Focus: ....

Action Steps: ....

....

....

....

Goal 4: ....

Deadline: ....

Vision: ....

....

Area of Focus: ....

Action Steps: ....

....

....

....

Goal 5: ....

Deadline: ....

Vision: ....

....

Area of Focus: ....

Action Steps: ....

....

....

....

MY COMMITMENTS

Take charge of yourself and make the choices you need to move forward.

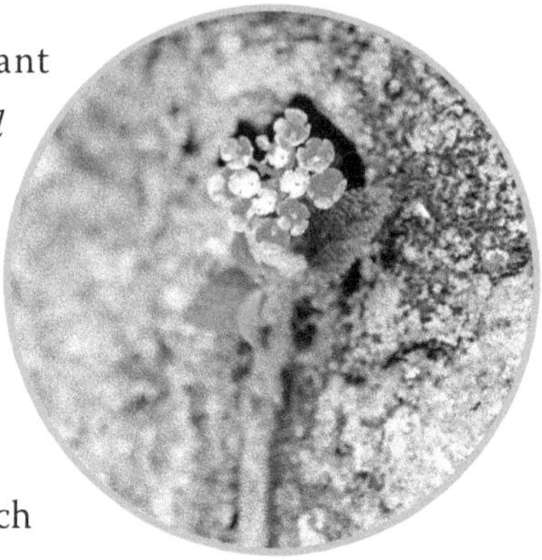

Ask yourself the important questions, such as: *Can I afford to avoid doing the things I really want to do? Should I live my life as others want me to? Is putting things off the way to live*? Chances are your answers will be: **Live . . . Be You . . . Enjoy**.

Take charge of yourself and live each moment for everything it's worth. The life struggles are pretty much the same for each of us. Disagreements, conflicts, and compromises are a part of being human. So are money issues, growing old, sickness, death, natural disasters, accidents, and relationship challenges.

Many forces in our society conspire against individual happiness, and thus you must trust in your own ability to feel, act, and commit to whatever you feel gives you joy and brings you peace.

You must commit to your own happiness. You are in charge. You don't need other people's approval.

Make a commitment now and choose. Affirm the following:

1. I ***choose*** how I feel.
2. I ***choose*** to be happy.
3. I ***choose*** health over sickness.
4. I ***choose*** to live in the present moment.
5. I ***choose*** to let go of all fear.

6 I ***choose*** to let go of perfection.

7 I ***choose*** to value myself.

8 I ***choose*** self-love over conceit.

9 I ***choose*** self-compassion.

10 I ***choose*** to love my body.

11 I ***choose*** to accept myself without complaint.

12 I ***choose*** positive self-image.

13 I ***choose*** whom to love.

14 I ***choose*** to break free from the past.

15 I ***choose*** to be free.

MY WINS

Track your progress and check in weekly. Make sure you're rewarding yourself as you take the important steps to make any kind of change. Celebrating small wins encourages you to keep going and to continue to build upon your successes. Remember, it's not about being perfect. It's about doing what you can with what you have. It's about loving yourself enough to want the best for yourself.

•WEEK 1•

What I've accomplished: ....

....

How I'm feeling: ....

My reward for taking care of me: ....

....

What I'm committed to improving over the next month:

....

....

....

•WEEK 2•

What I've accomplished: ....

....

How I'm feeling: ....

My reward for taking care of me: ....

....

What I'm committed to improving over the next month:

....

....

....

•WEEK 3•

What I've accomplished: ....

....

How I'm feeling: ....

My reward for taking care of me: ....

....

What I'm committed to improving over the next month:

....

....

....

•WEEK 4•

What I've accomplished: ....

....

How I'm feeling: ....

My reward for taking care of me: ....

....

What I'm committed to improving over the next month:

....

....

....

MY NEW STORY

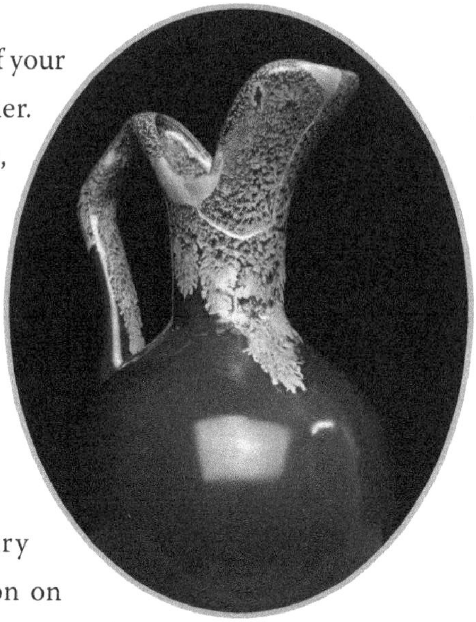

Now that you have all the pieces of your life, let's bring them all together. With the pieces in your hands, close your eyes and feel them. Know without a doubt that everything you want is possible. Imagine your new life. Feel it. Empty your mind of all else and focus on the here and now because it's impossible to do two things at once and do them well.

Creating something extraordinary requires that you focus all your attention on what this extraordinary thing is to you. Time and space don't exist. Your entire Universe is in your hands now, and in this precise moment, there is nothing but you and the pieces you hold in your hands. After all this time, after all your dedication and patience, you have arrived at this place.

Ceramics and life are very similar. Each are simultaneously fragile, strong, and beautiful. Each can break into a thousand pieces. But each can also be healed if you know how. The time has come to repair yourself, to put the broken pieces back together again. There is no need to hide your vulnerability because this apparent vulnerability has become your greatest strength. There is no reason to stop living life intensely and keeping alive all your hopes and dreams. You can do this.

Write down your new story. How has it changed from the time you picked up this book, when you decided to start this journey, when you answered your first question?

You've come a long way.

Something beautiful has been birthed. Acknowledge your efforts. Acknowledge and be excited about your new life.

You Did It!

I'm so proud of you for your commitment, focus, and relentless action. Making meaningful and lasting change to create an amazing life feels wonderful, doesn't it?

How good do you feel?

You're probably feeling on top of the world right now. Remember, this is only the beginning. You have so many new goals and experiences to look forward to, so continue on your journey. Don't stop. Make these changes into habits so they become your reality and stepping-stones to a lifestyle you're proud of.

Celebrate you!

"Your heart knows the way. Run in that direction."

—Rumi

Final Thoughts

> *"Have a mind that is open to everything and attached to nothing."*
>
> *—Tilopa*

A great quote, albeit one so easy to say but not as easy to do considering how many of our thoughts are influenced by outside factors—our past, our parents and caretakers, our culture, our society and our tribe, our religion, and even our geography.

We've been so conditioned all our lives to think certain thoughts, believe certain beliefs, and live the life we've lived. And if we made any fuss about going against this preordained conditioning, we were probably brought back in line to do things the way they were always done. Our many choices and wishes stayed buried and unexplored because "fitting in" superseded having a mind that was open to new ideas and new dreams.

If we continue to allow our perceptions to influence how we view the life we've lived, if we allow the past to dictate our thoughts, journey, and destination, then we are truly missing out on life. Yes, perhaps we were broken or even shattered, but understand that no matter the failure, hurt, despair, or addiction; no matter the abuse, the trauma, or the fear, our scars are just a part of us. Each time we fix ourselves to create a new beginning, we become stronger. The gold in our cracks are life bonds that are enforced through mending; the breaks are a place for beauty to transpire. Like the kintsugi bowl, we are in fact more beautiful for being broken.

And so, I invite you now to be willing to change your mind and adjust your perceptions. Move away from all that you believe have made you who you are and stop identifying with the person you were and what you accomplished. Hanging on to the past and blaming others for what happened, believing that you are what you do, labeling yourself by what and how much you have keeps you from doing what you want to do today.

As we reach the end of our conversation, I thank you for traveling with me on this journey across your highest mountains and lowest valleys. And on this journey, I hope I have been effective in holding your hand through the hours of my writing and your participation and engagement with this work. I have imagined you broken, but I've also imagined you putting yourself back together piece by piece, fighting a battle and emerging strong and whole again to step forward and live the life you desire and to live it intensely.

Your life is your obligation. Your experiences are not wasted but extremely valuable. They have allowed you to grow and become the strong person you are today. Now, you know yourself better and know what you are capable of, what your potential is. Make peace with the past and give yourself permission to move forward so you can create a beautiful life. The real you is so much more than the outer you that you reveal to the world.

Remember, you cannot always control others and how they choose to live, but you have full control over your own inner world. You can't give away what you don't have. You can't share your good if you don't have any to give, can you?

Doing good for others without doing good for yourself doesn't feel very good, does it? So fill yourself up first so you can share from the overflow. Resentments keep you small, so forgive often. Don't give away your power. Tap into your expansive inner world for the abundance that you seek. The real you is waiting to be recognized and released. Unleash your power and discover your beauty, love completely, and live brilliantly.

Having done this work, you have no more excuses, so stop looking for them. Nobody conditions us; we allow ourselves to be conditioned.

Now is the only sphere of life that you can live. Not the past, not the future.

You can only live in the present. But people tend to forget that. The past is memory. If it is memory, it is unreal. The future is vision. Vision is anticipation.

The future can only become real when it has become the present. The past is important, so is the future. The past is a memory that nourishes your now, your present, and the future is the vision that makes your now, your present, meaningful.

Even then, only now is real. Live in the moment!

Always remember this most valuable life lesson: The past is gone and you cannot change it. However, you can create a new present and a brighter and more fulfilling future, one in alignment with your God-given gifts and dreams.

You have the choice to piece together all the broken pieces of your past and make them whole, to make them beautiful, to fill the cracks with beautiful gold. You are a treasure, the jewel that is waiting to reveal itself. You have the power within you—you just need to move forward in faith.

Your work does not stop here. In fact, it has just begun. The world is waiting for you to start dancing so the party can begin. You have suffered enough, and there may be more suffering in the future, for such is life. Now you are wiser, you have the tools, and when your strength fails you, you'll know what you can do and how.

You've been in a sort of sleep, dreaming a dream in which you often felt confused about the rules of the game, in which evil is rampant and conflict is everywhere. Now it's time to wake up and remove all those blinders that have kept you from seeing all the colors, hearing all the sounds, and most importantly, feeling the love that you really are.

Bring energy and focus to how you live your life. Awaken to your true identity. Lift out of your illusions and wake up to the beautiful life that is waiting for you. As you claim your light, so is your world illuminated.

Finish strong and go out and live your life to the fullest. How you finish is even more important than how you start. Your wounds naturally want to heal, but your stories just get in the way. The in-between stage as the caterpillar transforms into a butterfly is the *chrysalis,* which is just goo. It unfolds naturally to either become a butterfly or cease to exist. It can't ever go back to being a caterpillar. You, too have moved past that caterpillar stage and are now ready to emerge into the beautiful butterfly. Allow yourself. Give yourself permission. Don't hold yourself back, don't stop the growth, just lean into the unknown. You must risk your past to seek your potential and courageously let go.

Give yourself the gift. You can do this. You're stronger and more worthy than you know. Today, open yourself to the Divine Will. Open yourself to opportunities for creative expression and feel how this wellspring empowers you.

My prayer for you is that you will love your life in a greater way, that you will understand your value and live with confidence. I believe today is a new beginning. Let go of the old; tell a different story and receive the new into your life. Remember, everything you see is the play of Divine Love.

Stay open to what is possible and live a life fulfilled and happy, with a mind that is open to everything and attached to nothing. Remember, lasting change is an inside job.

You are magnificent. And what makes you magnificent is everything that you've previously believed was wrong with you. Now, you are seeing the world beyond your mind to the perfection that exists that is constantly expressing itself in infinite ways through the process of Divine Play.

I leave you with my deepest wish that you recognize and claim your beauty, that you know your magnificence. Go forth and live a life of the kintsugi master and fill your cracks with gold!

Remember you are more beautiful for being broken.

Namaste.

"Many things must be left unsaid because it is late, but whatever conversation we have not had tonight, we will have tomorrow."

—Rumi

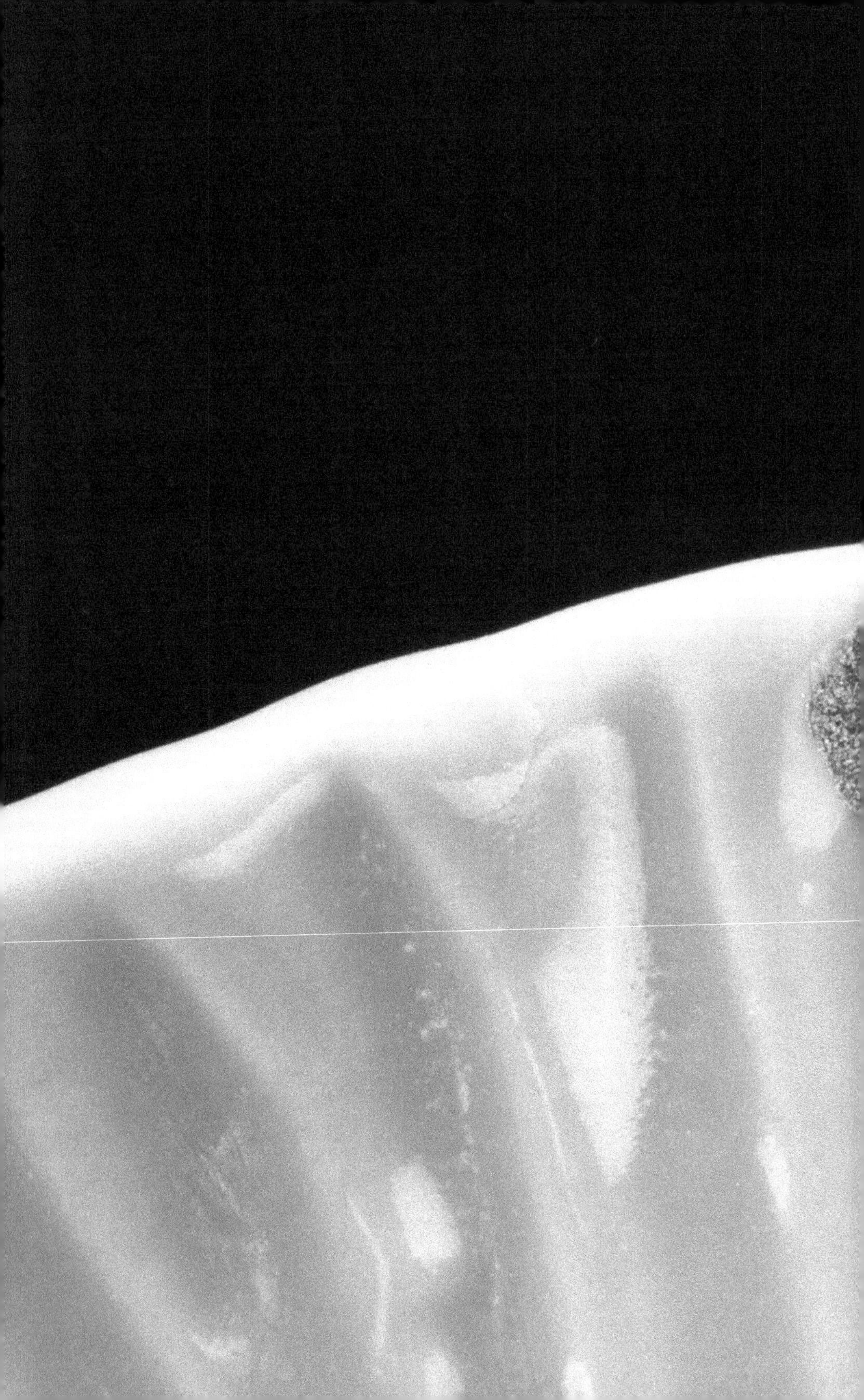

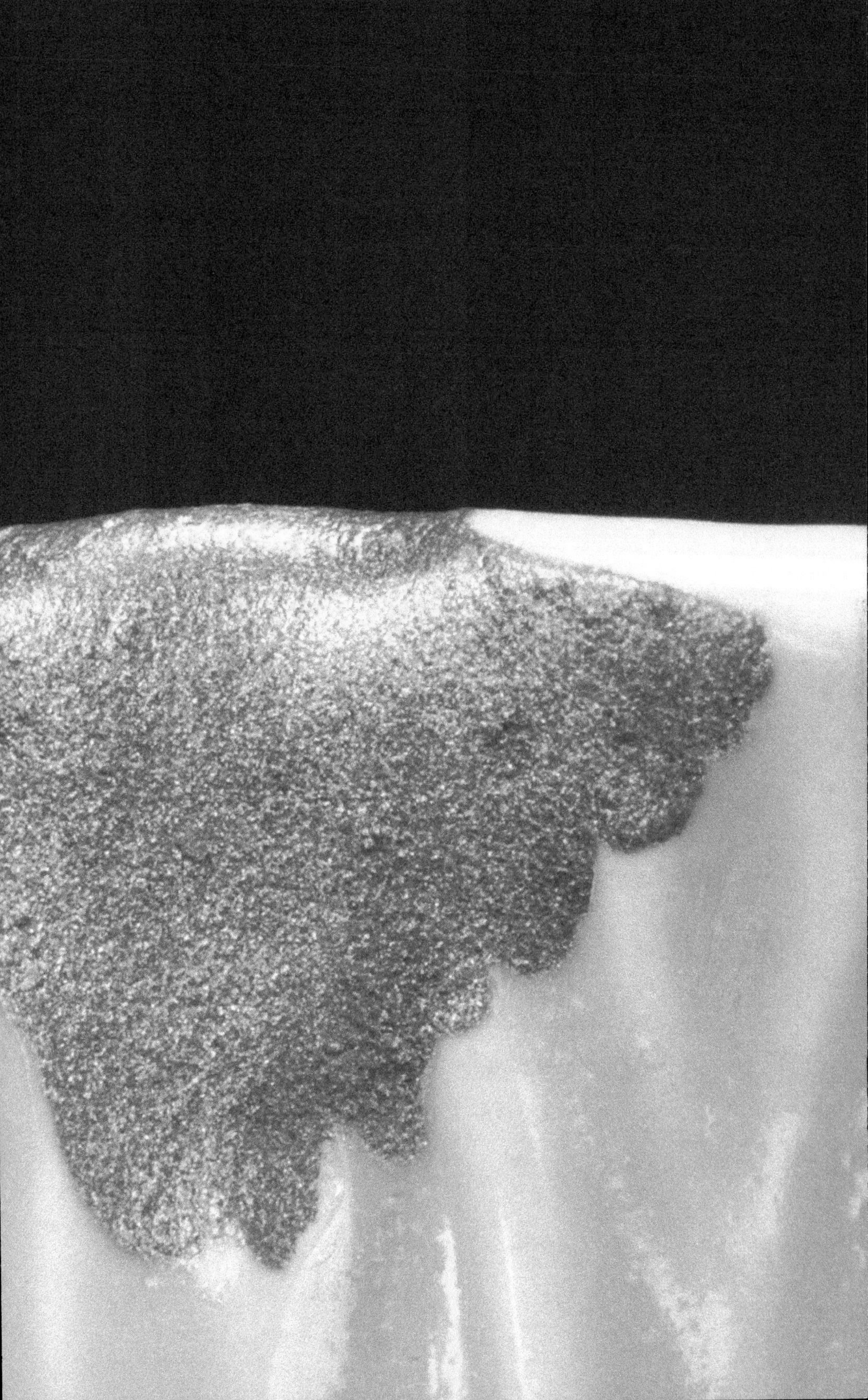

About The Author

Rani St. Pucchi is an international Bestselling Author, Inspirational Speaker, Success Coach, Image Consultant, and President and award-winning Designer of St. Pucchi, the internationally acclaimed bridal fashion house.

Rani began designing fashion at a young age. Growing up in Thailand in a culture of female oppression, and forced into an arranged marriage at the age of 18, Rani is well aware of the trauma girls and women often face, having lived the violence and suffered the pain and shame of domestic abuse. She found her only solace in design. In 1985 Rani launched her global bridal empire in the United States. Her vision was to create an avant-garde bridal couture line modern in styling, but classic in detail. Her vision was realized and her designs quickly gained celebrity attention and design accolades.

As the foremost designer to introduce exotic silk fabrics, hand embroidery and color to the United States bridal scene, Rani has been recognized on numerous occasions for her design talent. Rani's honors include being recognized as Style Innovator for five consecutive years before going on to win the Best Bridal Designer Award.

Rani's *St. Pucchi* collection is worn by the world's most discerning brides including celebrities, singer-songwriters, sports personalities and style icons, such as Olympic Gold medalist, Sanya Richards-Ross, Dallas Cowboys' quarterback Tony Romo's wife Candice Crawford, actress Tara Reid, Timbaland's wife Monique Idlett, Jason Priestly's wife Naomi Lowde, actress Candice Cameron and Grammy Award winning country music singer Alison Krauss who donned a specially designed Chantilly lace and silk gown at the Country Music Awards.

Rani's signature designs have been recognized in the media spotlight in high profile magazines such as *Harper's Bazaar, Town and Country, WWD, W, Cosmopolitan Brides, Bride's, Inside Weddings, Martha Stewart Weddings, The Knot, Town and Country,* on TV shows such as *E!, Entertainment Tonight, One Life to Live, Brides of Beverly Hills,* WE TV's phenomenal hit show *Girl Meets Gown,* and most notably, on the finale of *Friends,* as Phoebe captured the hearts of millions when she said "I Do" in a unique Lilac, corset bodice A-line St.Pucchi gown.

A car accident in 2015 shattered everything Rani took for granted. This near death experience left Rani with a heightened awareness of the fragility of life and an appreciation for the sacredness of her own body. During her two year recovery she experienced a spiritual awakening. She overthrew self-doubt and embarked on a new life of confidence and self-love.

Thus began her journey from acclaimed fashion designer to motivational speaker and author. After styling thousands of brides and A-list celebrities, Rani noticed an upsetting trend. Even the women who appeared to have everything–wealth, relationships, beauty–felt discontented and trapped in self-doubt. Standing in front of the mirror they could see only flaws in their reflections. Rani's position as bridal designer and stylist granted her an intimate perspective into this critical moment in her clients' lives and the power to make a positive difference. She began to see herself as not only a designer of fashion, but a designer of lives.

Rani believes that confidence must start with a woman's love and acceptance of her body and that when a woman is whole and fulfilled in herself, she makes better relationship choices.

Writing has always been Rani St . Pucchi's passion. Since she majored in English literature and poetry, it was inevitable that she would add the role of a number-one bestselling author to her roster of accomplishments.

In addition to the book you are reading now, Rani is the author of *Your Body, Your Style: Simple Tips on Dressing to Flatter Your Body Type.* Renowned for her savvy knowledge of a woman's form and fit, Rani shares her knowledge of more than three decades with all women so they can make better styling choices.

In her second book, *The SoulMate Checklist: Keys to Finding Your Perfect Partner,* Rani walks women through their journey to finding true soul mate love. She holds her readers by the hand, guiding them step by step on every phase of the path they must navigate before reaching that place of bliss.

In her third book, *Your Bridal Style: Everything You Need to Know to Design the Wedding of Your Dreams* Rani shares her expert advice on everything a bride needs to create a truly unforgettable day as she goes forward to plan the wedding she has always dreamt of and say "I Do" with ease and grace.

Her upcoming books include:

- ***Secrets About Success Every Woman Should Know***
- ***Unveiled: A Celebrity Fashion Designer's Story: A Memoir of My Life's Journey***

Today, Rani draws on her lifelong struggle against adversity and 30+ years in the fashion industry to help women break free of debilitating self-doubt and become the designers of their own lives. She coaches her clients to identify, weaken and replace limiting personal beliefs and embrace confidence as their greatest asset. Rani empowers thousands of women across the world with her message of body-positivity and self-love.

Rani's motto is:

LOVE YOURSELF
DISCOVER YOUR BEAUTY
LIVE BRILLIANTLY

Born and raised in Bangkok, Thailand, Rani now happily lives in Los Angeles, California. Learn more about Rani at www..ranistpucchi .com.

Also by Rani St. Pucchi

Your Body, Your Style:
Simple Tips on Dressing to Flatter Your Body Type

RANI ST. PUCCHI teaches you simple tricks on how to dress your body in a way that will enhance your best assets and camouflage areas that you feel uncomfortable about or find lacking in any way.

Elevate your self-confidence by defining your personal style and becoming clear on how you wish to be seen in the world.

Learn a simple process to determine what colors flatter you most and which ones to part with so that you may look more interesting, more assured, and in control.

Receive smart shopping tips, learn the importance of investing in the right lingerie, immerse yourself in simple style advice for your body type and more ...

Embrace your unique personality and shine with your body and your style.

The Soulmate Checklist:
Keys to Finding Your Perfect Partner

RANI ST. PUCCHI delves into the meaning of Soul Mate relationships as she guides you on a quest for love that lasts a lifetime.

Are images of the ideal relationship just fantasy, or do they have a basis in truth?

Does everyone have a perfect Soul Mate who is waiting to be found by him or her, or is a "perfect" relationship something that one must develop with oneself first?

Getting beyond the "in love" phase—will the relationship last?

Questions like these and many others are addressed here as Rani provides insights into the nature of personal relationships and Soul Mate love.

The *SoulMate Checklist* will help you avoid misconceptions about love, find the blueprint for coming to terms with your past, experience unconditional love, and find out what a Soul Mate is—and isn't.

Your Bridal Style:
Everything You Need to Know to Design the Wedding of Your Dreams

Your wedding day is possibly the most important day of your life, and your wedding dress may be the most important garment you will ever wear. Why not take control of the entire process of planning your ideal wedding – one that is fun, intimate and uniquely your own?

In Your Bridal Style, award-winning bridal designer Rani St. Pucchi shares her expert advice on everything a bride needs to create a truly unforgettable day, including:

- How to define your personal style based on your specific body type.
- Different wedding silhouettes and what is suitable for different venues and ceremonies.
- A helpful timeline for planning your wedding.
- Do's and don'ts for wedding dress shopping.
- Tips on choosing fabrics, colors, accessories and other finishing touches.
- How to avoid common wedding day mishaps.
- A FAQs section which answers 53 of your most pressing questions.
- Strategies for the photo shoot, and so much more.

This engaging, beautifully illustrated book is a treasure trove of ideas and inspiration. With this book in hand, any bride-to-be can design and create the wedding of her dreams.

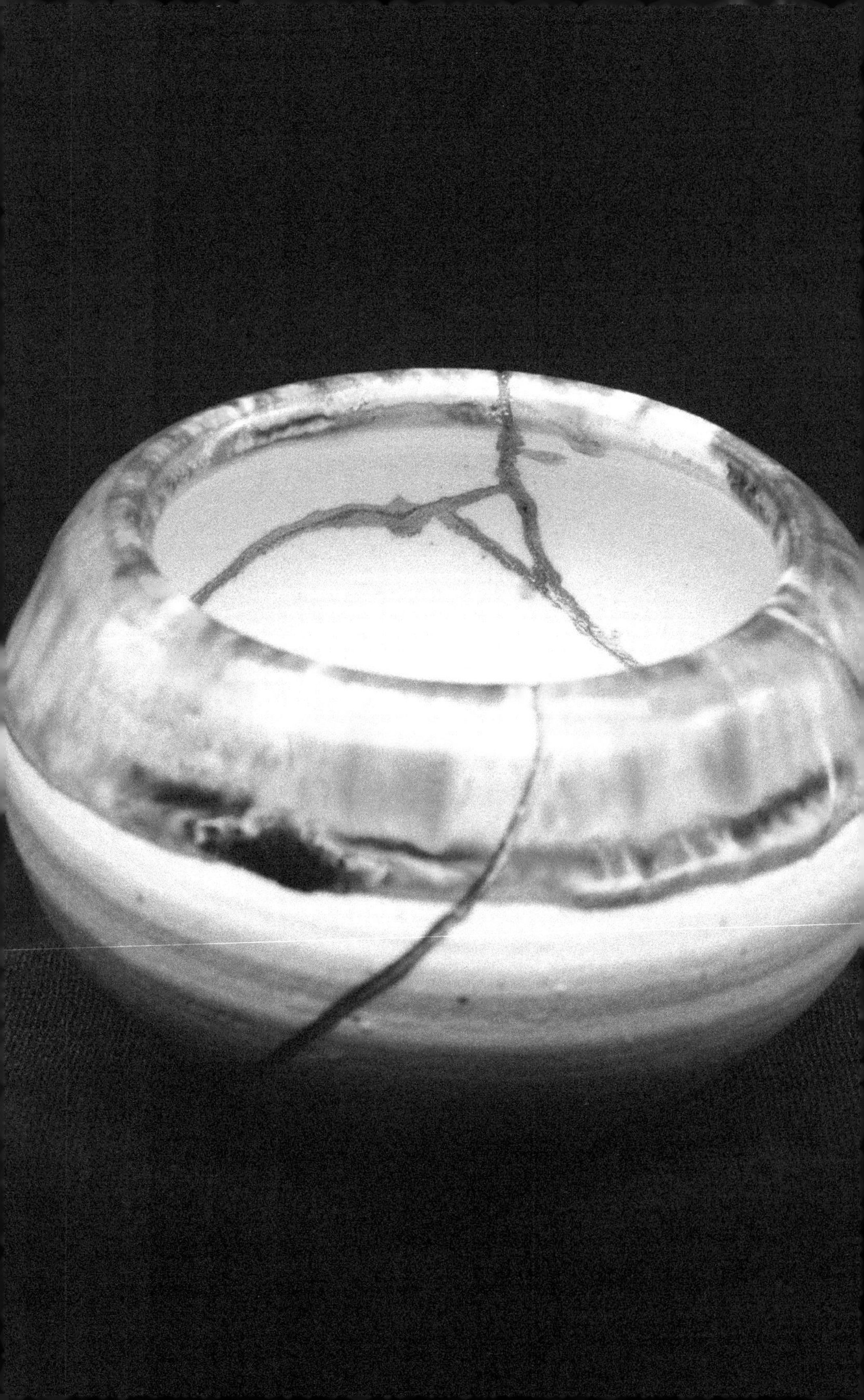

CPSIA information can be obtained
at www.ICGtesting.com
Printed in the USA
FSHW021740061118
53435FS